THE MANY FACES OF PLAY

Editor

Kendall Blanchard, PhD
Middle Tennessee State University

Associate Editors

Wanni W. Anderson, PhD
Brown University

Garry E. Chick, PhD
University of Illinois at Urbana-Champaign

E.P. Johnsen, PhD
University of Kansas

Human Kinetics Publishers, Inc.
Champaign, Illinois

ACKNOWLEDGMENTS

The 1983 TAASP annual meetings were a resounding success. Despite heavy snows in the Northeast that delayed the arrival of some participants, the event provided a combination of entertainment and intellectual exchange that made it one of the outstanding conventions in the Association's history. No one deserves more credit for this success than general program director Miles Richardson and local arrangements coordinator Anna Nardo. Also, AES program chair Edward Bruner provided several forms of assistance and made the initial arrangements that led eventually to Edmund Leach's agreement to present the TAASP keynote address.

The authors of the papers are to be thanked, especially for their polite cooperation and patience in responding to the editor's requests. Special thanks are reserved for the associate editors who were willing to take the time in the midst of other responsibilities to read, edit, make suggestions regarding the many papers submitted for consideration, and write introductory comments to the several chapters of the collection. Wanni Anderson, Garry Chick, and Pete Johnsen were gracious in their willingness to accept this responsibility, were thorough beyond the minimal demands of the task, and were both candid and conscientious in their suggestions.

Kendall Blanchard

Proceedings of the 9th annual meeting of The Association for the Anthropological Study of Play (TAASP) held February 11-16, 1983 at Baton Rouge, Louisiana

Library of Congress Cataloging in Publication Data
Association for the Anthropological Study of Play.
    Meeting (9th : 1983 : Baton Rouge, La.)
    The many faces of play.

    Bibliography: p.
    1. Play—Congresses.   I. Blanchard, Kendall,
1942-   II. Title.
GN454.A85   1983   790   85-30602
ISBN 0-87322-046-3

Developmental Editor: Gwen Steigelman, PhD
Proofreader: Ann Morris Bruehler
Typesetter: Bill Lewis
Cover Design: Jack Davis
Production Director: Ernie Noa

ISBN: 0-87322-046-3
ISSN: 0885-8764

Printed in the United States of America

10 9 8 7 6 5 4 3 2 1

Human Kinetics Publishers, Inc.
Box 5076 Champaign, IL 61820

CONTENTS

PREFACE

The ninth annual meetings of The Association for the Anthropological Study of Play, Reunion du Mardi Gras, were held in Baton Rouge, Louisiana, at the Prince Murat Hotel, on February 11–16, 1983. The meetings were held jointly with those of the American Ethnological Society (AES) and the Southern Anthropological Society (SAS). The time and site were chosen to coincide with the annual Mardi Gras celebration, and the program of all three organizations focused on play, ritual, and celebration themes (see 1983 AES Proceedings, "Text, Play, and Story: The Construction and Reconstruction of Self and Society," Stuart Plattner, editor).

The TAASP program featured a total of 80 papers, a keynote address by Edmund Leach, an invited address by Roger Abrahams, and a presidential address by Brian Sutton-Smith. Forty of the papers presented at the meetings were submitted to be considered for publication in the proceedings. These were reviewed by the editor and the associate editors, and 20 were accepted for publication, in addition to the presentations by Leach and Abrahams.

The papers included in this collection represent a broad range of academic disciplines, from anthropology and folklore studies to psychology, sociology, philosophy, and literature. They illustrate the growing importance of play studies as a legitimate area of scholarship. They also suggest new answers, new questions, and new possibilities as they provide one more important chapter in the continuing effort to understand human playfulness.

Kendall Blanchard
Editor

1

THE POSSIBILITIES

INTRODUCTORY
COMMENTS

Kendall Blanchard

The two papers in this section are slightly edited versions of the two major addresses delivered at the meetings in Baton Rouge. They illustrate as well as any paper in this collection the insight provided by the play perspective on human behavior.

Professor Edmund Leach is one of the giants of 20th-century scholarship and a dominant figure in British social anthropology. Perhaps best known among his many publications is the classic monograph *Political Systems of Highland Burma*, published in 1954. Although summarizing his theoretical contributions to the discipline in a few sentences is difficult, I think it is safe to suggest that his work has served two primary functions: to prod the intellectual and scientific consciences of anthropologists by reminding them of the limitations of grand schemes and elaborate speculations; and to bridge the gap between French sociology and the social anthropology in Britain while attacking the shortcomings and excesses in both.

Sir Edmund Leach was knighted by the Queen in 1975. This paper, the 1983 John Huizinga Keynote Address, is a playful, yet insightful, analysis of that event. Leach compares the British investiture ceremony with a headhunting ritual he observed in Borneo in 1947. In this context play is a convenient device for minimizing the differences between human societies and underscoring the universal "playful" quality that characterizes ritual behavior.

Professor Roger D. Abrahams is the Kenan Professor of Humanities and Anthropology at Scripps College. A major figure in folklore studies, Professor Abrahams is not a newcomer to play scholarship, having made many important contributions to the study of play and games.

In this invited address, Professor Abrahams describes the way in which playfulness affects the celebration of death in a West Indian agrarian community. The dialectic between those events viewed as nonsense or playful and those seen as respectable (i.e., not playful) is explained as a vital, creative process and a mechanism for dealing with the life-and-death dilemma.

Both the Leach and Abrahams papers are entertaining and insightful descriptions of human playfulness, particularly as play affects the rite of passage process. Together they highlight the significance of human play, underscore the vitality of play scholarship, and provide an appropriate introduction to an important collection of articles about play.

FIELDWORK IN BUCKINGHAM PALACE or ONCE A KNIGHT IS QUITE ENOUGH

Edmund Leach
Cambridge, England

Whatever may be the official definition used by members of TAASP, there must be great practical difficulties about how one draws the line between "play" and "nonplay." I am assuming here that play includes any form of activity which is entered into voluntarily and which is (at least potentially) enjoyed by the participants, but which leads to no immediate direct economic rewards. In particular, it includes the sort of thing that we will be seeing at Mardi Gras, when people dress up in bizarre costumes and generally conduct themselves as if a world of make-believe nonsense could temporarily be taken seriously.

My theme is the British institution of investiture, that is to say, initiation into knighthood. The underlying puzzle is why the British public at large takes these procedures seriously, for clearly, in manifest form they are just a piece of mildly comic play-acting. So, although I hope to entertain you, there is some serious anthropology at the back of what I say.

My qualifications for giving this account are personal and exceptional. Although there are parts of the city of London where British Knights of the Realm come two a penny, academic anthropologists of that ilk are uncommon. Among socio-cultural (as distinct from physical) anthropologists I can think of only four others besides myself: Sir Edward Taylor, the nineteenth century founder of British socio-cultural anthropology; Sir James Frazer, author of *The Golden Bough*; the late Sir Edward Evans-Pritchard; and his still-living contemporary, Sir Raymond Firth.

In this distinguished crew I seem to be quite alone in having seen the occasion as one in which, as a professional anthropologist, I had a kind of moral duty to act as a participant observer of an exotic ritual.

To avoid any possible misunderstanding, let me emphasize that my lecture is in no way intended as a sideswipe at the British monarchy. Symbolic heads of state play an important role in modern national and international relations, and our British version of that frustrating office has much to be said in its favor when compared with most of the versions which we encounter elsewhere. Also, the absolute distinction between symbol and reality which the British have achieved in their separation of hereditary monarch and prime minister has a great deal to be said in its favor. For example, it seems to me to have quite a number of advantages compared with your own system of elected presidents. In other words I am quite emphatically not one of the small band of British Republicans, though I am constantly surprised that more members of the British Royal Family do not opt out of what has become an entirely awful job.

My first teacher in anthropology was Bronislaw Malinowski. The key point about Malinowski's anthropology was his thesis that the fieldworker must use his eyes and his personal experiences rather than just ask "informants" about "customs" which, for all he knew, might be figments of their imagination. The data of anthropology come from real life, not from travellers' tales. My present exercise is given in this same spirit.

At a certain level of abstraction, initiation rites the world over exhibit a marked similarity not only of structure, but also of symbolism. For example, as in carnival, there is always some point in the proceedings when the participant actors doll themselves up in fancy dress. To demonstrate the structural part of this argument I shall shortly be making a comparison between a headhunting ritual which I observed in Borneo in 1947 and the induction into knighthood which I underwent in London in 1975. The crucial episode in the former affair was the sacrifice of a large pig; in the latter the initiate knight is himself the sacrificial pig.

In Britain an enthusiast can collect titles like other people collect postage stamps. Even if you are not a philatelist of this sort you are apt to accumulate these things one after another once you get onto the appropriate network. Some titles signify more than others. If a scientist is entitled to put the letters FRS (Fellow of the Royal Society) after his name, you can be sure he is a scientist of very great distinction, though the duties of most Fellows of the Royal Society, as such, amount to very little except to decide which other scientists shall be entitled to a like honor. By contrast, the letters FBA (Fellow of the British Academy), which I myself may append to my name, though they purport to be indicators of a like sort, indicate hardly anything except that you possess some influential friends.

The Royal Society and the British Academy are private institutions; the Monarch's Honours List is a different matter. Every six months, at New Year and on the Queen's Birthday (which needless to say is not her real birthday!), and sometimes more frequently if there is a change of government, an Honours List is issued in the Queen's name. Most such lists contain several hundred names, ranging in distinction from Peerages and Orders of Merit at the top to Police Medals for Bravery at the bottom.

The Peers are later inducted into office in a special ceremony in the House of the Lords, and Knights of the Garter and Knights of the Thistle have their own rigmarole in the royal castles at Windsor and Edinburgh. A fair number of people at the bottom of the list receive their badges of honor locally by delegation. However, the Queen herself deals with all the other more senior titles and a fair proportion of the minor ones. During 1975, when I myself received my knighthood, I reckon that she must personally have invested at least 500 of her faithful servants with their appropriate badges of honor. She clearly takes the job very seriously and does her homework. On the occasion that I am about to describe she inititated about 130 individuals and had something personal and more or less relevant to say to each of them.

Just precisely how the victims are selected is shrouded in mystery. A branch of the Prime Minister's Office known as the Office of the Patronage Secretary sifts the lists of nominees which are put forward by official bodies and by members of the general public. Senior civil servants and officers in the armed forces collect badges of honor almost automatically as they move up in rank, though there is a complex pecking order about the various sequences of letters. In the eyes of the recipient there is all the difference in the world between a KCB (Knight Commander of the Bath) and a KCMG (Knight Commander of St. Michael and St. George), though in the eyes of the rest of the public a knight is a knight and an oddity at that.

The acquisition of titles by unofficial individuals is more chancy. I have no idea just why I was nominated for a knighthood or by whom. But at the relevant date I was head of my Cambridge college and had been chairman of various university committees, and the network is such that any provost of King's College, Cambridge, is likely to fetch up with a title of some sort in due course.

If you are offered a title you can refuse, but I doubt if many people do; that would be taking matters too seriously. There are no perks except by accident. The only one that has come my way was that on one occasion a check-in clerk at London Heathrow Airport, noticing that I was "Sir," immediately sent me off to the first class lounge, where you get free drinks, even though I was travelling "tourist." Alas, it has never happened again!

However, I would not want to argue that titles have no personal consequences whatsoever. When my name appeared in the list, my immediate colleagues were simply amused. My daughter took it as an outrage against her political principles. My secretary, with whom I was on personal-name terms, took it as a boost to her personal pres-. tige, and from that day to this has made a point of referring to me as "Sir Edmund" on every occasion.

But tonight I will leave on one side the finer subtleties of the present-day social significance of British knighthood. My concern is simply with the ethnography of the rite of initiation.

Let me start then (if only briefly) with the head feast which was performed in the House of Penghulu Temenggong Koh on the Rejang River in Sarawak in September 1947.

On the basis that he had provided support for an expedition which claimed to have taken two Japanese heads in 1944, Koh was giving what anthropological literature describes as a Feast of Merit. He was celebrating, in the most ostentatious style, his assumption of a new title of honor, the highest rank that any Iban had claimed within living memory. The proceedings lasted for several days, with everyone dressed up in gorgeous regalia. The culminating event was the sacrifice of a large pig which was directly identified with Koh himself as donor of the sacrifice. This identity was indicated by the fact that Koh, who otherwise played a very passive role, placed his foot on the pig's back immediately before it was dispatched. The pig had lain all night and for most of the previous day under an awning on the longhouse verandah in front of Koh's dwelling room (*bilek*)[1] where it had received the tender attention of the women of Koh's domestic group. Behind the awning was a temporary construction of bamboo and decorative grass. This was described as "the seat of Lang," Lang being the name of the ancestor-headhunter-hero-deity to whom the pig was being sacrificed and whose blessings would, in return, bring beatitude to Koh and his household.

My first diagram shows this general layout (see Figure 1). Notice that the donor, sacrificial animal, and priests are in an area that lies midway between the members of the secular congregation, who were the witnesses of the deed, and the throne of Lang, which appears to ordinary human eyes to be empty.

After the pig had been killed, the donor withdrew and various things were done to the pig's blood and liver in order to take auspices. At the end of the day only a few token pieces of the pig's carcass were placed on Lang's shrine; the rest was removed and eventually distributed among the spectators. But these matters do not here concern us. Notice, however, the presence of an orchestra. The local equivalent of a Javanese *gamelan* played continuously throughout the sacrificial proceedings.

I have witnessed a variety of animal sacrifices in a variety of cultural contexts. The layout of the scene of action has always been more or less the same and included the following features: a shrine which, either in appearance or by name, was treated as a throne on which the deity had temporarily taken up his or her abode; a place of

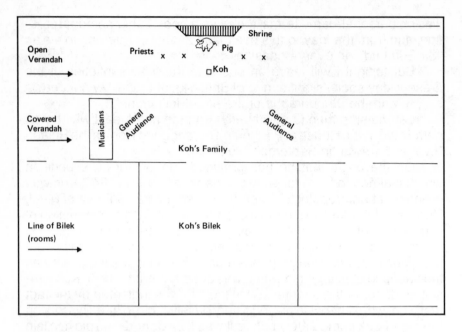

Figure 1. Layout of final episode of Penghulu Koh's Head Feast, Rejang River, Sarawak, September 1947.

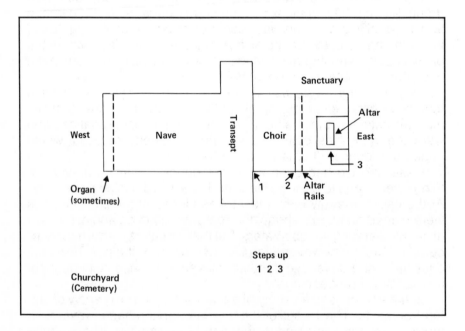

Figure 2. Layout of a typical English village church.

sacrifice, which was reserved for the priestly participants, including the donor and the victim; and a lay congregation of onlookers or witnesses.

The place of sacrifice was in every case located midway between the shrine proper and the congregation. Other common features were that the whole area in which the sacrificial proceedings took place was marked off from the ordinary everyday world by boundary markers of some kind, and the presence of some kind of noise-making machinery which also functioned as a marker of discontinuity with normality. The noise sources varied—orchestras, drums, firecrackers, shotguns, human singers. The scale of such arrangements may vary enormously, but the layout of a typical English parish church conforms to the general pattern and will give you an idea of what I am getting at (see Figure 2).

The church precincts as a whole, including the churchyard, is fenced off from "ordinary ground." The churchyard commonly functions as a cemetery and is often thought to be haunted on that account. It is "betwixt and between" the House of God and the World of Mammon.

When we get inside the church we find that it is again marked off into segments of differentiated sacredness. The main altar is ordinarily at the extreme east end. During church services this part of the church (the sanctuary) may only be entered by the officiating priests. It is separated from the rest of the church by a railing and often by a raised step. The nave, which forms the west end of the church, is occupied by the congregation, but most of the ritual action takes place in the intermediate area, the chancel, which lies between the nave and the sanctuary. This again is usually clearly demarcated by a raised step and was formerly separated from the nave by a screen.

The noise-making apparatus of the church, either a choir or an organ or both, is usually located in the chancel area, thus marking a separation of the sacred from the profane. But sometimes the organ (or the choir or both) is located immediately above the entrance to the church at the west end.

In various publications I have maintained that the principle that is involved here is extremely general. *Power is manifested at the interface of separable categories.* The principle applies whether the potency that is made manifest is physical—as in the case of electricity or other prime movers—sexual, political, or metaphysical. The real world is continuous. By the use of categories we separate physical and social space into areas of differentiated power potential, creating the illusion of discontinuity (see Figure 3). At the interface there is a region which belongs to neither category and yet to both. It is an area of danger, of taboo, of manifested power. You will see what I mean

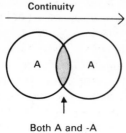

Continuity →

A   A

Both A and -A
discontinuity and ambiguity

Continuity →

This World   Other World

Liminal zone,
betwixt and between location
of ritual process

Real world of experience is continuous, but is cut up into discontinuous segments by our use of verbal categories. The boundary layer is ambiguous and becomes the focus of taboo.

Cosmos of imagination is likewise continuous but 'this world' is connected with the 'other world' by a liminal ambiguous zone in which ritual process takes place.

Figure 3. Real world of experience and the cosmos of imagination. Euler diagrams.

about power being "manifested at the interface of separable categories" if you clutch an electric power cable with your feet on the ground and without wearing rubber boots. But here we are discussing the potency of divinity and royalty.

In this frame of thinking, any shrine which is treated as a throne of an invisible deity is a source of potential metaphysical power. It is, for the time being, a part of the other world of immortal gods rather than of this world of mortal men. The penumbra of the shrine area, the betwixt and between region where most of the ritual action takes place, is both in this world and in the other world. The whole area is dangerous and loaded with taboo, but as you approach closer to the core, the throne of the deity, the ultimate source of power, the intensity of the taboo increases.

This model fits very well with my diagrams both for the Borneo head feast and for the English parish church; but how about Buckingham Palace? From my point of view no useful distinction can be drawn between the play-acting of religious performances and the play-acting of a secular entertainment such as a royal investiture. In structuralist terms what goes on in the Palace on these occasions confirms precisely to the general pattern of religious performances of which I have given you an outline. I will now try to show you how this works out.

Architecturally, Buckingham Palace is a real shocker. The building started out as Buckingham House, built by a Duke of Buckingham in the 18th century. It faced the other way around then, with the frontal to the west. Then the house was bought by King George III for his wife, and became known as The Queen's House. The present west front of the building, which opens onto extensive gardens, dates from 1825 when the architect was John Nash. But the present public aspect, which faces east, dates only from 1911 when it was redesigned as a backcloth for the outrageously hideous memorial to Queen Victoria which stands at the end of the mall.

The Victorian Memorial and Palace provide the destination for many grand formal processions of military type, but it is perhaps significant that the only London processions which contain "floats" in the style of Carnival have nothing to do with royalty. They form part of the Lord Mayor's Show which is held at the other end of town and which emphasizes the long-standing claims that the city of London has certain rights which are independent of the authority of the crown.

The Palace has been a regular residence of the reigning monarch since about 1850. One can only hope that the private apartments are more comfortable than the ornate splendors of the rooms which are open to the public.

The furnishings of these public rooms is quite comic in its ghastliness—a mixture of the guilded decadent baroque favored by George IV and the Victorians of the 1860s. The throne room, which is an immense rectangle 64 feet in length, dates from 1856 and retains all its original furnishings, including medallions of Prince Albert and the young Victoria worked into the panelling. In the labyrinthine passageways through which the visitor must pass on his way to the heart of things, the inevitable statuary consists largely of masterpieces of the 1850s, a truly astonishing period during which both British and American sculptors achieved the seemingly impossible feat of producing completely nude white marble ladies who are devoid of any semblance of sexuality.

All this is fairy-tale stuff; a proper setting for children at play. The "real" world of everyday life has been left far behind. In terms of the theory which I am propounding, this is very appropriate since these rooms and passages lie in an area of social ambiguity. At the time of the actual investiture, this imagery was intensified by the fact that the stairs and other points on the visitors' journey were guarded by sentries. The sentries were members of Her Majesty's Household Cavalry, on foot but otherwise dressed in their full regalia, which includes an armored breast plate appropriate to cavalry charges in the 17th century. The function of these sentries on the present occasion was to stand absolutely immobile for hours on end. As we went up the stairs I heard a small child whisper to its mother "Mummy, is it alive?" It was Alice's world behind the looking glass where everything was back to front.

As I remarked earlier, the investiture involved about 130 recipients of honors. At the head of the list came one recipient of an Order of Merit, (this really is a badge of distinction; there are never more than 24 at any one time and they come from all walks of life); then about a dozen knights of various grades; and then all kinds of lesser orders. What I have to say applies in the main only to the knights and, in particular, to the order of Knights Bachelor to which I myself, like most other civilian knights, belong.

The British institution of knighthood is very ancient; its history is mixed up with the emergence of European feudalism out of the remnants of Roman imperialism. In the battles of the 11th-century Crusades, armored knights on armored horses were the equivalent of the modern tank. But knighthood ceased to have any military significance at least as early as the middle of the 15th century. Ninety-nine percent of the present-day falderal, which is governed by an august body called the College of Heralds, was invented in the early part of the 19th century when the ravages of the industrial revolution produced (by dialectical reaction) an enthusiasm for antiquarian revivalism of all kinds. What we are talking about is a game invented by and played for the entertainment of adults.

In detail, I have no idea how Queen Elizabeth I initiated her knights at the end of the 19th century, but I feel pretty sure that, apart from changes in costume and other adjustments made necessary by the increased scale of the operation and the disappearance of most of the aristocracy, in 1975, Queen Elizabeth II was doing very much what her great-great-grandmother Victoria had done a century earlier. Just who invented the proceedings and what they had in mind when they did so is an interesting but largely unanswerable question. My concern is with the structure of the outcome, and to some extent with its mythology, but not immediately with its true history. As I shall explain presently, there are bits and pieces of the ritual which appear to be very old. But that is true of children's play-acting, too.

Although we do not know much about the details of the performances involved, we do know that the investiture of knights was originally an explicitly "religious" rite closely allied to the ordination of priests and the enthronement of bishops. In the late Middle Ages, one of the central issues in the struggle between the people and emperor was whether secular authorities had the right to hold investitures and thereby endow feudal knights with fiefdoms. The pope maintained that investiture was an exclusive prerogative of the church, but secular leaders successfully usurped this right and the patronage that went with it.

But enough of all this; let us get down to the ethnography. How does one become a knight?

The first thing that happens is that you receive a letter from the Patronage Secretary of the Prime Minister saying that the Prime Minister is minded to recommend to the Queen that you be appointed to a knighthood. Please sign on the dotted line to confirm that if so appointed you will accept the offer!

About a month later the actual list appears in *The Times*. At much the same time you receive a letter from some official in the College of Heralds asking for a subscription and instructing you to attend at the College to sign the roll. Once you have done this you are authorized to use your title. This however is a recent innovation; in the past you were not "actually" a knight until you had been dubbed by the monarch or her representative.

In due course you receive instructions from quite a different official about the date and procedure for the investiture at the Palace. The instructions specify time and style of dress and call for the names of guest witnesses, who can be any two persons, or three if two of them are your children. The dress instructions apply to the guests as well.

In the past when investitures were much smaller and confined to knights only, they were also much grander and more elitist and males were required to turn up in the fancy dress costume known as a "court dress." Even a generation ago this was usually hired for the occasion. The requirements are now much more lenient. Members of the armed services and the police appear in uniform, but civilians are simply advised: "morning dress or dark lounge suit."

In these plebeian days, "morning dress" for most people still implies a visit to a firm of dress-hire specialists. The ladies among the guests are advised to wear hats, but other details of dress are not specified. On this occasion they dressed to match their husbands; that is to say they put on costumes which they felt to be appropriate for a smart wedding. As to the males, a fair proportion of the guests, that is to say males in the audience, took advantage of the let-out and appeared in "dark lounge suits." However all the recipients of honors, right down the list (with one exception) appeared either in uniform or in morning dress. Appropriately, the one exception was the recipient of the highest honor of all, the Order of Merit. Since he had been through similar performances on a number of previous occasions, he was now so endowed with the potency of honor in his own right that he could ignore the rules altogether! He was dressed in a light-colored suiting appropriate to the hot summer weather outside.

And so on the appointed day, at 10 A.M., a queue of over-dressed local and national celebrities, with their spouses and offspring or perhaps less-legitimate associates, gathered outside Buckingham Palace on the east side. In due course they entered the Palace through a succession of courtyards appropriately decorated with 17th-century cavalrymen on foot (see Figure 4).

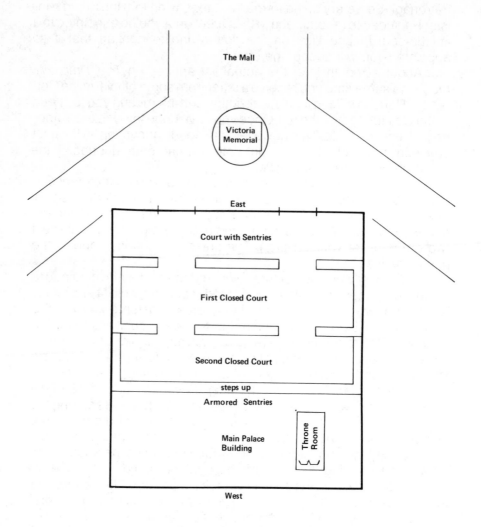

The Mall

Victoria
Memorial

East

Court with Sentries

First Closed Court

Second Closed Court

steps up

Armored Sentries

Main Palace
Building

Throne
Room

West

Present 'back' of Palace and Palace Gardens

Figure 4. Schematic layout of palace precincts.

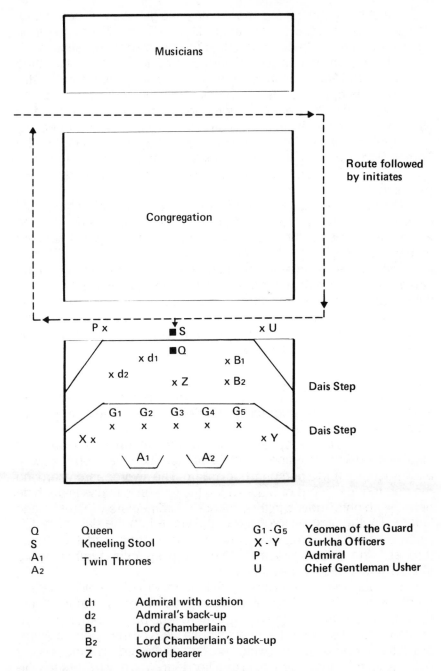

Figure 5. Layout of throne room for knight's investiture.

Once inside the Palace, the initiates and guests were separated. The guests proceeded directly to the Throne Room, where they took up seats which would be appropriate for the lay congregation in the nave of a parish church (see Figure 5). Secular light music dating from around 1900 was provided by the military band orchestra located at the opposite end of the room from the empty thrones. The initiates, meanwhile, were conducted to another part of the building where they were individually rehearsed in what they had to do.

At this point we need to look more closely at the layout of the Throne Room, bearing in mind the analogy with the general format of a sacrificial shrine and of a church to which I have already drawn your attention.

The band was placed in a kind of minstrels' gallery in what would have been the west end of a church. At the opposite end, located where the altar would be in a church setting, were the two ornate but empty thrones.

There are presumably certain grand state occasions when the Queen actually sits on her throne, though I don't know what they are. If this happened I feel sure she would be dressed in her full regalia— robes, crown, and all. But on this occasion the Queen was attired like an ordinary mortal; indeed, though elegantly dressed, she had clearly gone to some trouble not to upstage the female members of her audience. In terms of my general theory she was officiating as the priestess of a metaphysical divinity named "Sovereignty" whose unseen presence was symbolized by the empty thrones, but she was emphatically *not* masquerading as "Sovereignty" itself in her own person.

When the Queen appeared, she was accompanied by a covey of high-ranking service officers and Palace functionaries, together with a swordbearer and a personal bodyguard. The swordbearer, carrying the ceremonial Sword of State which the Queen is to use in dubbing her new knights, moved in the procession immediately in front of the Queen. By the time everyone was positioned on the dais area, the swordbearer stood midway between the Queen and the empty thrones. The sword, like the crown, is a specific symbol of the Queen's sovereignty (See Figure 5).

The bodyguard consisted of five members of the elite corps of much-bemedalled retired officers who form the Yeomen of the Guard, dressed in their splendidly picturesque but unauthentic 16th-century costumes, which resemble those worn by the Yeomen Warders of the Tower of London which are blazoned abroad by the posters of the British Tourist Agency. In addition there were two Gurkha Officers (Nepalese mercenaries). I don't know whether this is a regular feature or whether there was some special reason for their presence.

But the really interesting detail, from my point of view, was that when the members of the guard had taken up their stations on the daised area, they were quite clearly guarding the empty thrones and not the physical person of the Queen herself, who stood out in front (see Figure 5).

At the same time, the two Gurkha officers, a uniformed admiral, and the Chief Gentleman Usher of the Court took up positions at the four corners of a rectangle, thereby demarcating the limits of the sacred space within which the ritual process was about to take place. Notice carefully the arrangements within this rectangle.

Viewed from the Queen's orientation, the thrones are to the rear, the audience out in front. The initiates approach one at a time through a doorway to the right. They walk between the audience-congregation and the front of the defined ritual space.

Having reached the center of the room, the initiate then turns to face the Queen and the thrones and walks forward into the ritual space. He there kneels on a stool in front of the Queen, who is standing on the dais at a slightly higher level. The Queen dubs the kneeling knight on each shoulder with the flat of her Sword of State; he rises; she hangs the badge of his order around his neck (another recent innovation); they shake hands; the Queen says something appropriate to the particular initiate; the initiate bows, withdraws backward out of the ritual space and then moves off to the left.

Once he is outside the Throne Room, another functionary removes the badge of honor which the Queen has just bestowed, puts it in a case, and gives it back. The initiate then walks round to the back to join the audience.

On the dias on which the Queen is standing (which is a step lower than that on which the thrones are placed) are her various assistants. They are the Lord Chamberlain, holder of an office which dates back at least 700 years, whose function of this occasion was to read out the names of the initiates as they appeared; a checker, who seemed to be reading the same list to make sure that there was no slip up; another admiral in uniform, who handed the Queen the appropriate badges of honor, one by one, on a velvet cushion; and a backup for the admiral to make sure that *he* didn't get it wrong. The actual badges had been laid out on a table in advance.

All this is much as might have been expected. The Queen in her priestess role is a sacred person who cannot actually be touched even by an admiral. Hence the velvet cushion. Her role in the dubbing ceremony is to convey, by direct physical contact, an element of the power of sovereignty through the sword to the person of the initiate knight. But a detail which I had not appreciated until the performance was that the Queen would place the flat of her sword first on one shoulder and then on the other. In a symbolic sense the action is sacrificial. The priestess cuts off the victim's head.

I dare say that most of you will feel that this is just fantasy and I am sure that the Queen herself does not think of her action in that way. But from an anthropological point of view it makes a lot of sense. For here we are in the middle of a rite de passage and in such contexts, as is well known, the use of death and rebirth symbolism is extremely common. The initiate "dies" in his old status and is "reborn" in his new status. Moreover, sacrificial rites—the "making sacred" of the initiate—regularly form part of such initiatory proceedings. Where the sacrifices are real, the initiate dies vicariously because he is identified with the sacrificial victim, (as in the case of Temenggong Koh's Feast of Merit which I described earlier). In our present example no animal or human victim is actually killed, so it is appropriate that the symbolic killing should be directed against the initiate himself instead of against a vicarious substitute.

But if the dubbing implies the symbolic death of the knight to be, where is the symbolic rebirth? I shall come back to that point presently, but for the moment let me draw your attention to the several distinct sections of the Queen's performance: she dubs the kneeling knight with the sword; she hangs a badge round the neck of the standing knight; she shakes the knight by the hand; she says something—she exhibits the magical power of words; or in Malinowski's language, she utters a spell.

Another key point, which I shall elaborate presently, is that a knight's investiture is sometimes referred to as a "dubbing ceremony" and sometimes as "receiving the accolade." Contrary to some popular misconceptions, these are not just two names for the same thing; they refer to two distinct parts of a single sequence. The first is a symbolic slaying; the second a symbolic restoration to life.

For the present that is all I propose to say about the Buckingham Palace ethnography, but it seems to me that the structural parallels between my two cases, the Borneo slaughter of a pig as part of a Feast of Merit and the London investiture of a knight, are very close.

The key symbol in both cases is an empty throne, the seat of deity, the ancestor-hero Lang in the one case, the metaphysical concept of "Sovereignty" in the other. Both are viewed as sources of power. The purpose of the ritual performance is to convey some part of this power to the initiate, who thereby becomes properly qualified to assume his new title, his new social status.

The argument of course presupposes the appropriateness of Durkheim's formula which declares that, in the last analysis "God is society itself." In the London example, the sovereignty, which is exhibited in the symbols of the empty thrones and the sword and made manifest in the Queen's performance of her royal function is a very clear example of this principle.

But why should the 20th century British carry on in this way? Is the whole business just antiquarian, mediaeval, make-believe? Well, yes; this is play-acting but, as you all appreciate, play is a very serious business.

Indeed I would claim that in Britain it is from the validity of this symbolism that the legitimacy of the whole machinery of the state derives. This is Max Weber's point which he elaborated in particular with reference to the office of the Emperor of China. It was the *charisma* of the throne, rather than the individual emperor which was the ultimate source of the bureaucratic legitimacy of the Chinese *literati*. And so it is with the British except that, since the reigning monarch does not exercise any *actual* political power, it has become sociologically essential that the capacity of the monarch to legitimize status must be constantly reiterated by public demonstration.

A constitutional detail which is followed very punctiliously is that every new minister of the government of the day must attend personally at the Palace to "kiss hands." I have no idea what really happens on such occasions. But two points stand out: first, there is the clear implication that the legitimacy of the minister's authority as a servant of the Crown requires initiation by physical contact with the monarch; second, these ceremonials are private. Investitures, which, relatively speaking, are performed in public, are the counterpart of such private goings-on. Public approval of the play-acting of birthday and new year honors demonstrates indirectly a respect for the Constitution as a whole.

But enough of Durkheim and Weber. Let us get back to some contemporary anthropology. My ethnography bears on Victor Turner's association of rites de passage not only with liminality (as I have already done), but with what he calls "communitas," the breakdown of the hierarchical distinctions which separate the holders of public office in ordinary life.

Notice, for example, that the Queen was in ordinary dress, not ceremonial dress. She was separated from those who were seated at the front of her audience only by a passageway a few yards wide; she stood above them only by the height of the dais, a matter of 6 inches or so. She was representative of the throne, but in fact she was separated from the actual thrones by a line of guardsmen and a covey of functionaries. As a result she was among, or almost among, the ordinary people, or at any rate some of the more or less ordinary people. Nevertheless, she remained a sacred person. The badges of honor through which she conveyed the charisma of the Throne to the initiates had to be handed to her on a velvet cushion by an admiral.

But again, to emphasize the communitas angle, the various grades of initiate were all treated more or less alike. Only the knights were required to kneel and be tapped with a sword, and only the knights subsequently had their badges hung around their necks. In all the other cases the Queen simply pinned the badge on the initiate's left breast. The shaking of hands and the personal word of commendation were common to all. It is relevant here that it is only the knights who actually change their names and hence their social identity as a result of the ceremony. The others acquire an honor but not a new title.

This brings us back to the matter of the dubbing and the accolade and my improbable thesis that the dubbing symbolizes the cutting off of the knight's head.

As I said earlier, there are no grounds for thinking that the ceremonial which is now performed is ancient, though it does seem to contain ancient elements. Since at least the 17th century the expression "dubbing" has referred to the hitting on the shoulder of a kneeling knight with a sword held by the monarch. However, although the "accolade," which evidently refers to the neck (French *col*), was formerly described as an "embrace" or "kiss," this is not its present form.

In present-day England, shaking hands is the equivalent of the continental embrace around the neck, so I presume that both the shaking-hands element in the present ritual and the "kissing of hands" required of initiate ministers of state are derivative versions of the earlier accolade.

The earliest documentary reference to the dubbing of a knight goes back to 1085; unfortunately it is not clear what was involved. Initiate monks at that period were buffeted on each cheek by their ecclesiastic superior; the hitting of the initiate knight was the secular equivalent. The present practice of hanging a badge of office around the knight's neck is certainly very recent. It has the effect of reducing to a minimum the difference between the investiture of a knight and the investiture of lesser orders.

It seems possible that whoever invented the new procedure supposed that, since the knight's investiture needed to include an accolade, and an accolade has to do with the neck, then hanging a badge around the neck could serve as the accolade! If this is what happened then they were certainly misinterpreting the rules. The point about the accolade (if you accept my thesis) is that, in Van Gennep's language, it is "a rite of aggregation"; the initiate, having been "killed" in his old role, must be "restored to life" in his new one. To achieve this, the power of sovereignty must flow through the Queen to the initiate. It is the physical contact with the Queen's body which achieves this end. It is the shaking of hands which is the modern accolade!

But having asserted my opinion in this categorical way I need to consider a question which must be worrying some of you. What is the status of interpretations of this sort? None of the participants (other than the sole anthropologist present) had any conception that they were participating in a religious rite, and most of them would have been highly indignant if anyone had suggested that they were.

And by their criteria they were surely right. The band was not playing hymn tunes but music hall melodies of the era of "A Bicycle

Made for Two"! And anyway they would one and all have laughed to scorn my suggestion that the dubbing of a knight is analogous to a heathen animal sacrifice. So what is my justification for reshuffling the cards in this way?

Well, quite clearly my assertions are not scientific statements; they cannot be validated in any way; they cannot be disproved. They are more like the free associations of a patient on a psychoanalyst's couch. Yet they increase my insight into what was going on. I do not believe that people attempt to preserve "ye olde customes" just because they are old or just because they are customary; they do so because such behavior tends to give satisfaction to some kind of socio-psychological need. As Malinowski often asserted, all customary behavior is functional in the present; it is not just an odd survival from the past. The problem is to know what that function is. To say that it appeals to our need for play hardly seems adequate.

Opinions will differ here even among anthropologists of similar general orientation, but my own view is that an analysis of this sort, even though it may appear trivial, gives me a better understanding of why such archaic institutions as knighthood and investiture show the vitality that they do and why even cynics like myself can feel genuinely pleased, genuinely honored, by initiation into an office which carries with it no rewards or responsibilities of any kind.

And by feedback, I feel that this kind of mental and structural association tells me as a professional anthropologist something about the essential nature of sacrifice that I did not know before.

Van Gennep's insight concerning the three-phase structure of a rite of passage is penetrating and far reaching. In order to start again in a new role, the initiate must first escape from this world into a fairyland of the imagination where everything goes backwards. From that "land of the dead" where he loses his head he can then return to the real world "reborn."

The "other world" of the imagination can take many forms. In particular, it can be sedately archaic as in Buckingham Palace, or it can take on the aspect of a frenzied orgy as in the Rio de Janeiro carnival described by Roberto da Matta or the New Orleans Mardi Gras. But its function is the same in each case: it is other; it is the world of play; it is Alice's Wonderland seen backwards through the looking glass.

But of course my general point is much simpler. You do not have to go all the way to the Trobriand Islands or to Tikopia or to Sarawak either to observe the exotic or to practice anthropology. Right here in Louisiana will do very well.

Note

1. Koh's Longhouse was of the traditional Iban type, that is to say it was constructed wholly of bamboo and raised some 20 feet above ground level. The longhouse community consisted at

this time of 26 households, each with its own "room" (*bilek*). The *bilek* group was in effect the owner of the whole section of the longhouse (from back to front), which included their room. Seen from the front, the house consisted of three longitudinal sections: an uncovered verandah running the whole length of the house; a covered verandah also running the whole length of the house; a series of *bilek* rooms, each partitioned off from the next. The cooking area for each *bilek* was independent and tacked on to the rear of the sleeping area. Figure 1 is only schematic. The cooking area for Koh's *bilek* room (which was roughly in the middle of the string of 26 rooms) was "at the back," that is to say at the bottom of the diagram in Figure 1. The portion of the open verandah which included Lang's shrine and the sacrificial pig was considered to pertain to Koh's *bilek* room.

PLAY IN THE FACE OF DEATH: TRANSGRESSION AND INVERSION IN A WEST INDIAN WAKE

Roger D. Abrahams
Scripps College

When we play, we seem to alleviate the need to account for our actions. Diderot noted this with regard to the paradox of the actor on stage not having his performance motives or moves attributed to him off-stage. But the principle goes far beyond stage work and enters into the realm of any of those stumbling, embarrassing, harmful activities we find excuses for in everyday actions by saying that we were really "just playing." Borrowing from full-out play and its license, we say "I'm only joking," or "just kidding," all of which invoke play—or playfulness—as a social repair device. Whether or not we want to regard such rhetorical strategies as pointing to real play or not (and I think they don't), the fact that we have such hedges does indeed tell us something about that ontological state in which everyone agrees that play is going on.

Gregory Bateson (1977) showed us that playing does not operate successfully unless we can truly ask whether actions taking place on the stage, the playing field, or the festival grounds are really to be exempted from such judgment. The way Bateson put it was that all activities within the play frame must remind us that play is in process; at the same time, they must remind us to question whether it really is taking place. This carries the corollary question: Might we not as members of society find ourselves on some occasions asking this question directly of the players, as when a game seems to have turned into a grudge match, or even more, when actors play a part that carries a social or political message with which they have

My thanks to Brian Sutton-Smith for making the occasion of the presentation of this paper possible and especially for his outrageous introduction. Thanks also to Don Brenneis and Jay Edwards, and my wife Janet, for their critical readings.

been identified off-stage? This becomes especially problematic in situations of deep play, where the intensity, the investment in the exchange, the degree of focus, and the representative symbolic character of the activity are so profound that it is often difficult to draw the line between "just play" and deep seriousness.

The paradoxical conditions of play become all the more central when looking closely at play actually being carried off, because the relationship between the motives within the playing and the cognate activities outside will often provide clues to major cultural themes. This is an especially vexing question when the activity is not simple mimetic play but involves a transgression of social rules or cultural categories, whether in the form of simple noisemaking, drunkenness, and befouling the environment, or simply displaying selective trans-gressions regarding everyday values and practices. Invoking license "in play" often leads to the extension of that license to depict and explore motives that we are not permitted to examine through enact-ment outside that specially distanced, stylized, and intensified environment of the play-stage. To be sure, this inversive move is not the focus of the play, but a kind of by-product. But by drawing on such a vocabulary of moves once play goes on, such motives enter into the proceedings to intensify the occasion, thus making it more fun.

Such inversive motives, now exempted from full judgment on moral grounds, become the embodiment of the dark side of a cul-ture's vocabulary. And as a great many anthropological (as well as lit-erary) followers of Mikhail Bakhtin have demonstrated, to discover a culture's orders and values, it is necessary not only to detail its ideals but its transgressions as well (Bakhtin, 1968). This seems espe-cially so when the transgression with its subversive motives is deployed in traditional—and therefore repeated and repeatable— practices.

If play involves committing such transgressions even while we are saying "just kidding, only kidding, only kidding," it occurs to me that the study of the processes and the expressive repertoire of play-ing then provides a primary means of mapping the transgressions permitted and even encouraged by a group. To do so is to point out those places where the ordinary and the extraordinary, the most mundane and the most intensely attention-gathering, energetic, and creative activities come together in what becomes a no-man's land—a time-space or chronotope in which all meanings and values may be up for reassignment. The community agrees to the fiction that play is a liberating activity, but not because it represents a cultural retreat from being orderly or even moral. Rather, it is freeing because play establishes this zone of betweenness, one we could call a free-fire zone because of its enclosed dangers, or a fire-free zone because all the vegetation has been burned off ahead of time and or the creative growing that can arise because of its interstitial character.

Bakhtin (1968) designates just such an in-between location, the marketplace, as representing all such liberating transgressions, and refers to the process as the "carnivalization" of society and culture. Carnival represents to him the paradigmatic occasion for bringing marketing behaviors into performances, which he refers to as a gathering place for strangers, ones who come to enter into intense exchanges, whether in pursuit of trade (both products and services) of aesthetic energies between players and a potential audience, or through the coercive exchanges carried out by beggars or their king. Bakhtin's description of the role of the market as an in-between place of noise and of coercive interaction of rapid alteration between displays of high praise and decorum and low talk and cursing (and often by the same words with performers) conveys many of the most important characteristics of all such worlds of transgression.

Such symbolic play worlds can be created in other in-between places marked by permitted transgression. Indeed, many feasts and festivals and even rituals may draw on the cockeyed motive as a way of announcing that play is in process. Where this occurs in the midst of ritual, or some other condition of life passage, the messages delivered are especially complex, as in the situation I discuss here: the St. Vincentian West Indian response to a death in the family. Specifically, I discuss how storytellers stumble into such a cockamamie world and draw upon the undistributed energies that arise in the face of death. Such occasions encourage a jocular discussion of some of the most dearly held fictions by which family, community, and society are held together—by describing circumstances back when animals could talk about how things might, in fact, come apart.

On St. Vincent in the West Indies, many storytellers tell of the king who set a task for his two children, his son and daughter, that they must go from the king's yard and into the bush and collect flowers to bring back to him. Whichever of them returned with the most beautiful bouquet would get riches from the king. (In one version it is the kingdom that would be won.) They set off together, but took their separate ways. The boy, looking across the meadow, saw that his sister had found flowers much more beautiful than his, so he sneaked up behind her in the meadow where she was, hit her over the head and killed her, and buried her there, taking her flowers back to his father. There he and his parents waited for a long time for the young girl to come back, but return she did not.

One day a pasture-boy (for that is what they call shepherds there) and his dog were out tending the flocks, and the dog began to dig a hole under a large willow tree in the meadow. The dog brought back a bone to the pasture-boy. When the boy picked it up it began to sing:

Oh pasture-boy, oh pasture-boy
Take care the bone you blow
My brother has murdered me
And taken my flowers away
He dug a grave and buried me,
Beneath that willow tree.

The pasture-boy took the bone to the king, where it sang again, and the king called on his son to hold the bone, and it repeated the song of accusation. The king thereupon had his son killed for the terrible deed he had done.

Many of you will recognize this story, for it is very widely found throughout the Old World and New. In English we know it best through the ballad of "The Two Sisters," in which one woman's jealousy causes her to kill her sibling, pushing her into a mill-pond. When the body is fished out, a fiddler (or harper) passing by fashions an instrument out of the bones and hair, and it sings out its dreadful message (Child, 1965). To folklorists the story is known as "The Singing Bones," and it is reported as tale-type 780 in *The Types of the Folktale* (Aarne & Thompson, 1961).

By the fact that this story is so widely found does not begin to account for why it is oft-told and sung in this Afro-American island in the Caribbean. The fact that St. Vincent was for some time a French and then an English possession may explain how the story got there, but not why it took root. For, even though storytelling remains an important entertainment form and is placed at the center of the activities during one of their most significant events—the wake, or nine-night—a large proportion of the stories told there are of the sort more common to the African (spider-trickster, the name is a carry over from the Akan), who messes up everyone's lives for the sheer sake of self-interest. Indeed, all Vincentian stories are called *Nansi'tory*, even the one about the singing bone.

It is not immediately apparent how this serious moral tale told at a wake, an occasion of communal bereavement, is a device of play. But in the terms of Vincentians themselves, the story is a piece of nonsense and the nine-nights the most appropriate occasion for just such foolishness. In discovering this, I found myself revising my understanding of what play is, how it operates in non-Western contexts, and how important it is not to be intellectually fenced in by our own notions of play.

Moreover, the lesson has been especially hard won for me as a folklorist. Until recently, the members of our discipline have seldom brought to bear the notions of cultural context to our studies of the life of stories (or songs or whatever). Thus, the concept of cultural relativity has had little effect on our research. We have been concerned with texts in transmission, serving as cultural historians to the extent that we trace the career of individual items as they persevere in inter-national currency. I want to discuss some of the details of how this folklorist got from the comparativist tradition to one in which I operate more as an ethnographer.

Throughout my professional life I have collected, organized, and analyzed the folklore of play. I have not only worked in two methodo-logical traditions, the comparativist and the ethnographic, but in two culture areas, Afro-America and Anglo-America. However, I have not attempted to synthesize the two, other than to propose some theoretical notions regarding play that would account for the entire range of these ludic practices. As a comparativist folklorist I have worked with Western, mostly English-language materials, bringing together in dictionary form the accumulated texts of childlore, attempting to give a sense of the vigor and integrity of those specific performed items recorded in print (Abrahams, 1969; Abrahams and Rankin, 1980). These compendia make the commonsense assump-tion that there is a radical disjuncture between childhood and other sharable somatic states and that this lore illustrates just what childish concerns and practices are.

From the folklorist's perspective, childlore provides perfect examples of items in oral transmission, for the players are pre-literates. Thus, one can observe in children's songs, rhymes, games, riddles, tricks, and even certain formulaic stories the "pure" opera-tion of oral transmission over time and place. This is not the place to discuss the unexamined fictions that such a perspective relies upon. With or without the fiction, we are left with an immense body of such texts that have an integrity, a vigor, and an interest of their own. This Western perspective insists on this disjunction because in the main, we continue to identify play with childhood and the freedom of those of that age to enter into productive activities except as they enter into the development of skills. But, sad to report, the development of these dictionaries has not yet led to the larger kinds of analytic arguments by folklorists attempting to come to terms with those abundant data (but see Kirshenblatt-Gimblett, 1976; Stewart, 1980).

In a series of essays, on the other hand, I have made some initial attempts to explore "native" Western or American theory of play, both through discussing the ontological changes that occur whenever players use such traditional verbal devices to connect with each other, reminding all that play is taking place—or in the case of count-ing-out rhymes, about to take place—and by contrasting the term "play" itself with those for other display activities: games, per-formances, show, ritual (Abrahams, 1977, 1980, 1981, 1982).

But for such cultural semantic probes, in combination with the fieldwork I have carried out in Afro-American communities, it has become evident that the very word "play" may be employed in differ-ent contexts in other cultural settings, and that much of the discussion on ludic activities might be ethnocentric. Let me illustrate what I mean by comparing some differences in the Anglo-American and Afro-American employment of the term. In both culture areas, I have found play contrasted to work; but the dimensions of contrast differ. In Western cultures, especially America, work is what we do—that is, how we validate ourselves by employing our energies productively. It is also, therefore, what we like to talk about. In fact, the more professional we are in our work, the more license we seem to gather to ourselves to talk about what we do; thus the lesser need to actually spend time doing it. Play in this view is trivial precisely because it is deployed energies which need not be productive. In the black communities in which I have done fieldwork, I encountered a different approach to the work-play contrast. Work is not, in the main, a discussable subject; play is. Moreover, work tends to be private, play a public activity. One is known for how good, how effective a player one is, a subject for discussion concerning adults, youths, and children, and one that receives a great deal of attention. One's reputation may rely on how fully and enthusiastically one plays.

Obviously, in these communities, I found a number of activities that were regarded as play forms appropriate for only children to engage in. But the patterns and the vocabulary of play indicated a continuity between the various age groups. The word "play" itself is commonly used to refer to a wide-range of public activities throughout anglophonic Afro-America, from the casual verbal kicking up of the heels to entering into the more elaborate and prepared-for events like grand balls and fetes (widely called *plays*), and becoming a part of a group effort at festival time (one plays Carnival or Christmas sports, for instance). It is difficult to discern how important these differences really are, for the same sort of process may be a part of our Anglo-American cultural practices as well, but we have not looked to these continuities in how we describe and judge play.

"Play" has many synonyms in West Indian talk. The one area of playing that receives the greatest amount of discussion and elaboration relates to the idea of permitted disorders, inversions, and transgressions, variously referred to as foolishness, or even more commonly, nonsense. I propose to analyze this elaborate native concept by looking at the ways in which nonsense takes on meaning in the traditional tales told on one nonsense occasion, the "nine-night" or "wake," as it is employed in Richland Park, St. Vincent.

One of the most consistent features of African practices that has been maintained and indeed has proliferated in the New World is the high value placed on verbal facility expressed in competitive displays of wit. In its more casual eruptions especially characteristic of male gatherings it is called variously "signifying," "sounding," "woofing," and in its most tendentious forms, "playing the dozens" in the United States. As Henry-Louis Gates (1984) has argued, signifying is not only a set of devices of verbal play but an ironic and deconstructionist view of life, one that provides a critical perspective useful in developing adaptive strategies in the many different situations faced by New World Blacks here.

In the West Indies, a great many similar practices may be found in a number of settings. Best known perhaps are the satiric song-making traditions of the calypsonians on Trinidad (and now throughout the anglophonic islands, as well as in the West Indian outposts in the United States, Canada, and Great Britain) and the *sambistas* who rule Carnival in Rio.

On St. Vincent such signifying, whether of the everyday rumshop variety or the more extensive, stylized, and intense public display events, goes under the name of nonsense. Though obviously employed in the pejorative sense, nonsense is used as a synonym for play, and its practice is regarded as the creative heart of community life and highly valued as such. So long as nonsense is kept to the public places, especially areas where the men sit around "limin' and blaggin'," it is looked upon simply as an expression of male nature. In St. Vincent, as elsewhere in the West Indies, nature means statements about the Vicentian "way we are," as in: "That's the way we men are," "That's how children are; children are, you know, rude, rude, rude, rude!" and other such folk accounts for wild behavior. What is strange is that such wild and natural activity comes to the fore in the event of a death in the community. In such a situation, certain kinds of inversive activities that would commonly be seen as destructive of family continuity and respectability are actually drawn upon.

As many commentators have pointed out, West Indian life is, in a sense, biculturated; that is, two sets of situated behaviors are available. One is associated with respectability, order, stability, family continuity, females, older people, and the house-and-yard area in which private business is carried out. The other is the more public and expansive, energetic, and resourceful side of expressive life, associated with the marketplace, crossroad, rumshop, cricket field, males, the young, and the code of friendship-making or reputation.

For purposes of economy, I have provided a breakdown of content and interactional practices as they are played out in one domain or the other.

Each of these domains, the yard and the crossroad, have traditional events that are not only celebrated at such places but that explicitly spell out, in the content of the performances, the variety of language employed and the nature of the gestural systems, the "meanings" associated with the events. The major house and yard events are *thanksgivings, send-offs, baptisms,* and *marriage fetes.* Those held at the more public points of congregation culminate in Carnival, but include maroons (picnics held on Emancipation Day) and Christmas serenading (going from December 24 to January 5), as well as special national holidays. The following is a list of performance features that characterize each domain as they contrast with the other:

Yard	**Crossroads**
Private world.	Public world, keeping company.
Family (generational organization).	Friendship networks (peership organization).
Order, acting sensible.	License, being sporty, talking nonsense.
Decorum, behaving.	Rudeness.
Stability, passivity.	Mobility, activity.
Enclosed, protected.	Free, adventurous.
Circumspection.	Gregariousness, flash, keeping company.
Quiet harmony.	Noise to annoy, *vexation, boderation* (arguments, usually playful); making mock; giving fatigue (badinage).
Feminine values.	Masculine values.
Respectable maintenance (acceptance principle).	Reputation maintenance (heroic attitudes, superphalicism)
Truth, honesty, cooperation, loyalty.	*Gettin' on fas',* untrustworthiness, playful trickery, deceit.

Household Rites	**Road Festivities**
Performances in house.	Performances at crossroads, rumshops, open fields; yards only when invited.
Eating involved; drinking for toasts only within house; bottles passed into yard.	Drinking of rum emphasized.
Emphasis on sensible activities in speeches (truth, knowledge, continuity, respect).	Emphasis on nonsense in speeches, on lies and other foolishness.

cont.

Texts are logical in organization.	Texts often involve constant nonsequiturs, puns, other kinds of discontinuities.
Texts affirm social order and responsibility, focus on individual's acceptance on approved social role.	Texts often satirize social order, hypocrisy of individuals, focus on wrongdoings.
Performances emphasize the derivation from the past to these social roles, these roles are intensified through stylized actions and formal clothing.	Social disorder and license emphasized through rude behavior, motley or animalistic costuming; texts oriented toward inducing social confusion and embarrassment.
Texts emphasize progression in life. They invoke consciously mature motives by discussion of moving into one's place in the community.	Texts focus on regressive motives, emphasizing childish or "animal" or "underworld" (criminal or diabolical) behaviors.
Texts use complimentary address forms, emphasizing social harmony.	Texts are ego-centered, using stylized boasts, curses, argumentation.
Orderly performance presided over by chairman (master of ceremonies), who is responsible for maintaining flow of performance.	*Sporty fellow* seizes spotlight, makes as much noise as possible, acts rude.
Performers sit or stand rigidly; lack of facial animation (until in some cases, a joke is given at the end). No touching of other performers.	Much animation-walking, dancing, disjointed comic movement, menacing of crowd, beating. Much touching between performers, and performers and audience.
Performance coordination; everyone may perform serially when designated by leader.	Competitive, aggressive performances; much overlap of voices, movements; constantly shifting dramatic focus, as one or another performer or group intrudes themselves.
Performance speaking variety: *talking sweet, good, sensible.*	Performance speaking variety: *talking broad, bad, broken*

(from Abrahams, 1983)

The reality of this system resides in those events that do not subscribe to the contrasts in domain, content, or performance styles. On one occasion, for instance, the hanging, a public event, is made of private misdoings. In these mock trials and burnings in effigy, a song is sung about scandalous goings-on in a yard that have been brought to public notice. This provides the content and the point of departure for fun-making play carried out most commonly at the local cricket and football field.

Similarly, in tea meeting, ostensibly a public event taking place in a lodge hall or church school, speeches are made on timely subjects (e.g., Christmas, Easter, Emancipation Day) by the local chairmen and their young scholars. But here an active confrontation occurs between these men of words and the *rude boys* and strident market women who yell out curses, insults, and other kinds of nonsense talk in order to test the cool abilities of the actors.

But the anomaly in the system with which I am most concerned is the wake, for this takes place in the house and yard but calls for some of the deepest kinds of nonsense in the performance economy of the community. The nonsense of the yard and of the house, then, is play of a specially transgressive sort. Here trickster and his followers are not only allowed into this most private area; the events taking place are dedicated to him. Every organized activity held within the house during nine-night is called *Nansi 'tory*, whether it be riddling, game playing, or the actual tale telling. In the face of death, the most ludicrous variety of the impulse to play is called upon. All social bonds are held up to deep questioning without calling for any attempt to provide answers. The fabric of the community, already rent, is celebrated in a rags-and-tatters manner without any felt need to sew it back together. What seems to be taking place on this occasion is that energy itself is celebrated, whether in a life-enhancing or destructive form.

Let me survey the variety of perverse acts being carried out on this occasion:

- the valorized spaces and boundaries of the community are upended, reassigned their opposed values for the moment, the yard now serving in the place of the crossroad, the house now articulated as if it were rumshop;
- the activities within the house are all highly elaborated playings out of nonsense motives and in the deepest of nonsense talk, that is, in rapid-fire Creole;
- the performances depict and, through mimicry, may act out the most unrespectable kinds of behavior, thus bringing scandalizing to a high art, giving the impression that the respect-seeking motives that commonly are maintained in this place (and celebrated in all of the other house-based ceremonial events) are built upon the flimsiest of social fictions.

In this perhaps too neat division, the nine-night observation is extraordinarily anomalous. But like many anomalies, it is comprehensible within the terms of the overall symbolic system because of the self-conscious vocabulary by which departures are made from the norm. Of these, the realignment of symbolic spaces is underscored here not only to dramatize the range of inversive possibilities, but because the tales told in the name of *Compé Anansi* are themselves commentaries on this realignment. By this I simply mean that *Anansi 'tories* are, in the main, concerned with the strange behaviors that take place in people's yards.

Indeed, this is precisely the major theme of the singing bones story that I described earlier, the strange goings-on in the houses and yards of the powerful. Let me replay the plot in these more Vincentian terms for clarification and so that the process of the transmission of this European-style *märchen* (and others of the same sort) may be better understood. Something unusual is going on in the house of Massa King. In the first place, he has, in a supreme act of foolishness, demanded of his children that, acceding to his authority, they compete for riches by leaving the yard and going into the bush to collect flowers. From the Vincentian perspective this is a matter of testing nature—that is, the way people in specific roles are, rather than the way they are supposed to be. To Vincentians this nature is really a regression to wildness, to the animal side of existence. The King's son, then, follows his nature in this bush setting far away from the house and yard of Massa King in committing the unnatural act of murder. Discovery of the deed is brought to our attention by a figure, the "pashah boy," who at first blush seems to be an insignificant character in the on-going drama. But in the dramatis personae of *Nansi 'tory*, such figures are the instigators of action, the almost invisible members of the extended household who, acting from their marginal position, are able to engineer the revelation of the foolishness and the dissolution of the family bond. He is a member of the household but only marginally described as dirty, covered with ashes and sores, living with the animals and mostly in the bush. Bear in mind that in a tropical climate domesticated animals are constantly moved from place to place in the bush, usually by being staked at one place and allowed to graze only as far as the tether permits. The animals are seldom brought into the yard. The pasture boy in most households is commonly the one with the least power and is often the one too young or too foolish (*trupidy*) to perform any other task. Moreover, jokes are made about the sexual congress that purportedly goes on between the boy and the animals.

Thus, from the Vincentian perspective, the power alignment of Massa King's household is inverted and disfigured when it is the pashah boy who is the bearer of the bone and thus the agent of destructive revelations. It is not the murder itself that is reprehensible, but its discovery and subsequent republication. To put it in structural terms, the story begins with the pronouncement of the household arrangement of affection and authority, a situation in which the bond is broken first by a foolish test, then by a sibling murder, and finally by a revelation. It is a pattern of progressive dissolution of family and friendship relations, which characterize a great majority of the stories told on this occasion.

Another example that derives from the European tradition stems directly from the British cautionary ballad known as "Little Musgrave and Lady Bernard" in the Child Collection (where it is number 81) but is more commonly called "Little Mattie Groves" in American collections. This is a simple tale of adultery in which Lord Arnold's wife seduces her pageboy, Little Mattie. The Lord is informed of the deed, returns and catches them in bed together, and dispatches them, in common ballad form, by force of sword. In its Vincentian rendering, again, the basic plot is changed little. Miss Notty is married to a gentleman Master who goes off to work away from home. She is visited at night by another man, Garoleen. A parrot living there observes what is happening and warns the bedded pair that it is time to desist. He sings:

> If any man, if any man
> In another nex' man' home
> It is time, it is time,
> For to rise and go home.

But then he flies to where his Master is working and sings another song (to the same tune)!

> Oh master dear, oh master dear
> I don't tell you no lie.
> Miss Notty' dey (there), Miss Notty' dey
> On your bed with Garoleen.

The parrot then flies back and forth singing the two songs over and over, but the pair in bed heed him not. When they are caught, the Master shoots them both.

Again, in this story the action is carried on by three characters who are placed in a position of being shamed through the agency of an outside observer who, in terms of the outcome, has nothing to gain. In a sense, the pashah boy and the parrot represent society in calling attention to deep wrongdoings that need taking care of. They are instigators of action rather than actors themselves.

Most Vincentian stories have a character like this one who gets things going seemingly for the joy of seeing what will happen. This is precisely how Compé Nansi himself operates in most of the tales in which he is included as an actual character. To be sure, he is given greater motivation for instigating things, for in addition to being playful and childlike he is greedy, lusty, and in every way deceitful. Therefore, when he acts it is because he focuses on something that he wants to take away from others. But the outcomes of such stories are similar, for we witness in his doings the breaking down of all relationships and boundaries (Dundes, 1971; Edwards, 1978). He, too, insinuates himself into other people's yards (and the regular goings-on there) and manages to mess up everything, thus reminding us of his other name, Buh Nasty.

The strangest and most ubiquitous of these in-between characters, however, is one who emerges in a great many tales, the Old Witch Boy. Just as Compé Nansi betrays his imperfect character by his inability to talk correctly (he stutters and lisps), the Old Witch Boy is physically marred. He is also called the Jiggerfoot or Chiggerfoot Boy, and one foot is depicted as clubbed or diseased. This characteristic is the key to his social status as well, for he is part of the king's family yet he lives in the corner or under the bed, and is regarded as a filthy and *trupidy* figure.

Repeatedly the Old Witch Boy becomes involved in the drama of Massa King's family whenever a suitor arrives and wins the hand of the favored child, the King's Beautiful Daughter. (None of the royal family is commonly given names other than these generic labels.) Usually, the daughter is kept hidden, falls in love with someone she happens to see passing by, sneaks out and runs away with (or marries) him. But the Jiggerfoot Boy has discovered through his witching powers that this man is really an animal, devil, or *jumbie* (ghost). Often, he tries to tell the Queen, but is sent away to his usual place of shame. After the new couple go back to his home, the Old Witch Boy follows them, discovers the source of the man's phallic ascendency, and finds a way to reveal or defeat it and bring his sister back home. There is seldom any suggestion that his lot has changed because of this good deed, other than to remark that the daughter sometimes cleans his feet for him. Thus, his position in these stories, while more sentimentally affecting because of his place of rejection in the family, differs little from the instigator role of the pashah boy or the parrot.

Looking at it this way, the wake on St. Vincent is a totally liminal event, one not only played in the name of trickster but invigorated by this character or other characters who stir things up just to see what will happen. Playing in the face of death is the deepest kind of play. It rebuilds the social and natural world for the moment, reduces life to an operation of nature, and revises our very notion of how stories may successfully embody meaningful motives. Under these extreme conditions, we see not only that Anansi will have his time, but that from a folkloristic point of view, stories that are told in the Western tradition as morality tales centering on the doings of heroes and villains are translated into laughable nonsense, narratives that are as concerned with publicizing strange doings as with the doings themselves. It is under such special cultural conditions that tales in the wide circulation undergo extreme changes, producing oicotypes or special local renderings of international tales (Von Sydow, 1948).

Both the tale of the singing bones and that of the discovered lovers illustrate how such oicotyping operates. They emerge from traditions in which the driving force of the story revolves around a violation-discovery-punishment narrative structure, and in these West Indian renderings they may be interpreted this way. But being seen as *Nansi 'tory* puts them in a different light, as evidence of a different structure operating simultaneously in which it is not the violation but the discovery that is the most important narrative "move" (or, as folklorists put it, "motifeme"). Here the work of Dundes, Haring, and especially Edwards has been of great assistance in seeing the alternative pattern characteristic of African and, by extension, Afro-American trickster tales. Edwards' (1981) latest rendering of the paradigm phrases it most usefully with regard to the oicotyping process:

> Unlike the majority of European folktales, Afro-American (trickster) tales terminate in a condition of disharmony between two principal actors caused by a violation of an agreement and an unreciprocated exchange of values. These characteristics . . . are not . . . (ones) which predominate in many tale-telling traditions. (p.160)

Edwards focuses here on the trickster tale alone. If one extended the notion beyond these tales about Anansi or Brer Rabbit, however, a slightly different reading of Afro-American oicotypical patterns begins to assume shape. When one of the two major characters in the action is trickster, the contract violation pattern is to be almost universally discovered. But when *märchen* or some other Indo-European pattern is found in the Afro-American repertoire, where the interloper is not one of the major interactants, one finds such a role elaborated upon. A marginal creature is placed in the position where all secret goings-on can be revealed. Again, "disharmony" is the result, though such a chaotic move is not necessarily the only way in which a story may be ended. Here, the occasion and social condition of the telling becomes all important for an understanding of this oicotyping tropism. These stories are told within the nonsense environment of the wake, one in which enigmatic and confrontational motives have become the expected (if not the norm). Dissolution of friendship and family certainly are interesting motives and patterns to put into play on the wake occasion.

In the construction of these Nansi stories, then, within the context of the wake, we are forced to confront a basic enigma: Why is it that at the very time when one might reasonably expect narratives with a transcendental message we are given narratives that underscore disruption and distrust? Moreover, they are stories told in the house-and-yard complex that represent the silliest and most reprehensible actions, the very kind that are the subject of gossip were they to occur in everyday life, inasmuch as they dramatize patterns of social dissension and dissolution.

Because this is a nonsense occasion, answers to such basic questions do not come easily, precisely because the goings-on in the house and the yard have already become public with the death. With the introduction of such a disjunction in the household, to place the power on inversion in the doings of structurally insignificant members of the family seems meaningful but difficult to "read" precisely because the doings themselves are laughed at and regarded as special to occasion. I have argued in the past (Abrahams, 1983) that the nine-night provides an occasion for the enigma of death to be named and given a laughable projection, thus underscoring the need of the community to consign the body and soul to its appropriate resting place.

The structure of the Anansi stories and the instigating role of outcast figures seem to be entering a different strategy of presenting life and death and the threat that death brings to the surface with regard to family relationships. Perhaps all comment on such matters is compromised by the inversions that occur on this occasion. Not least of these complicating factors is that these stories concern themselves with non-normal families insofar as the older male (especially in the stories about Massa King and his family) represents the ordering power of the household, which is hardly the common case in the Vincentian family. When one adds to this the fact that some informants indicated that they envisaged Massa King as a white man, the interpretive questions become all the more profound. What may be said without question is that under the conditions of license on this nonsense occasion, all manner of social realignments come into the ludicrous discussion, not least of which are the strange things that can be discovered going on in people's yards and houses once one is allowed to go through the gates. The stories belong to trickster, after all, and perhaps we must interpret them as such, as the world depicted from the perspective of the margins, the nooks and crannies, when these laughable characters are finally brought to the center of family and community and given their nine-nights.

Play, then, in the form of a trangressive attitude, a willingness to test, mess around, or rearrange, enters into Vincentian affairs in a way that reminds the community of life's vigor and continuity. This amplifies our vision of how play engages with the largest movements of life, serving not only as a way of testing social and cultural boundaries in the pursuit of personal and social development, but maintaining the sense of open passage between the worlds of the dead and living. To do this, the world of the living is rearranged and revalued, at least for the moment of the wake. Here, then, life-and-death matters are subjected to investigation in play, play in the very face of death, but in a world of laughter.

REFERENCES

Abrahams, R.D. (1969). *Jump-rope rhymes: A dictionary.* Austin: University of Texas Press.

Abrahams, R.D. (1977). Toward an enactment theory of folklore. In W. Bascom (Ed.), *The frontiers of folklore* (pp. 79-120). Washington: AAAS.

Abrahams, R.D. (Ed.) (1980). *Counting-out rhymes: A dictionary.* (with L. Rankin). Austin: University of Texas Press.

Abrahams, R.D. (1981). In and out of performance. In *Folklore and oral communication* (pp. 69-78). Narodna Umjestnost, Yugoslavia.

Abrahams, R.D. (1982, June). Play and games. *Motif 2* (1), 5-7.

Abrahams, R.D. (1983). *The man-of-words in the West Indies.* Baltimore: The Johns Hopkins Press.

Aarne, A., & Thompson, S. (1961). *The types of the folktale: A classification and bibliography* (2nd ed.). Helsinki: Suomalaineu Tiedeakatemia.

.khtin, M. (1968). *Rabelais and his world* (H. Iswolsky, Trans.). Cambridge, MA: MIT Press.

Bateson, G. (1977). *Steps to an ecology of mind.* San Francisco: Chandler Publishing Company.

Child, F.J. (1965). *The English and Scottish popular ballads* (Vols. 1-5). New York: Dover Reprints (Original work published 1882-1898).

Dundes, A. (1971). The making and breaking of friendship as a structural frame in African tales. In P. & E. Kongas-Maranda (Eds.). *Structural analyses of oral tradition* (pp. 171-189). Philadelphia: University of Pennsylvania Press.

Edwards, J. (1978). *The Afro-American trickster tale: A structural analysis* (Monograph 4). Bloomington, IN: Folklore Publications Group.

Edwards J. (1981). Structural analysis of the Afro-American trickster tale, *Black American Literature Forum, 2,* 155-164.

Gates, H.L. (1984). The Blackness of blackness: A critique of the sign and the signifying monkey. *Critical Inquiry.*

Haring, L. (1972). A characteristic African folktale pattern. In R.M. Dorson (Ed.), *African folklore* (pp. 165-182). Garden City, NY: Anchor Doubleday.

Hill, D. (1977). The impact of migration on the metropolitan and folk society of Carricou, Grenada. *The Anthropolgical Papers of the American Museum of Natural History, 54.*

Kirshenblatt-Gimblett, B. (Ed.). (1976). *Speech play.* Philadelphia: University of Pennsylvania Press.

Stewart, S. (1980). *Nonsense.* Baltimore: The Johns Hopkins Press.

Turner, V.W. (1982). *From ritual to theater.* New York: Performing Arts Publication.

Von Sydow, C.W. (1984). *Selected tales on folklore.* Copenhagen: Rosenkilde and Bagger.

2

CHILDREN'S PLAY IN PSYCHOLOGICAL PERSPECTIVE

INTRODUCTION

E.P. Johnsen

Traditionally, psychology has tended to avoid investigating global and amorphous human experiences like play and love. These universal phenomena do not lend themselves to assessment by thoughtfully constructed test items, nor to the operational definitions so revered in the mainstream of American psychological thinking. Nevertheless, the psychological community has in the last 10 years overcome its work-ethic resistance to studying play and produced a wide variety of books and articles on the topic.

The studies included in this volume reflect some of the interests in the field today: the relationship between play and intellectual activities; the nexus between undirected or creative behavior and play; and the concern about the child's knowledge about play itself. Even with thousands of pages currently in print, only the surface has been scratched.

Christie and Johnsen review studies that attempt to tease out the sequential and/or causative relationship between play activities and intellectual aptitudes measured by intelligence tests. Their review suggests that engaging in playful episodes is not likely to account for measured advances in intelligence test scores. On the contrary, the intellectual competence of children may be guiding the structure of children's play.

Johnsen and Christie approach a similar question but focus on the developmental rather than the psychometric aspects of intelligence, using Piaget as a frame of reference. A selected number of studies are reviewed and criticized for design flaws. Piaget's view of play as reflective of the development of cognitive rather than causative functions is not seriously challenged by these studies.

Dansky attacks the difficult task of trying to relate two illusive psychological constructs — play and creativity — in a review that includes several of his own studies. While concluding that some data suggest that play facilitates an increase in creative problem solving, he is less sanguine about the long-term effects of play on producing the creative player.

Reifel, Briley, and Garza present a descriptive study of children's phenomenological impressions of play in a school setting. While the youngest children in the study included play as part of their description of school activities, differences in metaknowledge about play appeared across age groups. These results suggest a developmental trend in children's perception of the meaning of play itself in ordinary daily activities.

While psychologists are sure that play is a correlate of developmental activities occurring during the first 6 years of life, definitive answers about the effects of play remain illusive. As Rubin, Fein, and Vandenberg[1] have pointed out, play may be the context for those important growth-oriented events that mark the developing psyche of the young child. To explore this hypothesis, improvements in the design of research on play, including improving assessment techniques to include blind controls, controlling for the effects of social interaction, and consistently utilizing functional and social categories of play, are necessary. In addition, investigations of children's differences beyond social class, sex, and imagination will be needed to fill the gaps about the why and how of play. Children's interpretations of their own play and that of their peers may help resolve finally the perennial problem of trying to define this baffling but engaging phenomenon.

Note

1. Rubin, K., Fein, G., & Vandenberg, B (1983). Play. In P.H. Mussen (Ed.), *Handbook of child psychology; Vol. 4. Socialization, personality, and social development* (pp. 693-774). New York: John Wiley.

PRETEND PLAY AND LOGICAL OPERATIONS

E.P. Johnsen
and James F. Christie
University of Kansas

Considerable interest has been shown recently in the relationship between play and changes in intellectual functioning during the early years. Developmental theorists like Piaget, Vygotsky, and others have accorded very specific roles for play activity during this period of rapid change. Practitioners, concerned about the role of social agencies as they affect the mental life of children, look to scientific findings to resolve questions about public policies and educational practice. Applied psychologists have analogous interests and are impatient to have these theoretical roles validated by evidence and to determine a scientific foundation for policy suggestions and instructional advancement.

This paper is concerned with a selective view of play and its relationship with intellectual development as measured by Piagetian tasks—those restricted forms of problem-solving tasks that require children to demonstrate a solution involving a logical transformation and then offer a verbal rationale for their solution. First, we comment briefly on the theoretical statements that have generated studies to test the assumptions of the theories. Then, we review a few exemplary research studies, including one often neglected in the research literature, and offer some cautions regarding their conclusions.

Piaget (1962) has outlined the development of symbolic play over the first several years of life. Moving beyond the sensorimotor exploration of the first year or so of life, children allegedly reflect in their play the emerging symbolic competence of representing events in their world. For example, Fein (1979) describes the process of object substitutions where, by the late preschool period, children use nonrealistic objects as substitutes for life-like events in evoking fantasy play. Many studies reaffirm this pattern of symbolic changes—actions and objects become psychologically differentiated, symbols become at least partially emancipated from the concrete objects they represent, and sociodramatic play becomes more common (Fein, 1979).

The point here is to emphasize what others have lucidly described about Piaget's thinking: play is seen as a process reflective of emerging symbolic development, but contributing little to it. Symbolic play, in essence, distorts cognitive activity and is a transitory period in mental life marked by the strong urge to bend reality to the limited symbolic system of early preschool period. Thus, one witnesses the charm of a child immersed in a pretend sequence where the rules of adult logical reality have no force. Quite soon, this phase declines and the emergence of games and cultural rules becomes apparent, once again as a reflection of the preschooler's semi-logic being replaced by more sophisticated questions.

Of course, not all researchers have adapted Piaget's view of the role of pretend play. In particular, Lev Vygotsky (1967) regarded play as a facilitator of development. Sutton-Smith (1979) noted: "One might think that the development of substitute objects in play (toys, etc.) is a precursor to the development of symbolic thought in general. This is the approach Vygotsky has taken" (p. 12). Thus, Vygotsky regards play, not as a passing fantasy dependent on a logical timetable, but as means of aiding a child's construction of symbolic thinking no longer dominated by the context of current events and concrete objects. Rather than being replaced, play lingers as a parallel process to sophisticated logic, a refuge where symbols and ideas can be manipulated and where higher steps of development can unfold (Gardner, 1982).

The following studies of logical thinking seem to be in the tradition of Vygotsky's claims about the effect of play on advanced logical skills (see Table 1). Fink (1976) investigated the effect of a variation of Smilansky's (1968) sociodramatic play training procedure on kindergartners attainment of several types of conservation, the understanding that certain properties of objects and relationship remain invariant in spite of perceptual transformations. Funk hypothesized that, because pretend play requires children to "conserve" the identities of objects and persons in the face of make-believe transformations, training children in dramatic play might facilitate their performance on conservation tasks. During the training sessions, an adult introduced play themes, assigned roles to children, and modeled sociodramatic play behaviors. The results were mixed. The play training group did show a significant gain over controls on a social perspective-taking task (e.g., a man can be a teacher and a father at the same time). However, no significant differences were found for either conservation of quantity or conservation of number. Fink attributed these differential effects to the content of the training procedure. Sociodramatic play training places heavy emphasis on social roles and role-taking skills, content that is obviously more closely related to social role conservation than to conservation of number or amount.

Table 1. Design Features of Studies on Play and Logical Skills.

Study	Subjects	Treatment conditions	Treatment Assignment	Duration	Other Variables
Rubin & Maioni (1975)	16 middle-and lower-middle-class children selected from one Canadian preschool	n/a[a]	n/a	n/a	Classification Empathy Perspective taking Play quality Popularity
Fink (1976)	36 middle-class children selected from one kindergarten	1. Sociodramatic play training 2. Play, no training 3. No treatment	Randomized matching	Eight 25-minute sessions	Conservation of number Conservation of quantity Play quality Social role conservation
Golomb & Cornelius (1977)	30 upper-middle-class children selected from three preschools	1. Pretense-explanation training 2. Construction play training	Matching	Three 15-minute sessions	Conservation of quantity
Guthrie & Hudson (1979)	30 middle-class preschoolers	1. Pretense-explanation training 2. Construction play training	ns[b]	Three 15-minute sessions	Conservation of quantity
Golomb & Bonen (1981)	60 lower-middle-class children selected from three kindergarten classes	1. Pretense-explanation training 2. Verbal rule training 3. No treatment	Random within the experimental groups Control ns	Three 15-minute sessions[c]	Conservation of quantity

[a] n/a = not applicable, correlational study.
[b] ns = not specified.
[c] Not specified for the verbal training treatment.

Golomb and Cornelius (1977) attempted to develop a play training strategy to foster logico-mathematical forms of conservation. Their procedure, which might be called "pretense-explanation training," involved engaging a child in pretend play and then maneuvering the child into explaining the make-believe transformations that had occurred in the play. For example, after encouraging a child to pretend that a bean bag was an animal, the experimenter would point out that it was really just a bean bag. This was done in order to prompt children to explain that objects can be used in a make-believe manner and still retain their real-life identities. Golomb and Cornelius hypothesized that making children aware of this type of quasi-reversible transformation from fantasy to reality would facilitate children's attainment of conservation of quantity.

Thirty upper-middle-class 4-year-olds were divided into experimental and control groups. Prior to the training period, none of the subjects in either group gave acceptable conservation responses. However, after only three 15-minute sessions, 10 of the 15 subjects in the experimental group gave conservation responses with acceptable explanations as compared with only one control subject. Golomb and Cornelius (1977) caution that the play training may not have resulted in the creation of new cognitive structures; rather, it may have merely activated "pre-existing structures in the child" (p. 251). This seems reasonable, given the short duration of the treatment.

It should also be noted that pretense-explanation training only indirectly involves play. A key element in the strategy is the questioning by the examiner that calls the child's attention to the implicit reversibility in make-believe transformations. The child's verbal responses to these questions may also have been an important factor. Howard Gardner conjectured:

I think it's not the pretend play but rather the going outside the frame of pretend play and getting the child to talk about what something is and what it appears to be. I think it's the part that trains the correct conservation response . . . it's not necessarily the case that if you pretend play with kids a lot, they therefore conserve more quickly. (Sutton-Smith, 1979, p. 80)

A partial replication casts doubt on the generalizability of Golomb and Cornelius' findings. In this replication, Guthrie and Hudson (1979) used Golomb and Cornelius' pretense-explanation training but made several changes in the experimental procedures:

- Middle-class rather than upper-middle-class 4-year-olds were used as subjects.
- Multiple experimenters conducted the training and testing sessions, permitting "blind" assessment.
- A 2-week delayed posttest was added to determine if the training effects were lasting.

Guthrie and Hudson's results were much less impressive. On the immediate posttest, only 1 of 15 subjects in the play training group offered a conservation response with an appropriate explanation, even this modest gain disappeared on the delayed posttest. Guthrie and Hudson offered several reasons for the discrepancy between their findings and those of the earlier study. The most likely of these explanations is that Golomb and Cornelius' upper-middle-class 4-year-olds were at a more advanced cognitive stage than the middle-class subjects in their study. Golomb and Cornelius' subjects may have already acquired the congitive structures needed for conservation, whereas Guthrie and Hudson's may not. Given individual differences in rate of cognitive development, it is possible that pretense-explanation training may not be effective with the majority of children at 4 years of age.

Guthrie and Hudson noted that their control group's performance actually improved on the delayed posttest, with more subjects making conservation responses without explanations than on the immediate posttest. This finding led the investigators to conjecture that the conservation tests themselves may have contributed substantially to the children's acquisition of conservation. This argument, however, requires one to accept verbal responses without justifications as a valid criterion of conservation attainment, which is a questionable practice.

In an extensive replication of the 1977 study, Golomb and Bowen (1981) randomly assigned 36 children who failed to benefit from one direct verbal training episode on a solid and liquid conservation task given to two groups. One group received the same pretense-explanation training mentioned above for six 15-minute episodes on 3 successive days. The other group received 3 days of additional training on verbal rules with the researchers demonstrating correct conservation responses with justifications. Twenty children who received no training constituted control subjects.

Conservation tests given after the training, 3 days later and again after 2 weeks revealed interesting findings. While there were no immediate differences, after 3 days the verbal conservation-training group scored statistically higher than the control group, and on the delayed (14-day) posttest, both the play training and the verbal training group scored statistically higher than the control group.

The strengths of this study are that training was more extensive than in the prior study, that posttests were delayed and included some transfer tests (i.e., tests using materials not included in the original training), and the majority of the children were from a lower economic category. A careful examination of the training results, however, yields some concerns over several issues. While the results yielded statistically different outcomes mentioned above, actual differences in the scores were minimal. Students in the training groups had potential scores of 340 to 360 points on each of the posttests. Raw scores, however, averaged between 64 and 78 points, less than 4 points out of a possible 20 for each subject. Such total scores could be accounted for by a very few subjects within each group.

Testing itself seemed to have an effect on the experimental groups in that performance seemed to improve toward the last items in each testing situation. No equating of time between the experimental groups was mentioned, an unfortunate oversight because of the extensive involvement of adults (tuition) with children in the play training condition. No exact percentages were reported on the socio-economic classifications of the subjects, nor was the method of classifying parent economic status described. Children in this study nearly reached an average age of 6, about 18 months older than subjects in the 1977 study. Many children at this age level would typically exhibit conservation or be described as transitional (i.e., possessing the intellectual competence to think logically) and thus be quite responsive to any environmental suggestion to perform. Finally, only one person was involved in the testing who also conducted all of the training. She is described as highly motivated and, "personally determined to make the training experience of value to *all* the participating children and to accomplish what she perceived as an important education goal" (Golomb & Bonen, p. 155). These confounding conditions raise serious questions about casual relationships among the variables under study.

Rubin and Maioni (1975) classified the free play of 16 Canadian preschoolers according to Smilansky's (1968) play categories: functional play, constructive play, dramatic play, and games with rules. All children were administered a series of cognitive measures, including subsections of Kofsky's (1966) classification scale. Classification is the consistent application of defining properties (e.g., physical properties like form, functional properties like pain inducement, connotative properties like science-fiction stories, etc.) to group together events in a set, based on similarities and differences. Some knowledge of the concepts all, some, and none is also required for a mature grasp of classification. Results revealed a positive correlation between classification and dramatic play that approached significance ($r = .49, p < .06$). Classification was negatively correlated with functional play, which is considered to be less mature than dramatic play ($r = .58, p < .05$).

Dramatic play often involves social interaction and peer conflict. For example, children may argue about who gets to adopt a popular role or about what should happen next in a dramatic sequence. Rubin and Maioni hypothesized that this type of peer interaction may require children to take other people's points of view, resulting in a better understanding of reciprocal relationships. Because classification involves reciprocal concepts such as part-whole relationships, such peer interaction may lead to improved classification skills. Due to the correlational nature of the study, the casual direction of the relationship between dramatic play and classification cannot be inferred.

In analyzing the outcomes of these few studies, let us direct our attention to commentary by Greta Fein (1979) in a review on play and symbol development:

When children play different roles, they are, in a sense, using what they already know. But when they reverse or change roles, old information is used in an unusual way and a new problem is posed. The new problem may encourage the inference that roles have the characteristic of reversibility and substitutability, but the role-playing person stays the same. From a developmental perspective, the issue may be conservation of self over varied transformations. Pretend roles might provide 'pivots' for the separation of self from others and the shift from an egocentric to a sociocentric perspective. (pp. 219-220)

Our interpretation of the literature would be quite different from Fein's. While the descriptive literature (e.g., Fein, 1981) provides substantial evidence for a systematic change in these two parallel systems (i.e., the structure of pretend play and changes in symbol use), drawing causal relationships seems premature, perhaps because of play's effect on social knowledge (Johnsen and Christie, 1982) and its impact on the development of logical thinking.

When play effects seem to occur, other sources of influence compete. The social context remains a potential explanation for such effects, as noted by other authors (Sutton-Smith, 1979). Peer interaction and adult-child exchanges are confounded with the play experience. The process of assessing logical skills may influence subsequent testing by sensitizing children to the procedure (i.e., a reactive effect to testing practice). Other design issues such as convenience sampling, the use of matching subjects rather than random assignment to treatments, and the frequent absence of blind assessment present difficulties in interpreting outcomes.

In summary, our interpretation is that there is little evidence to suggest that play training alone as designed by these researchers facilitated young children's competence in conservation, a logical skill considered significant by many developmental theorists. Piaget's view that play, per se, does not result in new cognitive structures remains a viable hypothesis.

Rubin, Fein, and Vandenberg (1983) have noted in reviewing Piaget's theory of play that little is known about the process of consolidation during play episodes. Consolidation refers to processes whereby children achieve the organization of important life experiences; they impose a constructed meaning on the collective symbolic prototypes that emerge during pretense. Perhaps researchers might attempt to direct their efforts along this line of inquiry to focus more on the consolidation of knowledge and less on the acquisition of new structures like conservation.

Play in the broadest sense does not seem to be unrelated to other indices of cognitive functioning such as creative productions or nondevelopmental measures of intelligence. Studies that examine a greater variety of play experiences, that sample more widely from populations varying in age and background, that design assessment procedures more carefully, and that separate the effects of the context from the playful acts themselves will help us to understand these relationships more fully.

REFERENCES

Fein, G. (1979). Play and the acquisition of symbols In L.G. Katz (Ed.), *Current topics in early childhood education,* Vol. 2, (pp. 195-225). Norwood, NJ: Ablex Publishing.

Fein, G. (1981). Pretend play in childhood: An integrative review. *Child Development, 52,* 1095-1118.

Fink, R.S. (1976). Role of imaginative play in cognitive development. *Psychological Reports, 30,* 895-906.

Gardner, H. (1982). *Developmental psychology* (2nd ed.) Boston: Little, Brown and Co.

Golomb, C., & Bowen, S. (1981). Playing games of make-believe: The effectiveness of symbolic play training with children who failed to benefit from early conservation training. *Genetic Psychology Monographs, 104,* 137-159.

Golomb, C., & Cornelius, C.B. (1977). Symbolic play and its cognitive significance. *Developmental Psychology, 13,* 246-252.

Guthrie, K., & Hudson, L.M. (1979). Training conservation through symbolic play: A second look. *Child Development, 50,* 1269-1271.

Johnsen, E.P., & Christie, J.F. (1982), April). *Play and social cognition: The score-board.* Paper presented at the meeting of The Association for the Anthropological Study of Play, London, Ontario.

Kofsky, E. (1966). A scalogram study of classificatory development. *Child Development, 37,* 191-204.

Piaget, J. (1962). *Play, dreams and imitation in childhood.* New York: Norton.

Rubin, K.H., Fein, G.G., & Vandenberg, B. (1983). Play. In P.H. Mussen (Ed.), *Handbook of child psychology: Vol. 4. Socialization personality and social development* (pp. 693-774). New York: John Wiley & Sons.

Rubin, K., & Maioni, T. (1975). Play preference and its relationship to egocentrism, popularity and classification skills in preschoolers. *Merrill-Palmer Quarterly, 21,* 171-179.

Smilansky, S. (1968). *The effects of sociodramatic play on disadvantaged preschool children.* New York: Wiley.

Sutton-Smith, B. (1979a, June). *Piaget play and cognition Revisited.* Paper presented at the meeting of the Jean Piaget Society, Philadelphia.

Sutton-Smith, B. (Ed.), (1979b). *Play and learning.* New York: Gardner Press.

Vygotsky, L. (1967). Play and role of mental development in the child. *Soviets Psychology, 5,* 6-18.

PLAY AND PSYCHOMETRIC APPROACHES TO INTELLIGENCE

James F. Christie and E.P. Johnsen
University of Kansas

People who work in educational settings describe their students as bright or slow, genius or handicapped. What do these labels mean? Is intelligence the number of facts one knows or how creatively one utilizes knowledge? Even without consensus on the meaning of intelligence, society places great value on mental ability, measuring it through the use of IQ tests and recording differences in test outcomes in some relatively permanent fashion.

All such attempts at measuring mental ability have their roots in Binet and Simon's early-20th-century creation—collection of tasks allegedly tapping a variety of skills such as understanding words, immediate memory, everyday facts, reasoning, abstraction, and the time it takes for individuals to respond to questions.

Years of data collection and sophisticated analysis have polished these techniques but not changed them substantially. The tests are still used (and misused) in about the same way: they function to compare children of the same age and to assign labels of average, above average, and below average. Whatever the skills that these tests measure, they do predict patterns of success and failure for children, particularly in school-related tasks like classifying according to a taxonomy, making calculations, manipulating abstract but artificially construed stimuli, and engaging in some aspects of hypothetical thinking (Sharp, Cole & Lave, 1979).

Debate continues to rage over the nature-nurture issues in examining what influences the occurrence of varying levels of IQ. Naturists like Arthur Jensen (1969) have argued for an overwhelming genetic component, referring to a within-species variability principle; the chance pairing of parental gene complexes together with a "regression towards the mean" (offspring of very bright or dull parents tend to be less extreme in levels of talent) produces a "normal" distribution of mental ability. It is further suggested that not only are these abilities relatively immutable but that patterns of IQ can be determined on the basis of ethnic or racial factors.

The overwhelming response of the professional community has been to disagree with the naturists, maintaining that the content and the language of IQ tests have a strong middle-class, white bias. The strong positive association between social class and IQ has suggested to many that there is an informal curriculum in the middle-class home that promotes performance on these tests. The use of symbols, including language, the promotion of conventional literacy, the stress on intellectual accomplishment—all result in a training forum in this social milieu that may appear hereditary at first glance, but may just as likely be a socially induced phenomenon.

Schools as institutions of formal education have been required by the society to increase the likelihood of success for all children, especially for those who have suffered from social and economic inequities. A variety of training programs, perhaps the most notable being Head Start, have attempted to provide low-income children with experiences comparable to this theoretical curriculum that some have suggested promotes school success. The measure of success of these programs in the short term has often been the IQ test, a relatively accurate predictor of academic progress.

While many such "remedial" programs have miniaturized tasks typically performed by older children in school, a few researchers have shown interest in process rather than product. They have suggested an open-ended method of schooling, encouraging preschool experiences that are more home-like rather than hurrying children through packaged academic lessons typical of later grades. Play experiences obviously are of interest here, as play is conceived of as a joyful, spontaneous, and naturally occurring social experience in the life of the young child.

Play may be related to the intellectual abilities measured by IQ tests in two ways. Garvey (1977) and others have documented that advanced forms of make-believe such as sociodramatic play require children to use role abstractions, symbolic transformations, "frame breaks," and many other higher-order cognitive activities. A certain level of intelligence may be required in order for children to engage in these advanced forms of play. It is also possible, on the other hand, that engaging in such play may promote intellectual growth. Smilansky (1968) has argued that engaging in sociodramatic play stimulates language development, enhances symbolic capabilities, broadens concepts, and leads to the acquisition of new knowledge.

This paper examines research that has addressed the issue of play and mental ability as measured by intelligence tests. Correlational studies are reviewed first, followed by play training experiments.

CORRELATIONAL STUDIES

Johnson (1976) observed the free play of 63 low-SES preschoolers and classified their play into three categories: nonfantasy play, nonsocial fantasy play, and social fantasy play. The children were also administered the Peabody Picture Vocabulary Test (PPVT), the picture completion subtest of the Weschler Preschool and Primary Scale of Intelligence (WPPSI), and several measures of divergent thinking. Results showed that social fantasy play was related to IQ scores, while nonsocial fantasy play was not. This finding probably reflects the fact that group make-believe play has higher cognitive and linguistic demands than solitary fantasy activity.

Johnson's results revealed that the correlations between social fantasy play and IQ were quite modest but significant ($r = .25, p < .05$). Examination of the play scores of children with mental ages above and below the median revealed that half of the children with above-average mental ages engaged in social fantasy play and half did not. Children with mental ages below the midpoint rarely engaged in this complex form of play.

Johnson (1976) interpreted these findings to indicate that a certain level of intelligence is required for social fantasy play to occur. However, he also noted that "intelligence appeared to be a necessary but not sufficient condition for social make-believe play" (p. 1200). Half of the above-average children did not engage in this form of play. The finding that measures of divergent thinking were moderate predictors of social fantasy play ($r = .35-.52$) suggests that a certain level of creative thinking may also be an important prerequisite.

Johnson, Ershler, and Lawton (1982) analyzed the free play of 34 middle-class preschoolers in terms of cognitive and social play categories. The subjects were also given the Raven Progressive Matrices, and Peabody Picture Vocabulary Test, and five Piagetian conservation tasks. Factor analysis yielded three play factors: dramatic-interactive, functional-constructive, and parallel. The authors labeled the first factor as sociodramatic play, and their analysis revealed a modest but nonsignificant correlation ($r = .22$) between this type of play and a factor that included the IQ test scores. This finding contradicted Johnson's (1976) earlier findings, even though the magnitudes of the correlations in both studies are quite similar. A constructive play factor (e.g., using objects to build things) was found to be positively associated with the IQ factor ($r = .41$), leading the investigators to speculate that make-believe play may not be the only type of play with "important cognitive consequences" (p. 115).

Freyberg (1973) gave the vocabulary subtest of the Stanford-Binet Intelligence Test to 80 low-SES kindergartners, and observed their free play. She found low correlations between the children's IQ scores and the imaginativeness ($r = .22$), affect ($r = .26$), and concentration ($r = .18$) observed in their play. The statistical significance (or lack thereof) of these correlations was not reported. It is interesting that, even though pretend play was analyzed in a very different manner, Freyberg's play level/IQ correlations are very similar in magnitude to those reported in the two studies by Johnson and his associates.

Steele (1981) divided 52 middle-class preschoolers into two age groups: younger (35 to 53 months) and older (54 to 74 months). The children were administered several cognitive measures, including the Stanford-Binet Intelligence Test. Their free play was also observed and classified, and the frequency of pretend/fantasy play was determined. As in the previous studies, results revealed low correlations between IQ scores and the level of make-believe play. It is noteworthy that the pretend play/IQ correlation was higher for younger children ($r = .33$) than for older ones ($r = .15$). Steele also examined sex differences and found that make-believe play was more highly related to IQ scores in boys ($r = .36$) than in girls ($r = .20$). However, none of these correlations was statistically significant.

One other investigation, though not a correlation study, should be noted. As part of her pioneering play training experiment, Smilansky (1968) administered the Stanford—Binet tests to 782 low-SES Israeli children prior to the onset of training. IQ was used only as a pretest measure and was not a dependent variable in the study. While Smilansky found no overall relationship between pretraining IQ scores and the subjects' response to her sociodramatic play training treatment, she did note that play training was totally unsuccessful with children whose IQs were in the 50 to 70 range. This finding led her to conclude, like Johnson, that at least a minimal level of intelligence is required for children to engage in sociodramatic play.

TRAINING STUDIES

Correlation studies, by their very nature, cannot determine the causal direction of any relationship such as that between play and intelligence. Therefore, such investigations cannot supply evidence that play promotes intellectual growth. This has prompted several investigators to conduct experimental training studies using IQ as a dependent variable. Table 1 summarizes the major design features of these studies, most of which used pretest-posttest control group designs. The rationale behind these training studies is as follows: if children receiving play training show significantly larger gains in both play level and IQ scores than controls, then one can attribute the IQ gains to the enhanced levels of play brought about by the training. This assumes, of course, that rigorous experimental controls are

Table 1. Design Features of Experimental Studies on Play and IQ

Study	Subjects	Treatment conditions	Duration	IQ measures	Other variables
Hartshorn & Brantley (1973)	12 children selected from two second-grade and two third-grade classrooms	1. Sociodramatic play 2. No treatment	Daily half-day sessions for 11 weeks	Items selected from the WISC and Stanford–Binet	Empathy
Saltz & Johnson (1974)	75 low SES children selected from four preschool classes in one school	1. Thematic–fantasy training 2. Dimensionality training 3. Combination (1 & 2) 4. Listen to stories	Three 15-minute sessions per week for 16 weeks	Subtests of the WPPSI and ITPA	Picture and object memory Play quality Story memory Story telling
Saltz, Dixon, & Johnson (1977)	146 low SES children selected from one preschool over a three year period	1. Sociodramatic play training 2. Thematic–fantasy training 3. Story discussion 4. Nonfantasy activities	Daily 15-minute sessions for 7 months	PPVT (first year) PTI (second & third years)	Empathy Fantasy judgment Impulse control Play quality Sequential memory Story interpretation
Smith, Dalgleish, & Herzmark (1981)	77 low SES children selected from four classes in two British preschools[a]	1. Play tutoring 2. Skills tutoring	Daily 40-minute sessions for 8 weeks	Subtests of the WPPSI	Creativity Play quality Perspective taking
Christie (1983)	20 lower-middle class children selected from two classrooms in one preschool[b]	1. Sociodramatic play training 2. Skills tutoring	Weekly 20-minute sessions for 9 weeks	PPVT	Creativity Play quality

[a]65 subjects remained at the 8-week delayed posttest.

[b]17 subjects remained at the 12-week delayed posttest.

employed to insure that play is the only difference between the experimental and control treatments, and that reliable and valid measures of the variables are employed.

Harshorn and Brantley (1973) used a posttest-only control group design to evaluate the effects of an 11-week training program that attempted to teach social studies concepts through sociodramatic play. The subjects were 12 second- and third-grade students who displayed low verbal and social skills. The six subjects in the experimental group constructed a miniature city, chose roles in the community, and engaged in sociodramatic play. After the training period, the subjects were given items, selected from the Weschler Intelligence Scale for Children (WISC) and the Stanford-Binet, that involved solving social and practical problems. Results showed that the experimental group scored higher on these IQ test items than did the controls. The experimenters concluded that dramatic play had enhanced the children's problem-solving abilities. However, the extremely small sample size, the selective characteristics of the sample (low achieving), and the nonrandom method of selecting subjects and assigning them to treatment conditions all cast doubt on the validity of this conclusion. In addition, the experimental treatment involved many other variables besides sociodramatic play (e.g., discussion sessions, field trips, and selected readings), any one of which may have been responsible for the obtained gains.

In a more controlled study, Saltz and Johnson (1974) assigned low-SES preschoolers to four treatment groups, two of which received thematic-fantasy play training. This training involved the role-playing of familiar fairy tales such as *The Three Pigs*. Results showed that this type of play training resulted in higher levels of dramatic play and in significant gains in composite scores on several subtests of the WPPSI and the Illinois Test of Psycholinguistic Ability (ITPA). The investigators, however, urged caution in interpreting the intelligence estimate results because a complete intelligence test was not administered and, due to time constraints, only a random subset of less than half the subjects completed the posttest IQ measures.

In a series of related studies, Saltz, Dixon, and Johnson (1977) compared the effects of thematic-fantasy training (enacting fairy tales) and sociodramatic play training (enacting real-life situations) on a number of cognitive variables, including intelligence. A fantasy discussion group, in which children heard fairytales, and a nonfantasy activity (e.g., cutting and pasting) group were used to control for the effects of verbal stimulation, maturation and history. For purposes of replication, the same experiment was repeated three times over a period of three years. No significant differences were found between the thematic-fantasy and the sociodramatic play groups on IQ. However, the combined play training groups did show a significant gain in

IQ scores as compared with the combined control groups. A significant interaction was found between the subjects' pretraining IQ scores and the experimental conditions, with most of the beneficial effects of both play training procedures occurring with children whose pretraining IQ scores were above the median for the sample. This supports Smilansky's (1968) earlier suggestion that play training is only effective with children who are already functioning at a certain level of intelligence.

In reviewing the play training literature, Smith and Syddall (1978) suggested that adult tuition, rather than enhanced levels of play, may have been responsible for the cognitive gains brought about by play training:

The other studies did involve one or more control groups which experienced extra interaction with an adult of some kind or another. However, no measurements were made of the amount or kind of interaction with the tutor in the different conditions, so the control, being based at best on gross time available, is not a satisfactory one . . . . Differential improvement of competence by children in the play group may be due to qualitative and quantitative differences in adult contact in the tutoring, rather than to the differential increase in play levels. (p. 316)

Christie (1982) has pointed out another limitation of play training studies: the lack of follow-up assessment. In the studies reviewed above, assessments were only conducted before and immediately after training. The studies could not determine, therefore, if play training had lasting effects on children's IQ scores. This is an important issue because research has shown that the effects of many early childhood intervention programs are short lived (e.g., Moore, 1977).

Smith, Dalgleish, and Herzmark (1981) investigated both the adult-tuition and permanency-of-training-effects issues in an extensive play training study conducted in England. Low-SES preschoolers were assigned to two treatments: play tutoring, which involved children in sociodramatic play; and skills tutoring, which included art projects and academic games that did not involve fantasy. The amount and type of adult-child interaction in the two treatments were carefully monitored via observers and audio recordings. These observations revealed that tutor contact was roughly equivalent in both conditions. The experiment was repeated independently at two separate preschool centers, and an 8-week delayed posttest was included to determine the permanency of training effects.

Results showed that the play tutoring and skills tutoring treatments resulted in equivalent gains on four subtests of the WPPSI and that these gains still remained at the 8-week follow-up assessment. The only differences favoring the play treatment were found on measures of fantasy play and social interaction. Smith et al. (1981) concluded that play tutoring led to stable gains in intelligence, but that these gains were probably caused by adult contact rather than by play.

A smaller study was conducted by Christie (1983) in the United States, with comparable results. Low-SES preschoolers were divided into play tutoring and skills tutoring groups similar to those used by Smith et al. Immediate posttest results showed that both treatments led to significant gains in scores on the Peabody Picture Vocabulary Test. These gains were also maintained on the delayed posttest 12 weeks later. No differential effects were found between the two treatment groups, supporting Smith and Syddall's (1978) adult tuition hypothesis.

DISCUSSION

Results of the above research indicate that a certain level of intelligence is necessary for children to engage in advanced forms of make-believe play such as sociodramatic play, and that some minimal level of intelligence is required for children to profit from training in these types of play. These findings probably reflect the advanced linguistic and cognitive skills needed for children to plan and carry out cooperative dramatizations.

Several investigators reported low correlations between IQ scores and level of make-believe play, suggesting that intelligence, as estimated by IQ tests, is not the only prerequisite for pretend play. Johnson's (1976) finding that measures of divergent thinking were stronger predictors of social fantasy play suggests that creative thinking ability is also an important element. Certain social skills, such as cooperation and turn-taking, may also be needed to engage successfully in group make-believe play.

Most of the correlational studies focused on the relationship between pretend play and IQ. Johnson, Ershler, and Lawton's (1982) finding that constructive play was positively associated with intelligence suggests that future studies on play and IQ should investigate other forms of play as well.

Training studies have shown that play tutoring can lead to stable gains in children's IQ scores. There are, however, several constraints on this generalization:

- A confounding variable, adult-child interaction, makes it difficult to determine the extent to which play itself is responsible for these gains in IQ. In fact, some evidence suggests that the adult-contact variable is the major causal component in play training procedures.
- The studies used a variety of different measures to assess intelligence. In particular, some of those that employed subtests rather than total scores are open to criticism in terms of the reliability of their findings with relatively limited numbers of quite young subjects.

- If play is a spontaneous, fun, anxiety-free activity occurring in relatively familiar surroundings (Weisler & McCall, 1976), have training studies satisfied these essential elements of the definition? Future training studies should attempt to demonstrate that the quality of induced play experiences is somewhat equivalent to those initiated by children.
- Most of the above studies used children from limited SES backgrounds as subjects. Replications with children from a variety of social and economic backgrounds would help determine how generalizable the results are.

Perhaps future studies will reveal that play training enhances mental test scores only for relatively able children who come from economically impoverished backgrounds. Such a finding would only reinforce the notion that middle-class families use a subtle or hidden curriculum during the early years. Emphasizing the use of arbitrary symbols, encouraging dialogue and explanation in social settings, orienting children toward social roles relevant to agencies like schools—these and other similar activities may constitute the tuition apparent in what we have addressed as "training to play."

In summary, the research reviewed above sheds some light on the nature of the relationship between play and intelligence. Findings support the notion that a certain level of intelligence is necessary for children to engage in group make-believe activities. There is less evidence, however, that merely engaging in play facilitates intellectual gains.

From a social perspective, utility may be the most convincing factor in applying these findings to real-life situations. Educators are likely to ignore the ancient debates over the stability of IQ and the role of nature in limiting the effects of environmental alterations. They will probably be satisfied with the simple fact that play training appears to be a worthwhile activity for promoting greater success for large numbers of children entering the educational system. In addition, play training may offer some balance, even with substantial adult involvement, to the restrictive emphasis on what in this decade is called the basics.

REFERENCES

Christie, J.F. (1982). Play: To train or not to train? In J. Loy (Ed.), *The paradoxes of play* (pp. 122-129). West Point, NY: Leisure Press.

Christie, J.F. (1983). The effects of play tutoring on young children's cognitive performance. *Journal of Educational Research, 76,* 326-330.

Freyberg, J.T. (1973). Increasing the imaginative play of urban dis-advantaged kindergarten children through systematic training. In J.L. Singer (Ed.), *The child's world of make-believe: Experimental studies of imaginative play* (pp. 129-154). New York: Academic Press.

Garvey, C. (1977). *Play.* Cambridge, MA: Harvard University Press.

Hartshorn, E., & Brantley, J.C. (1973). Effects of dramatic play on classroom problem-solving ability. *Journal of Educational Research, 66,* 243-246.

Jensen, A. (1969). How much can we raise IQ and scholastic achievement? *Harvard Educational Review, 39,* 1-123.

Johnson, J.E. (1976). Relations of divergent thinking and intelligence test score with social and nonsocial make-believe play of preschool children. *Child Development, 47,* 1200-1203.

Johnson, J., Ershler, J., & Lawton, J. (1982). Intellective correlates of preschoolers' spontaneous play. *Journal of General Psychology,* (1977). 106, 115-122.

Moore, S.M. (1977). The effects of Head Start programs with different curricular and teaching strategies. *Young Children, 32,* 54-60.

Saltz, E., Dixon, D., & Johnson, J. (1977). Training disadvantaged preschoolers on various fantasy activities: Effects on cognitive functioning and impulse control. *Child Development, 48,* 367-380.

Saltz, E., & Johnson, J. (1974). Training for thematic-fantasy play in culturally disadvantaged children: Preliminary results. *Journal of Educational Psychology, 66,* 623-630.

Sharp, D., Cole, M., & Lave, C. (1979). Education and cognitive develop-ment: The evidence from experimental research. *Monographs of the Society for Research in Child Development, 44* (1-2, Serial No. 178).

Smilansky, S. (1968). *The effects of sociodramatic play on dis-advantaged preschool children.* New York: John Wiley.

Smith, P.K., Dalgleish, M., & Hermark, G. (1981). A comparison of the effects of fantasy play tutoring and skills tutoring in nursery classes. *International Journal of Behavioral Development, 4,* 421-441.

Smith, P.K., & Syddall, S. (1978). Play and non-play tutoring in preschool children: Is it play or tutoring which matters? *British Journal of Educational Psychology, 48,* 315-325.

Steele, C. (1981). Play variables as related to cognitive constructs in 3-to-6-year-olds. *Journal of Research and Development in Education, 14* (3), 58-72.

Weisler, A., & McCall, R. (1976). Exploration and play: Resume and redirection. *American Psychologist, 31,* 492-508.

PLAY AND CREATIVITY IN YOUNG CHILDREN

Jeffrey L. Dansky
Eastern Michigan University

Among the numerous functions and adaptive consequences that have long been attributed to play, enhanced flexibility and creativity may be the most common (Bruner, 1972; Dansky & Silverman, 1975; Feitelson & Ross, 1973; Lieberman, 1977; Singer, 1973; Smilansky, 1968; Sutton-Smith, 1972, 1977; Sylva, 1977). For example, Sutton-Smith (1979) claims that, "the major cognitive consequence of play is an increase in cognitive alternatives available to the player, as well as the flexible management of these" (p.316). Vandenberg (1981) claims that, "Play generates behavioral diversity that enhances the long-term adaptive capabilities of a species" (p.359).

The fact that so many scholars have repeatedly asserted this relationship between play and creativity in unequivocal terms over such a long period of time seems to imply that play does promote creative behavior. However, it has been argued that even in those studies where a causal link has been established between play experiences and posttest scores, variables other than play may be responsible for the shift in scores (Rubin and Pepler, 1980). It has also been argued that "any directional influence that might exist between cognitive ability and imaginative play goes from cognitive ability to imaginative play and not from imaginative play to cognitive ability" (Johnson, Ershler, & Serlin, in press). It is clear that complex activities like dramatic play necessarily presuppose the earlier development of certain cognitive skills, and it seems sensible to assume that play and cognition are continuously intertwined and exert bidirectional influences on one another. However, a case can be made for the position that play contributes to creativity or, stated more precisely, that some forms of play facilitate behaviors commonly associated with creativity. A review of research supporting this contention is summarized below.

SCOPE OF THE PAPER

The primary focus of this review is on studies of children's play whose dependent measures involve divergent problem solving. This decision was made, in part, because of the inherent difficulties involved in defining creativity. However, there were other more prominent considerations. First, while very young children may frequently engage in behaviors that are novel, unusual, or even imaginative, they rarely (if ever) produce the kinds of artistic, scientific, or literary products that can unequivocally be labeled creative. Second, this writer agrees with Guilford's (1957) contention that, "It is in divergent thinking that we find the most obvious indications of creativity" (p. 112). Finally, several of the studies that most directly test the hypothesis that children's play enhances their creativity have used measures of divergent thinking (e.g., the alternative-uses test) that several investigators have established as being both relatively independent of intelligence and significantly correlated with various indicators of creative functioning (Dansky & Silverman, 1973; Kogan & Pankove, 1972; Singer & Whiton, 1971; Wallach, 1970; Wallach & Wing, 1969).

CORRELATIONAL STUDIES

The first systematic investigations of the relationship between play and creativity were reported by Lieberman (1965) and Sutton-Smith (1967). Lieberman (1965) constructed a scale for rating playfulness and found that kindergarten teachers' ratings of their students' playfulness were significantly correlated with three divergent thinking measures adapted from the work of Torrance (1960) and Guilford et al. (1951). Sutton-Smith (1967) took advantage of certain naturally occurring variations in children's toy preferences and found that kindergarteners gave more alternate uses for toys with which they were most familiar and fewer uses for toys normally receiving less of their attention during free play. Although both Lieberman's and Sutton-Smith's findings were consistent with the hypothesis that play (or playfulness) is related to creativity, both studies had methodological shortcomings that allowed alternative interpretations (Dansky & Silverman, 1973).

Support for a relationship between fantasy play and creativity can be found in studies reported by Hutt and Bhavnani (1967) and Johnson (1976) in which divergent thinking was positively correlated with measures of pretense, and in Schaefer's (1969) finding that adolescents who recall having had imaginary playmates when they were children score higher on tests of creativity. These correlational studies all support the belief that play is related to creativity. However, none of these studies were designed to permit inferences about causal relationships between variables. In fact, each study is as consistent with the assumption that divergent thinkers prefer fantasy as with the assumption that fantasy play facilitates divergent thinking.

MANIPULATIVE PLAY AND INNOVATIVE TOOL USE

Before proceeding to experimental studies of play and divergent thinking, brief attention will be given to a line of research that has established links between free play opportunities and one form of convergent (but innovative) problem solving. In their now classic studies, Kohler (1926) and Birch (1945) showed that chimpanzees who are given opportunities to freely manipulate sticks will later succeed at solving problems that require the telescopic joining of those sticks to serve as tools to retrieve attractive lures. The lack of such freely manipulative activity led to failure at these problems. More recently, several investigators have revived, refined, and extended the lure-retrieval paradigm to determine the extent to which manipulative play influences such innovative problem solving in young children (Sylva, Bruner, & Genova, 1976; Smith & Dutton, 1979). Collectively, these studies show that free play with sticks does facilitate solution of lure-retrieval problems. However, in the context of the present paper, the most noteworthy finding of these studies was that play opportunities appeared most beneficial for solving the more complex problems that required the most innovative transfer (Smith & Dutton, 1979).

PLAY AND ASSOCIATIVE FLUENCY'S EXPERIMENTAL STUDIES

The first study to be summarized in this section provided an experimental test of Sutton-Smith's (1967) contention that time spent in playful activity should increase a child's associative fluency as measured by the number of ideas produced in an alternate uses test. To test this hypothesis, Dansky and Silverman (1973) randomly assigned preschoolers to one of three treatment conditions: free play, imitation, or control. Immediately after engaging in their respective activities, each child was given an alternate uses test. As predicted, preschoolers who were given opportunities to play with various objects subsequently gave more unusual uses for those objects than did children involved in either of the two nonplayful activities. This study also provided evidence of a relationship between play and "broad attention deployment," a cognitive disposition that Wallach (1970) claims is crucial for creative productivity. In a follow-up to this study, Dansky and Silverman (1975) showed that play also has a general facilitating effect on associative fluency. That is, free-play opportunities not only increased the number of uses given for objects played with, but also for objects that were not present during play.

Dansky and Silverman's (1973, 1975) findings strongly support the position that playful activity enhances processes associated with creativity. However, "play" is a heterogeneous behavior category, and "free-play time" can provide children with opportunities for engaging in a wide range of behaviors. Thus, the studies cited so far do not permit firm conclusions about the nature of the particular behavioral mechanisms that mediate the relationship between free-play opportunities and subsequent increases in associative fluency. This writer believes that the relationship between free-play opportunities and enhanced associative fluency depends on the occurrence of symbolic make-believe during the free-play period. This hypothesis is founded on the observation that there are certain similarities between Piaget's (1951) characterization of symbolic play and the cognitive processes that Wallach (1970) associates with creativity. Specifically, it seems that the free combination and mutual assimilation of schemes that characterize Piaget's (1951) account of symbolic make-believe constitute a playful analogue of the tendency toward broad attention deployment and nonevaluative ideational productivity, which Wallach considers central to creative thinking.

The studies summarized in the remainder of this section provide further support for the proposition that play enhances creative processes, include tests of the hypothesis about make-believe discussed above, and reflect a constructive trend that has become increasingly prominent in the psychological literature on play in recent years. This is a trend away from initial attempts to find global relationships between play and social or cognitive variables and toward an examination of the ways in which various elements and forms of play may be differentially related to a variety of dependent variables. (For illustrations of this trend in areas not included in this review see Cheyne & Rubin, in press; Pepler & Ross, 1981; Saltz, 1980).

In an attempt to test the hypothesis that, "it is the make-believe aspect of play which may be associated with divergent thinking," Li (1978, p. 35) modified Dansky and Silverman's (1973) object play design by adding an experimental group that was explicitly encouraged to make believe. Thus, Li's (1978) design included four experimental groups: imitation, free play, make-believe play, and control. As in previous studies, play subjects later gave more uses for objects than did controls. Li (1978) also found modest support for her conclusion that introduced make-believe elements in the instructions can have a "greater facilitating effect [on associative fluency] than just asking subjects to play with the objects" (p.35). However, Li's make-

believe subjects scored significantly higher than her free-play subjects on only one of the four posttest objects she included. This rather
modest support for the make-believe hypothesis may be attributable
to a weakness in her experimental manipulation. The only difference
between her free-play and make-believe conditions was that children in the latter group were given a moment of verbal encouragement to make believe prior to receiving the same instructions as the
free-play group. Thus, Li's make-believe subjects may have
engaged in no more make-believe than her free-play group. Unfortunately, Li did not report having made any systematic observations of
the behaviors displayed during the experimental sessions to check
the effectiveness of her manipulation.

In order to test more adequately the hypothesis that it is make-
believe that mediates this relationship between free play and associative fluency, Dansky (1980a) combined the techniques of
naturalistic observation and experimental manipulation in the following study. After unobtrusively observing 146 preschoolers during
free-play time in their nursery schools, it was possible to categorize
96 of the children as either "pretenders" or "nonpretenders." Pretenders spontaneously displayed make-believe quite often; nonpretenders spent less than 5 percent of their time in make-believe. All
subjects were then randomly assigned (in pairs) to either a free-play
condition or one of three control conditions (imitation, problem-
solving, or no treatment). The children were observed again during
the experimental free-play sessions. As expected, the children who
were pretenders engaged in make-believe during the experimental
free-play sessions and the nonpretenders did not. All subjects were
given an alternate-uses test immediately after their experimental
sessions.

The only group whose uses scores differed significantly from
any other group was the group of children who engaged in make-
believe during free-play. They gave significantly more unusual uses
than children in every other group. The results of behavioral observations made during the experimental free-play sessions themselves
also support the conclusion that the relationship between play opportunities and enhanced fluency depends primarily on the occurrence
of make-believe. Specifically, the data showed that the amount of
make-believe displayed during the 10 minutes just prior to testing
was directly correlated with the number of unusual uses given.
Finally, it was noted that make-believe enhanced fluency irrespec-
tive of the particular form it took (i.e., sociodramatic episode, solitary
nonliteral play with objects, or interactive nonliteral play with objects).

The various findings of this study show that,
merely providing children with play materials and encouraging
them to play will not necessarily enhance fluency. Thus, the relationship between play and fluency cannot simply be attributed to a

relative sense of freedom or perceived lack of situational constraints inherent in the unstructured context of a free-play setting.
These situational variables interact with specifiable individual differences among children (pretender/nonpretender) to yield a particular mode of activity (make-believe) which then has
implications for the level of associative fluency displayed.
(Dansky, 1980a, p.587)

This writer has recently completed another study designed to
clarify the nature of the relationship between free play and associative fluency. This study was stimulated by two informal and unpublished failures to replicate this relationship between free play and
enhanced fluency (Dansky, 1983). A post-hoc analysis of these two
failures to replicate suggested that, although both studies differed
from each other and from earlier studies in several ways, they were
similar in that neither insured that all children would be tested for
fluency immediately after playing. All previously published play/
fluency studies had posttested immediately. Therefore, the present
study was conducted to test carefully the hypothesis that a short
period of free play would have a temporary facilitating effect on associative fluency, and that this effect would be diminished significantly
by simply redirecting the child's cognitive set. This was accomplished by randomly assigning 108 middle-class preschoolers
(mean age = 4.7 years) to the three conditions originally used by
Dansky and Silverman (1973; i.e., free play, imitation, or no-treatment
control). Each experimental group was then randomly assigned to
either an immediate or a delayed posttesting condition. The delay
lasted only 2 minutes, during which time the children were occupied with a reverse digit span task. This is a serious task that requires
careful (nonplayful) attention to the experimenter's directions. This
manipulation allowed a comparison of the fluency levels of children
with a playful set (immediate posttesting after play) and a nonplayful
set (digit span delay).

Briefly, the results of this study are twofold. As in earlier studies,
play significantly enhanced associative fluency. However, when play
subjects were tested after a brief, nonplayful delay, they performed
no better than the controls did. These findings suggest that the facilitating effects of play on associative fluency may be attributed to the
activation of a temporary cognitive set that is also conducive to the
production of many imaginative associations. These findings and this
cognitive set interpretation seem to raise questions about the meaning (or significance) of this entire line of research. However, it should
also be noted that these experimental investigations of the effects of
play on associative fluency have all involved relatively brief (10-
minute) periods of play. Evidence suggesting a more enduring connection between play and creativity in situations more reflective of
children's everyday lives is examined in the next section.

CONCLUSIONS

Prior to Lieberman's (1965) investigation of the relationship between playfulness and divergent thinking, many writers had authoritatively claimed that playing enhances one's creativity; however, they did so on the basis of no systematic research. Just a few years ago, Rubin and Pepler (1980) still maintained that, despite much promising data, "the theoretical basis for arguing that play serves a causal role in growth and development is stronger than the empirical support for such a position" (p. 220). Although this writer might still agree with them, the gap between speculation and evidence in this area has closed considerably. In fact, on the basis of the research reviewed thus far in this paper, it would seem reasonable not only to conclude that play and playfulness are associated with various measures of divergent thinking, but that when young children engage in make-believe play, one clear outcome is enhanced associative fluency.

The fact that the rigorous experimental demonstrations of this causal relationship may only reflect a short-term phenomenon should not be surprising. In their initial paper on this topic, Dansky and Silverman (1973) emphasized that no claim was being made regarding a permanent increase in the creative abilities of the children studied. They state,

> The brief experimental manipulation employed here was not intended to train children to be more creative, but rather to permit a controlled examination of some of the processes which several theorists have attributed to both playful and creative behaviors . . . An inquiry into the enduring effects of play on children's creative abilities, or any enduring aspect of cognitive functioning, would require a considerably more powerful experimental manipulation (e.g., extensive work with the children under each condition over a long period of time). (Dansky & Silverman, 1973, p. 43)

Actually, some progress in this direction has been made. Two studies have been reported in which children who initially displayed little or no make-believe in their spontaneous play have been taught to engage in dramatic play in extensive sessions over a period of several weeks and were later posttested on a variety of tasks involving divergent thinking (Feitelson & Ross, 1973; Dansky, 1980b). In both of these studies, children were randomly assigned to training groups that controlled for factors such as adult involvement, warmth, verbal interaction, and tuition. The kindergarteners in Feitelson and Ross' (1973) study were pretested with three subtests from the Cincinnati Autonomy Test Battery (task initiation, curiosity box, and dog and bone) and the picture completion subtest of the Torrance (1960) "Thinking Creatively with Pictures" test. Torrance's picture completion subtest yields three measures labeled fluency, flexibility, and originality. After 10 thematic (make-believe) play training sessions, the play-trained group improved on four of the six measures noted above. Feitelson and Ross (1973) concluded that their study, "did succeed in establishing a causal relationship between an increase in level of thematic play and improved performance on conventional tests designed to measure innovative and original behavior" (p. 218). However, it should be noted that, due to their small sample size (six play-trained children), only one of the four improvements reached statistical significance (i.e., the originality score on the Torrance test). Thus, Feitelson and Ross' (1973) call for further, more-substantial studies seems prudent. Only one similar study addressing this issue has been reported thus far (i.e., Dansky, 1980b).

The only other play training study to examine the effects of play on creativity (Dansky, 1980b) has provided strong support for Feitelson and Ross' initial conclusion. Dansky's (1980b) preschool-aged subjects were trained in sociodramatic (make-believe) play and later posttested on numerous tasks, including four measures of divergent thinking. The play training effect generalized to the children's everyday free-play activities. Compared with randomly assigned control subjects, play-trained children displayed significantly more and more imaginative make-believe activity during daily free-play periods. Enhancing the quantity and quality of the children's spontaneous sociodramatic play also resulted in significantly higher scores on all four measures of divergent thinking. In the context of the present discussion, it is important to note that one of these measures was an alternate-uses task identical to the dependent measures of the studies described in the previous section. Thus, engaging in make-believe play has both a temporary and an enduring impact on a child's associative fluency. The actual facilitating mechanisms in both cases may involve the same processes proposed earlier in this paper, with enduring changes appearing as a cumulative result of repeatedly engaging in the freely assimilative functioning characteristic of make-believe play.

Finally, although evidence continues to accumulate in support of the notion that play may be "an ultimate source of novelty" (Sutton-Smith, 1972), unanswered questions remain concerning the extent to which the novelty and behavioral diversity generated in play become integrated into long-term adaptations of the player and society. Only if further research can show that such adaptations do emanate from play will we be able to go beyond the claim that play enhances processes associated with creativity to the conclusion that playing makes the player a more creative person.

REFERENCES

Birch, H.G. (1946). The relation of previous experience to insightful problem-solving. *Journal of Comparative Psychology, 38,* 367-379.

Bruner, J.S. (1972). Nature and use of immaturity. *American Psychologist, 27,* 687-708.

Cheyne, J.A., & Rubin, K.H. (in press). Playful precursors of problem-solving in preschoolers. *Developmental Psychology.*

Dansky, J.L. (1980a). Make believe: A mediator of the relationship between free play and associative fluency. *Child Development, 51,* 576-579.

Dansky, J.L. (1980b). Cognitive consequences of sociodramatic play and exploration training for economically disadvantaged preschoolers. *Journal of Child Psychology and Psychiatry, 20* 47-58.

Dansky, J.L. (1983, May). *Immediate and delayed effects of free play and fluency training on associative fluency.* Paper presented at the meetings of the Midwestern Psychological Association, Minneapolis.

Dansky, J.L., & Silverman, I.W. (1973). Effects of play on associative fluency in preschool children. *Developmental Psychology, 9,* 38-43.

Dansky, J.L., & Silverman, I.W. (1975). Play: A general facilitator of associative fluency. *Developmental Psychology, 11,* 104.

Feitelson, D., & Ross, G.S. (1973). The neglected factor of play. *Human Development, 16,* 202-223.

Guilford, J.P. (1957). Creative abilities in the arts. *Psychological Review, 64,* 110-118.

Guilford, J.P., Wilson, R.C., & Christiansen, P.R. (1951). *A factor analytic study of creative thinking: Hypotheses and test descriptions.* (Reports of Psychological Laboratory, No. 3). Los Angeles: University of Southern California.

Hutt, C., & Bharnani, R (1976). Predictions from play. In J.S. Bruner, A. Jolly, & K. Sylva (Eds.), *Play: Its role in development and evolution* (pp. 216-129). New York: Basic Books.

Johnson, J.E. (1976). Relations of divergent thinking and intelligence test scores with social and nonsocial make-believe play of preschool children. *Child Development, 47,* 1200-1208.

Johnson, J.E., Ershler, J., & Serlin, R. (in press). Developmental changes in imaginative play and cognitive ability in preschoolers. *Child Development.*

Kogan, N., & Pankove, E. (1972). Creative ability over a five-year span. *Child Development, 43,* 427-442.

Kohler, W. (1926). *The mentality of apes.* New York: Harcourt Brace.

Li, A.K. (1978). Effects of play on novel responses of preschool children. *Alberta Journal of Educational Research, 24,* 31-36.

Lieberman, J.N. (1965). Playfulness and divergent thinking: An investigation of their relationship at the kindergarten level. *Journal of Genetic Psychology, 107,* 219-224.

Lieberman, J.N. (1977). *Playfulness.* New York: Academic Press.

Pepler, D.J., & Ross, H.S. (1981). The effects of play on convergent and divergent problem-solving. *Child Development, 52,* 1202-1210.

Piaget, J. (1951). *Play, dreams and imitation in childhood.* London: Routledge Kegan Paul.

Piaget, J. (1962). *Play, dreams and imitation in childhood.* New York: W.W. Norton.

Rubin, K., & Pepler, J. (1980). The relationship of child's play to cognitive growth and development. In H. Foot, J. Smith, & T. Shapman (Eds.), *Friendship and childhood relationships* (pp. 209-233). London: John Wiley.

Saltz, E. (1980). *Pretend play: A complex of variables influencing development.* Paper presented at the meetings of the American Psychological Association, Montreal.

Schaefer, C.E. (1969). Imaginary companions and creative adolescents. *Developmental Psychology. 1,* 747-749.

Singer, D.L., & Whiton, M.B. (1971). Identical creativity and expressive aspects of human figure drawing in kindergarten-age children. *Developmental Psychology, 4,* 366-369.

Singer, J.L. (1973). *The child's world of make-believe.* New York: Academic Press.

Smilansky, S. (1968). *The effects of sociodramatic play on disadvantaged preschool children.* New York: John Wiley.

Smith, P.K., & Dutton, S. (1979). Play and training in direct and innovative problem solving. *Child Development, 50,* 830-836.

Sutton-Smith, B. (1967). The role of play in cognitive development. *Young Children, 6,* 361-370.

Sutton-Smith, B. (1972). *Play: The mediation of novelty.* Paper presented to the Scientific Congress, fur die Spiele der XX Olympiade, Munich.

Sutton-Smith, B. (1979). Play as metaperformance. In B. Sutton-Smith (Ed.), *Play and learning* (pp. 295-322). New York: Gardner Press.

Sylva, K. (1977). Play and learning. In B. Tizard & D. Harvey (Eds.), *The biology of play* (pp. 59-73). London: SIMP/Heinemann.

Sylva, K., Bruner, J.S., & Genova, P. (1976). The role of play in the problem-solving of children 3-5 years old. In J.S. Bruner, A. Jolly, & K. Sylva (Eds.), *Play: Its role in evolution and development* (pp. 244-257). New York: Basic Books.

Torrance, E.P. (1960). *Assessing the creative thinking abilities of young children.* Minneapolis: University of Minnesota Press.

Vandenberg, B. (1981). Play: Dormant issues and new directions. *Human Development, 24,* 357-365.

Wallach, M.A. (1970). Creativity. In P.H. Mussen (Ed.), *Carmichael's manual of child psychology,* Vol. 1, (pp. 1211-1272). New York: John Wiley.

Wallach, M.A., & Wing, C.W., Jr. (1969). *The talented student: A validation of the creativity-intelligence distinction.* New York: Holt, Rinehart & Winston.

PLAY AT CHILD CARE: EVENT KNOWLEDGE AT AGES THREE TO SIX

Stuart Reifel, Sandy Briley,
and Margaret Garza
University of Texas, Austin

Play activity occupies a large proportion of daily experience for children in most early childhood programs. Much of the scheduling and equipment in preschool programs is oriented to play. Earlier research has documented the frequency of different types of play in early education programs from the point of view of an adult observer (e.g., Bott, 1928; Shure, 1963). The purpose of this project is to investigate children's descriptions of their play experience in an educational setting. Specifically, the study looks at children's narrative descriptions of their own play experiences in a full-day child care program.

Child care is expanding rapidly as mothers see the need to return to the work force. In the United States alone, it is estimated that 15 million preschool children need child care and that this number will increase by 50 percent in the next 7 years (Grossman, 1980). With so many children enrolled in child care, there is a tremendous need to know more about what happens in programs and about the effects of programs. The current study addresses that need.

There is a growing awareness among those who study children that we have overlooked the child's own point of view in research (e.g., Cole, Hood, & McDermott, 1978; Mishler, 1979). This awareness has prompted those with a concern for the child's experience in educational settings to seek ways of assessing how the child understands the situations we observe from our "objective" position as researchers; what we see may or may not be experienced by the child as an example of what we choose to call it. This paper takes one step toward answering the question: What is the nature of children's own views of play activity in an educational setting?

Earlier work has looked at the actual behavior of children as they play in the classroom. Shure (1963) used time-sampling to ascertain the number of appearances by children in five different free-play areas (art, book, doll, game, block) in the preschool. She found that block play and art attracted children most frequently, with boys going to the blocks more often and girls going to art most often. Boys in block play tended to remain there for longer periods of time, as was the case for both boys and girls looking at books. Games and dolls tended to produce play of short duration.

In an earlier attempt to document indoor play habits in a nursery school, Bott (1928) observed the frequency, duration, and social patterns associated with use of different types of materials. Categories for material types were empirically generated. Data revealed age-related material preferences, with 4-year-olds selecting "Pattern Toys" (beads, puzzles, peg boards) more often than do younger children, younger children selecting "Mechanical Toys" (wind-up and battery operated cars, robots) more often, and "Locomotor Toys" (trains, tricycles, doll carriage) being used at a similar rate for both ages. These observations documented actual material selections, but the author could not make statements about social play or children's descriptions of what they did.

More recently, King (1979) looked at kindergartners' distinctions between work and play in the classroom. After observing children in a variety of activities, King interviewed the children to determine whether they were working or playing. Children indicated that they were playing when they freely chose the activity, whereas they were working when the teacher directed them to an activity, even if that activity was a game or "fun" activity. Teachers defined many more classroom activities as play than did children. King's study takes a major step toward understanding children's views of play in schools by seeing how they define activities in which they have been observed.

The current study differs from the work described above in that we attempt to have children generate and describe the experiences that they view as play in child care. We are especially interested in those on-going activities that form children's knowledge of play experience. We will rely on the concept of script to explore children's knowledge of play experience.

CHILDREN'S EXPERIENCE: A SCRIPT APPROACH

One approach to documenting children's experience has been presented by Nelson and her colleagues (Nelson, 1978; Nelson and Gruendel, 1979, 1981). They rely on the idea of a cognitive script as an organizing device for daily experience, building on the idea of script used in cognitive science (Abelson, 1981; Shank and Abelson, 1977). Experiences come to be organized into structures by a person. These structures come to guide behavior, by providing information on what typically is associated with experiences. These structures also come to shape expectations by virtue of the fact that structural relationships imply the presence of elements in any given experience. For example, on the second day of kindergarten, children already expect a sequence of acts including "coming in," play, group meeting, class work, lunch, and "going home" (Fivush, 1982). Additonal acts were added to this structure by the 2nd week of school, at which point the script for kindergarten stabilized to a large extent. This script formed the children's expectations for the school day and directed their behavior accordingly.

Two elements are characteristic of script formation. First, there must be a statement about acts, which are memories for events as experienced. For example, a group of children questioned about lunch at school responded with statements about cleaning up for lunch, setting the table, serving food, eating food, and cleaning up (Nelson and Gruendel, 1981). These acts comprise the event of school lunch. Earlier research has found consistent statements of acts for children as young as 3 (Nelson and Gruendel, 1981) who have had as little as one day's previous experience with an event (Hudson and Nelson, 1982).

The second element of script formation is the language form used to state acts. Scripts are expressed with either "we" or "you" (in the sense of "one") combined with the timeless present tense (e.g., We go outside to play. You go to sleep at nap time.). This form suggests the regular, on-going nature of the acts presented in the script.

METHODOLOGY

Data were gathered as part of a larger study of children's experience in child care. The larger study investigated narrative script formation with regard to the entire day's events, including events such as meals, nap and story times, and indoor and outdoor play activities. Fourteen children between the ages of 3 and 6 participated in the study. Every child in the center participated in interviews, if they were capable of seeing and verbally responding. This included all of the nonhandicapped, English-speaking children in a small (27-child), federally funded, full-day care program housed in the College of Education at the University of Texas at Austin. The children represented a number of ethnic groups. Children were interviewed individually by the first author, who was familiar to all the children as director of the center.

The interview began with a request to "Tell me what you do at school each day." As reported in another paper (Reifel et al., 1983), all the children responded spontaneously saying they played at school as well as participating in other events. None of those children mentioned playing outdoors at school. Illustrative examples of responses are given in Tables 1, 2, and 3. When the child completed responding to the first request for information, a series of specific requests were made about events, such as "Tell me more about what you play," and "Tell me what you like at school." Examples of those responses are also included in the tables. The interviews were tape recorded and transcribed by a graduate student who was unfamiliar with the project.

Table 1. Responses From a Girl, Age 58 Months

A: I'd like you to tell me what you do at school each day.
C: Play with toys.
A: Is that all you do? No?
C: Sleep, play with all the toys, and eat.
A: Go to sleep, play with toys, and eat.
C: And sleep with the toys.

        *   *   *

A: Still, tell me all the things you do at school.
C: Play with toys, and play with toys ... and everything.

        *   *   *

A: Tell me more about the things you do at school.
C: Play with stuff.
A: Play with stuff.
C: And go to the table and "write."
A: Tell me more about what you play.
C: Play with dolls ...
A: What happens when you go outside?
C: Play.
A: Tell me ...
C: With scooters and play houses.
A: Scooters and play houses. Tell me more.
C: And play with, play with, play with everything.

Table 2. Responses From a Boy, Age 63 Months

A: Could you tell me what you do at school each day?
C: I eat lunch.
A: Is that all you do:
C: No. I eat breakfast, too.
A: Tell me all that you do at school each day.
C: I go outside each day, and I go to sleep each day.
A: Tell me about it from the beginning. What's the first thing you do when you get to school?
C: When I get to school and eat breakfast?
A: Yes.
C. And . . . I, when I get through with breakfast, we go outside. And, and I like going outside.
A: Tell me more.
C: When we come in, when we come in we do our activity: and we sing; and, and, uh, and we, uh, and we, uh, and we play with toys; and, and we clean up; and we, uh, and we, uh, cook; and, and we make stuff.

*　　　*　　　*

A: What happens when you go outside?
C: We run.
A: Yes?
C: And we play with toys.

Table 3. Responses From a Girl, Age 67 Months

A: I'd like to find out what you do at school each day.
C: I go outside and play.
A: Is that all you do?
C: No. I eat breakfast.
A: Tell me all the things you do at school.
C: Okay. I go outside, go outside to play, and I . . . I have to go in to eat . . . to eat . . . to eat lunch.
A: Yes.
C: And then we go to school now: and then eat snack, and then we

*　　　*　　　*

A: What happens next?
A: We go outside and play.
A: Tell me what happens when you go outside to play.
C: We run, we . . . and we go outside and play.
A: Go outside to play? Is that all that happens when you are outside?
C: I, I play with my sister, Vicky.

The transcripts were independently inspected by the junior authors, who coded, respectively, for instances of play activities mentioned and for the language forms used to describe the acts. To assess the reliability of their coding, both independently recorded four of the other's transcripts. Interrater reliability for coding the play acts was .79, and was .84 for the language forms.

PLAY ACTS FINDINGS

Across the 14 transcripts, we found a total of 125 acts of play given by children. Twenty-six of these acts were simple statements affirming the act of play, such as "We play," "And then I play." Among the other play acts mentioned, there was a wide range of responses. Only one activity (using scooters) received as many as six mentions, with books receiving five mentions, outside play five mentions, puzzles four mentions, and unspecified "toys" four mentions. The remaining responses ran the gamut from playing with mud to duck-duck-goose, with some mention given to dolls, trucks, blocks, friends, and pretending to be girl scouts.

The wide range of responses necessitated the creation of an organizing scheme for considering the play acts mentioned by the children. Originally, categories for play types were generated from earlier systems developed by Piaget (1951/1962) and by Buhler (1930). An initial scan of the data suggested that materials and social activities were a significant dimension to consider, which led to the four categories presented in Table 4. It is apparent that these categories are not as refined as those developed by Piaget and others and that there are not as many possible gradations as had been elaborated by earlier theorists. These categories serve as a means of distinguishing between types of statements made by the children, rather than as a description of what they actually did in an activity. For example, a child might play with dolls with a friend, but say only that she played with dolls.

Table 5 summarizes the figures on the frequencies of different play acts, broken down into categories. These figures are further broken down by age groups. Clearly, for most of the children in this setting, play is remembered in terms of manipulative activities (e.g., playing with scooters, puzzles, on trees, with blocks) and of dramatic play without materials (playing with friends, "with people," pretending to be girl scouts or in jail). Manipulative play acts were not described as social activities or to be done with friends. Dramatic play acts did not include any reference to materials. These two categories accounted for nearly all the acts, although a small number of children at all ages made reference to pretend activities with materials. It is no surprise that rule-bound play was mentioned only by the oldest chil-

dren, even though teachers reported that all children actually participated in games with rules.

Table 4. Categories of Play Acts

I.   Play with Materials, without People

    A. Pretense

        Pretending, with the use of material props, including the
        symbolic use of materials (e.g., feeding dollies, playing house
        [with house equipment or dolls], pretending to sleep)

    B. Manipulation of Materials

        Practice or manipulation of materials with no mention of other
        motive. There may be more to the activity than purely motoric
        activity, but the manipulation of material is all that is
        mentioned (e.g., riding scooter, looking at books, playing with
        blocks, puzzles, wagons, mud, toys)

II. Social Play

    A. Dramatic

        Make-believe, or pretending, or social activity, but with no ref-
        erence to specific materials (e.g., playing house with friends
        outdoors, pretending to be girl scouts, playing in general)

    B. Games

        Collective games, with rules (e.g., duck-duck-goose, hide-
        and-seek)

Table 5. Play Acts Provided by Children

	Totals N=14		Younger n=7		Older n=7	
	#	%	#	%	#	%
Materials						
Pretend	7	5.6	2	4.1	5	6.6
Manipulation	50	47.2	23	46.9	36	47.4
Social						
Dramatic	57	45.6	24	49.0	33	43.9
Games	2	1.6	0	0.0	2	2.6
Totals	125		49		76	

The summary figures reported above are further refined by considering summaries of each child's responses. A proportion of each child's total number of responses for each category was averaged across children. These findings are summarized in Table 6, revealing a slightly different pattern than in Table 5. The total figures for the entire group do not change much, but one age difference emerges. Older children in the group tend to include a greater number of manipulative play activities than do younger children.

Table 6. Mean Proportion of Play Act Types Per Child

	Pretend	Manipulative	Dramatic	Games
Younger Children n = 7	2.74	40.25	45.72	0
Older children n = 7	5.95	51.36	40.65	2.04
Total N=14	3.75	45.51	41.68	1.02

Note. Average proportion figures will not total 100%.

LANGUAGE FINDINGS

That children produced instances of play acts from their school day is necessary, but not sufficient, evidence for the existence of scripts for play. Further evidence can be found in the language children use to express their knowledge of play acts. Specifically, we look for the use of a general present tense: you (in the sense of "one") or we with present tense (e.g., "You play with dolls;" "We play duck-duck-goose."), as opposed to I with any verb tense (e.g., "I rode on the scooter; "I like puzzles."). In most cases, present tense with "we" or "you" gives a sense of habitual, regular activity.

Of the 125 acts of play given by the children, roughly half were in the general present tense and half were in present tense with a non-general pronoun (usually I, they, or no pronoun). There were very few cases of the use of a tense other than present. Again, to compare the figures on language form used across children, the proportion of each language form used was averaged (see Table 7). The age differences in language form indicate a developmental progression toward a script-like description of play experiences. For younger children (ages 3 and 4), there is a tendency to see play activities as personal, on-going activities (e.g., I play with a doll). Older children (ages 5 and 6) are more likely to see play as regular activities that everyone (we, or "one") participates in (e.g., We play with toys).

Table 7. Mean Proportions of Language Forms

| | Present Tense | | Other Tense |
	We, You	I, They, No Pronoun	
Younger Children			
n=7	29.27	68.53	2.20
Older Children			
n=7	65.43	30.87	3.70
Total			
N=14	47.35	49.70	2.95

DISCUSSION

The data presented here suggest that, by age five, children have formed general-knowledge scripts of play activities in child care. By that age they use language forms that indicate regular, daily participation in play activities, usually with materials (such as scooters or dolls) or with friends (pretending games). Play events fit into the child's overall structure of the child care day, as an expected component of daily experience. Play activities complement other activities in child care such as meals, story, and nap time.

It also appears to be clear that children associate play with both indoor and outdoor times at child care. Play takes place for children during certain indoor periods (i.e., when they are not eating, resting, or hearing stories) and apparently all the time outdoors (e.g., "We go outside and play"). Play is associated with certain parts of the temporal child care day and with all the spatial areas that they describe. This is apparently more likely among the older children than among the younger.

Even the youngest children include play as part of their scripts, although their descriptions are somewhat less differentiated and elaborated. They included fewer descriptions of play acts, even though the profile of acts they did describe resembles that of the older children in many ways. While it is less clear for the younger children in this sample, it appears that play is seen mostly as manipulations of toys (with no mention of people) and as dramatic play (with friends but not with materials). Formal games with rules emerged only in the scripts of the older children. The latter finding is especially interesting in light of the fact that all the children did play games with rules.

While the interview method used here only begins to scratch the surface of children's descriptions of play, it is interesting that the children here described play either in terms of materials or of people, but seldom both. Teachers and other observers would confirm that most of the children's play was both social and with materials (e.g., groups of pretend motorcycle cops on scooters; "families" of children playing house with dolls). Why do these children form their descriptions based on either materials or people? It is possible that their descriptions are a function of the interview and its questions. It is also possible that children of this age do not tend to think of play as having multiple, simultaneous dimensions. They may be centering on one aspect of play, in Piaget's sense of the term centering (Piaget and Inhelder, 1966/1969). It is possible that their spontaneous descriptions will remain centered until children reach the stage of concrete operations. It is also possible that these spontaneous descriptions accurately reflect these young children's perceptions and preferences for play at this time.

There are many refinements to be made in interviewing techniques with young children. There are benefits to be had from such work, especially benefits from gaining the child's point of view. In many cases, how adults see and define play behaviors may not be consistent with the child's sense of the play. An example would be the child riding on a scooter, who can be understood as participating in gross motor play (Buhler, 1930). The child may, in fact, be pretending to be a motorcycle rider, and the play would more accurately be described as dramatic. A child building a block house would appear to be involved in construction play. It may be the case that the child is creating a place for a doll family to live, so is really involved in planning for dramatic play. The child's description and perspective are necessary in these situations to clarify the meaning of the observed activity.

The same argument may hold true for children's descriptions of their experience in child care. Are they experiencing what the adult teachers intend that they experience? Do the children and adults share a common view of daily events? In this study we have attempted to learn more about the child's construction of play experience in child care. From the teacher's point of view, the children are expressing knowledge of some events they plan for and value. The children may be developing a sense of play and other school events that approximates the teacher's view. Exploring children's scripts of events may help us understand more about their socialization into child care, school, and other environments.

REFERENCES

Abelson, R.P. (1981). Psychological status of the script concept. *American Psychologist, 36,* 715-729.

Bott, H. (1928). Observation of play activities in a nursery school. *Genetic Psychology Monographs, 4,* 44-88.

Buhler, K. (1930). *The mental development of the child.* New York: Harcourt, Brace and Co.

Cole, M., Hood, L., & McDermott, R.P. (1978). *Ecological niche picking: Ecological invalidity as an axiom of experimental cognitive psychology.* Unpublished manuscript, University of California at San Diego.

Fivush, R. (1982). *Learning about school: The development of kindergartener's school scripts.* Unpublished doctoral dissertation, City University of New York.

Grossman, A.S. (1980). Working mothers and their children. *Monthly Labor Review, 104,* 49-54.

Hudson, J., & Nelson, K. (1982). *Scripts and autobiographical memories.* Unpublished manuscript, City University of New York.

King, N.R. (1979). Play: The kindergartener's perspective. *The Elementary School Journal, 80,* 81-87.

Mishler, E.G. (1979). Meaning in context: Is there any other kind? *Harvard Educational Review, 49,* 1-19.

Nelson, K. (1978). How young children represent knowledge of their world in and out of language. In R.S. Siegler (Ed.), *Children's thinking: What develops?* (pp. 255-274). Hillsdale. NJ: Erlbaum.

Nelson, K. & Gruendel, J. (1979). At morning it's lunchtime: A scriptal view of children's dialogues. *Discourse Processes, 2,* 73-94.

Nelson, K., & Gruendel, J. (1981). Generalized event representations: Basic building blocks of cognitive development. In M.E. Lamb and A.L. Brown (Eds.), *Advances in developmental psychology,* Vol. 1, (pp. 131-158). Hillsdale, NJ: Erlbaum.

Piaget, J. (1962). *Play, dreams and imitation in childhood* (C. Gattegno & F.M. Hodgson, Trans.). New York: Norton (Original work published in 1951.)

Piaget, J. & Inhelder, B. (1969). *The psychology of the child* (H. Weaver, Trans.). New York: Basic Books. (Original work published in 1956.)

Reifel, S., Garza, M., & Briley, S. (1983). *Child care as script: Children's descriptions of daily experiences.* Unpublished manuscript, The University of Texas at Austin.

Shank, R.C., & Abelson, R.P. (1977). *Scripts, plans, goals, and understanding.* Hillsdale, NJ: Erlbaum.

Shure, M.E. (1963). Psychological ecology of a nursery school. *Child Development, 34,* 979-994.

3

CHILDREN'S PLAY IN ETHNOGRAPHIC PERSPECTIVE

INTRODUCTION

Wanni Wilsbulswasdi Anderson

The relationship of play to the socialization experiences and cognitive functioning of children is well recognized. As a shared system of ludic knowledge and interactional rules of behavior, the play of children can be regarded as a subculture, a children's culture. To date, the goals of children's play ethnography have included multi-faceted approaches, multi-dimensional studies, intracultural investigations, or cross-cultural inquiries. In response to these objectives, the methodological approaches used to analyze children's play data are becoming increasingly sophisticated as the descriptive, qualitative approach, rich in content and contextual meanings, is combined with the controlled, quantitative approach, bringing together the insights of anthropology, sociology, folklore, and literature, as well as developmental psychology.

The papers in this chapter exemplify the trend. Western and non-Western, urban and rural cultural settings are the backdrops of Katz, Forbes, Yablick and Kelly's paper, and Harkness and Super's paper. Whereas Katz et al. employed video-taping of the free play activities of 5-year-old American children in the laboratory setting, Harkness and Super's method is based on spot observations of Kip sigis children, ages 1 to 9 years old, in their natural setting. The focus of Katz et al.'s paper is on children's pretend play in relationship to children's interactional behavior and the construction of reality. Pretend play is here seen as a fantasy drama with a dramatic sequence of acts and scenes in which children, as actors, used behavioral norms within the culture as arguments, believed to be the reality shared by all children. Harkness and Super, on the other hand, apply the concept of "developmental niche" to analyze Kipsigis play activities in their physical and cultural context in relationship to the cultural concept of child rearing. The effect of Kipsigis socialization is observable in the acceleration of work over idleness and play activities of children from the age of 4 years old on up.

Vandenberg's theoretical paper "Mere Child's Play" poses a challenge to the future of the ethnopsychology of emotions in play research. Vandenberg feels that, rather than looking at the roles of children's play from the standpoint of adults' cultural values and developmental theories, play scholars should devote more attention to looking at play from the perspective of children's experience. Children's emotional experience of excitement, of hope, and of expectation are cited here as examples. Vandenberg also emphasizes the importance of the scholar's own orientation, for it is his cultural values and objectives that direct the way the questions are framed and where and how the answers are sought.

The ethnography of children's play—how to decode its meaning and how to provide insights that give full breadth and depth of its dynamism in a particular culture and across culture—continues to be a challenge. It is hoped that the challenge will stimulate further sophisticated research and insights into the world of play. Scholarship will be all the richer for such endeavors.

THE CULTURAL STRUCTURING OF CHILDREN'S PLAY IN A RURAL AFRICAN COMMUNITY

Sara Harkness and Charles M. Super
Harvard School of Public Health

Anthropological interest in children's play, as with many other aspects of child life in different cultures, has traditionally centered on its relationship to adult life. As described by Schwartzman (1978) in her comprehensive treatise on the anthropology of children's play, the idea that children's play has the important function of serving as practice or rehearsal for adult activities has become "one of the most commonly accepted explanations in the literature" (p. 100). Schwartzman (1978) quotes Malinowski (1944), who, in propounding this theory of play, also seems to express his own feelings about the process of childhood socialization in general:

> The foundation of all synthetic knowledge, the first elements, that is, of the scientific outlook, the appreciation of custom, authority, and ethics, are received within the family. Later on, the growing child enters the group of his playmates, where, once more, he is dulled towards conformity, obedience to custom and etiquette. (p.100)

More recently, Lancy (1976) has tested the validity of the "practice" theory of play through an examination of relationships between children's play and aspects of adult life among the Kpelle. In his review of play behavior among Kpelle children, he notes that children's play in that society can be related to adult life along several dimensions, including learning specific technologies, social and sociolinguistic skills, and cultural values.

The study of children's play as it relates to knowledge necessary for successful functioning as an adult in a particular culture, especially as developed in detailed studies such as those carried out by Lancy, holds promise for enhancing our understanding of what Schwartz (1981) has referred to as "the acquisition of culture." In these studies, the general orientation of the researcher may take either one of two basic directions. The first, as in earlier functionalist studies, is to view the activities of childhood with a long-range focus on the roles of adult life. The second orientation is simply the reverse and uses knowledge of the culture in general to interpret the structuring of children's play.

Research by the authors in a rural Kipsigis community of Kenya has taken something more akin to this latter orientation. In studying many diverse aspects of child development and family life in this community, the goal has been to gain a greater understanding of the interactions between universal processes in human development and functioning, and the specific environments that different cultures provide for their expression. In order to describe the environmental side of this interface, we have elaborated the idea of the "developmental niche." An understanding of how experience is structured for individuals at different developmental stages is necessary, we believe, not only for an adequate theory of child development but also for the analysis of cultural systems.

The developmental niche can be conceptualized in terms of three basic dimensions. The first consists of the physical and social settings in which the child lives, including, for example, aspects of daily routine such as where he or she spends different amounts of time, in whose company, and engaged in what kinds of activities. A second dimension consists of culturally regulated systems of child care and rearing or, in other words, the repertoire of strategies that parents and other caretakers call on in meeting the needs of children. The third dimension of the developmental niche is the psychology of the caretakers, or the beliefs and values that inform the ways in which parents and others both structure and respond to behavior in children. The "developmental niche" has provided a useful theoretical framework for considering various aspects of childhood socialization and development, including the development of sleep in infancy and the socialization of affect (Harkness & Super, 1984, Super & Harkness, 1982).

The idea of the developmental niche may be particularly helpful in considering relationships between the child's environment and universally recognized elements of behavior. In these cases, the process of environmental shaping of children's behavior is more evident than in those areas where it is not quite clear whether the behavior is in some sense the product of the environment in the first place.

Play would seem to be a good candidate for status as a universally recognized construct. Although, as Schwartzman (1978) notes, students of play have yet to agree on a single definition, the idea of play would seem to be a familiar folk concept in all cultures. Even for those of us whose lives are too dominated by the Puritan ethic, the notion of play is at least honored in the breach. Yet the confusion—if such it is—over what the real definition of play is may indicate (among other things) an important aspect of this construct: namely, that play may be a very different kind of phenomenon depending on the context in which it takes place. This paper will offer some considerations of how the nature of play is shaped by its function in the developmental niches of children among the Kipsigis of Kenya.

The sample community, called Kokwet, is a Kipsigis settlement in the western highlands of Kenya. The Kipsigis, who refer to themselves as belonging to the Kalenjin grouping, are a highland Nilotic people whose subsistence base is cattle herding and swidden agriculture. Like other highland East African peoples, the Kipsigis are patrilineal and traditionally used age sets as the basis of military organization. Today, male and female circumcision ceremonies remain the focal point of cultural solidarity. Kokwet, the location for our anthropological and psychological research for 3 years (1972 to 1975), consists of 54 households established on land repatriated from the British in 1963. Although as a government-sponsored "settlement scheme" Kokwet was intentionally modern in some agricultural practices, the community remained traditional in many significant respects: most adults had little or no schooling, few men worked at salaried jobs away from the homesteads, cows were still used for the customary brideprice, and virtually all adolescents still chose to undergo the traditional circumcision ceremonies.

Many features of child life in Kokwet, as elsewhere, are derived from the economic and social organization of adult life. The work of mothers in Kokwet includes farming on the family fields as well as gathering firewood and bringing water from the river, preparing food, and being responsible for the care of the children. Fathers are in charge of the cows, plowing the fields when new crops are to be planted, major repairs around the property, and the important political business of the community. The cultivation of crops is intensive and more successful the more hands that are available. Perhaps for this reason, the traditionally preferred form of marriage was, and still is for many men in the community, polygyny.

But the labor of women is not sufficient to accomplish all the tasks of the household; children are also important contributors to the economic equation. Children are used to help take care of younger siblings, the cows, the gardens, errands, and in general help around the homestead. One striking aspect of these childhood tasks is the age at which children are expected to carry out important responsibilities. It is not unusual, for example, to see a child of three chasing a calf out of the garden. The children responsible for taking care of babies are usually 8 to 10 years old, and may be as young as 5 or 6.

Data on children's daily routines in Kokwet comes from an adaptation of the "spot observation" technique developed by the Munroes (1971). Over the course of a year, all 54 households were visited 10 times (each during a period of 2 to 3 weeks) at randomly assigned hours of the day from 9:00 a.m. to 6:00 p.m. At each visit, the observer noted the location and activities of each family member who could be seen around the homestead, and gathered a report from someone present on the location and activities of those others who could not be directly observed. Taken as a whole, these "family spot observations" provide a profile of the daily lives of people of different ages in Kokwet.

In order to obtain a schematic measure of how children aged 2 to 9 years spend their time, the activities listed for them on the family spot observations were grouped into three major categories: play, idleness, and work. These three major categories accounted together for approximately 80 percent of the children's observations, with eating and school accounting for most of the remainder. The play category consisted of the subcategories of active or quiet play alone or with others, while the idleness category included resting, sleeping, watching others, or just sitting around either alone or with others. The work category included a long list of chores, including processing food, cooking and tending the fire, collecting firewood and bringing water, taking care of the animals, and caring for young children.

As can be seen in Figure 1, at age 2 play seems to be the activity occupying the greatest proportion of the children's time (almost 40 percent), followed by idleness (about 25 percent), and then work (about 12 percent). Starting at age 3, however, the trends in children's activities begin to reverse themselves, with the work category climbing sharply to age 6 while the play and idleness categories drop off. At age 9, children are spending over 50 percent of their time in work activities, and 10 percent or less in play and idleness.

This profile of children's activities might seem a bit grim, except that it is not the whole story. Although the family spot observations provide data on activities that were actually observed, they also include reports of activities to which the children were assigned. As such, they contain two different kinds of information. First, the family spot observations tell us a great deal about settings for children's social and individual behavior, including play. A game of tag could take place in the context of watching the cows, for example, and a child might climb a tree while looking after a younger sibling. Secondly, the family spot observations give a good indication of the kinds

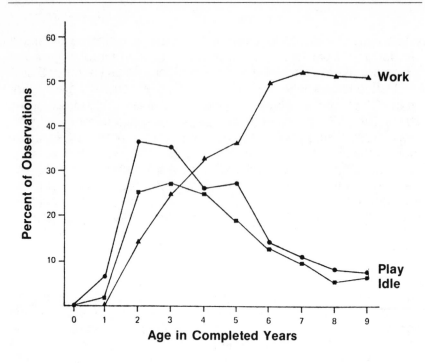

Figure 1. Amount of time spent in play, idleness, and work for children aged 2 to 9 years. *Note.* From "The cultural construction of child development: A framework for the socialization of affect" by S. Harkness and C.M. Super, 1983, *Ethos,* **11,** 226. Copyright by University of California Press. Reprinted by permission.

of socialization pressures to which children in Kokwet must respond as they pass through successive stages of child development. Specifically, it seems clear that socialization is toward work, not play, for these children.

The structuring of the developmental niche for children in Kokwet should have a number of implications for the nature of children's play. For present purposes, we will briefly present some material that supports the idea that elements in the developmental niche are reflected in the sequencing of children's play episodes as well as in the content of mother-child interactions.

Information on children's play episodes comes from a large collection of running records of children's naturally occurring behavior, which were written and later coded using the system developed by Beatrice Whiting (1971). Although episodes of play often occur in these protocols, it seems that they are usually interspersed with other activities or curtailed in some fashion. This aspect of sequencing is illustrated in the following example, constituting all of a 20-minute observation was a 4-year-old girl whom we shall call Chebet. Other people present were her mother (Obot Chebet), her 8-year-old sister (Chepkemoi), her 7-year-old brother (Kiprotich), her 2-year-old brother (Kibii), and the observer, a young woman from the community. The observation took place at home, probably in the space defined by the family kitchen hut on one side and the maize storehouse on the other.

The observation began with Kiprotich asking Chebet who was coming (presumably a reference to the observer). Chebet answered, "I don't know."

Kibii asked Chebet if he could see the mirror that she was holding. Chebet tried to run away, but Kibii grabbed her dress. Chebet shouted, "It's mine!"

Kiprotich asked Chebet to let Kibii see the mirror. Chebet replied, "He won't return it."

Kiprotich said, "I will make him return it," so Chebet handed over the mirror to Kibii.

Chebet followed Kibii around saying, "He took my mirror." Kiprotich asked Kibii to return the mirror, but he refused. Kiprotich tricked the mirror away from Kibii and gave it back to Chebet.

Chebet admired herself in the mirror, then stared at the observer, then listened to a donkey cry in the distance.

Obot Chebet asked Kiprotich to play with Chebet. Kiprotich came over and embraced Chebet, then whispered to her, "Mummy said that we should play."

Chebet replied, "Let me put away my mirror first," and went into the hut to put it away.

Chebet and Kiprotich wrestled with each other, but stopped when Obot Chebet told Kiprotich not to put Chebet down on the grass.

Chepkemoi invited Chebet to play tag, and Chebet agreed. She chased Kiprotich, who pushed her down. Chebet sat on the grass, crying, "You pushed me!"

Kiprotich invited Chebet to tag him. Chebet chased him but was not able to catch him so she stood aside.

Chepkemoi called to Chebet to tag her, and Chebet chased after her but soon asked her not to run so fast. Chepkemoi slowed down and let herself be tagged. Chebet then tagged Kiprotich and announced, "I have tagged you both!"

Obot Chebet told Chebet not to run because she was coughing. Chebet sat down. Obot Chebet then asked her to call Chepkemoi, which she did. Kiprotich invited her to play again, but she ignored the request.

Kiprotich again invited her to play tag, which she did. Being unable again to tag Kiprotich, however, she sat and chewed on a blade of grass.

This behavior observation contains episodes of what might be called individual play, involving a mirror, by both the target child and her younger brother. It also contains a game of tag. Both of these instances of play occur within a larger framework of responsibilities of older members of the family for younger members. In the case of the mirror, the older brother intervenes first with the target child on behalf of her younger sibling, then on behalf of the target child to get it back from the younger child. At the mother's directive, the older brother then initiates play with the target child: a wrestling match. The mother immediately intervenes in prohibiting the older brother from putting the target child down on the grass (presumably because she has a cough, as is indicated later in the observation). The older sister then initiates a game of tag. This game is sporadic in its development, as the target child stops when pushed by her older brother and again when she is unable to tag her older siblings. The game is again curtailed at the mother's directive; she then asks the target child to do a quick chore (calling her older sister). The observation terminates with another very brief episode of tag.

We suspect that this kind of sequencing in and around episodes of play may be more common than one might gather from reading reports whose focus is the play itself, not its context. Nevertheless, the sporadic quality of play activities recorded in observations such as the above may also be due to the general orientation of families in Kokwet toward work, not play. One way in which socialization pressures are expressed may be in the development of behavior sequences toward longer and more complex strings. If this is true, then we would expect that in a setting such as Kokwet sequences of work for children would become longer and more complex, while sequences of play would tend to remain short and relatively undeveloped.

The orientation of socialization pressures should also be reflected in the topics around which parents interact with their children. In carrying out a study of child language development in Kokwet, we found that it was difficult to obtain even small samples of mothers talking with their 2- and 3-year-old children, as such communications tended to be brief at best. Mothers, when asked, reported that they did not believe that it was their role to play with their children. This was the responsibility of the child caretakers (who were usually older siblings, as in the observation described above). Thus, it is not surprising that in 2-hour recordings of child language at home in naturally occurring situations for a sample of 21 children, there are no instances of mothers playing with their children. What we find instead is mothers reprimanding their children for work not done, directing dialogue around an episode of sweeping the house (with the help of the toddler), or training the young child in doing errands — this last episode being the closest we come to a "play" interaction.

In conclusion, it seems that parents in different cultures choose different domains for developing desired characteristics in their children. These choices imply the assignment of children to setting (see

B. Whiting, 1980), or the structuring of the developmental niche. In Kokwet, children's play very often takes place in the context of work. To say that the opposite is true of our American culture, though over simple, may not be far from the truth. Although we personally do not have systematic data on this subject, we would like to offer one anecdote as an illustration of our perceptions as parents. The other day, one of us asked our 2-year-old daughter to go upstairs to tell her sisters that supper was ready. Her response seemed to indicate a toddler's first attempts to express the cultural principle that, for American children at home, play comes before work. Her words were, "First have watch TV, Mommy."

Note

The research reported here was supported by funds from the Carnegie Corporation of New York, the William T. Grant Foundation, and the National Institutes of Mental Health (grant No. 33281). All statements made and views expressed are the sole responsibility of the authors.

REFERENCES

Harkness, S., & Super, C.M. (1984). The cultural construction of child development: A framework for the socialization of affect. In S. Harkness & P.L. Kilbride (Eds.), The socialization of affect. *Ethos, 11,* 221-231.

Lancy, D., & Tindall, B.A. (Eds.). (1976). *The anthropological study of play: Problems and prospects.* New York: Leisure Press.

Munroe, R.H., & Munroe, R.L. (1971). Household density and infant care in the East African society. *Journal of Social Psychology, 83,* 3-13.

Schwartz, T. (1981). The acquisition of culture. *Ethos, 9,* 4-17.

Schwartzman, H.B. (1978). *Transformation: The anthropology of children's play.* New York: Plenum Press.

Super, C.M., & Harkness, S. (1982). The infant's niche in rural Kenya and metropolitan America. In L.L. Adler (Ed.), *Cross-cultural research at issue* (pp. 47-55). New York; Academic Press.

Whiting, B.B. (1971). *A transcultural code for the study of social behavior.* Unpublished manuscript, Laboratory for Human Development, Harvard University.

Whiting, B.B. (1980). Culture and social behavior: A model for the development of social behavior. *Ethos, 8,* 95-116.

DISAGREEMENTS DURING PLAY: CLUES TO CHILDREN'S CONSTRUCTIONS OF REALITY[1]

Mary Maxwell Katz, David Forbes, Gary Yablick, and Victoria Kelly

Laboratory of Human Development
Harvard Graduate School of Education

Many psychological studies of children's pretend play delineate the cognitive and social competencies expressed in play without referring to the content of play themes in any detail (cf. Fein's 1981 review). Yet to researchers with an ethnographic orientation, the content of play themes is of great interest not only as a window to children's thinking about the world, but also because an understanding of the specific meaning of themes to the participants is considered essential to an interpretation of the behavior of individuals in any social interaction. This study describes a method being developed for the systematic examination of play themes—their structure, their potential as clues to children's constructions of reality, and their role in social interactions.

Our own interest in play themes has been stimulated by preliminary observations of pretend play episodes of 5- and 7-year-old children from Cambridge, Massachusetts, that suggest that children in social pretend play are occupied by three closely intertwined agendas—the thematic, the social, and the communicative. It appeared that each of these agendas may have cultural conventions whose reference and manipulation together create the particular meaning of play sequences. We wished to consider further the problem of whether and how thematic conventions constrain or orient children in play in the way that others have pointed out for social and linguistic conventions.

Recently, a number of developmental psychologists have noted the importance of conventional schemata or scripts in children's pretend play (e.g., Garvey & Berndt, 1977; Nelson & Gruendel, 1979) and others have acknowledged the centrality of shared knowledge or mutual understandings between participants in analyses of play episodes (Franklin, 1983; Brenner & Mueller, 1982). The present study is consistent with these concerns and also builds upon the work of scholars who have noted the dramatistic or metaphoric qualities of both play and social custom (Bateson, 1956; Goffman, 1974; LeVine, 1982; Schwartzman, 1978, 1982; Sutton-Smith, 1979). As for the methodological approach, perusing the methods for identifying thematic elements and examining relations between them suggests that more guidance is available in anthropology, literary analysis, and cognitive science than in developmental psychology. The methodological approach of this study draws on a sampling method familiar to ethnographers and on a content coding system inspired by the work of Kenneth Burke (1969).

The sampling method—observation of instances of interpersonal distress or conflict — is well known to ethnographers working in unfamiliar settings, although not necessarily articulated by them as a specific method. Analysis of disputes and disagreements in daily life is an efficient means to identify cultural and individual beliefs, because at these times the interactants usually make explicit references to norms and values. Several studies of children's disputes have already shown that a common behavior in these episodes is the offering of reasoned arguments or explanations that make reference to cultural beliefs and norms of various kinds (Brenneis & Lein, 1977; Eisenberg & Garvey, 1981; Much & Shweder, 1978; Walton & Sedlack, 1982). The analysis of social pretend play in particular, however, allows additional leverage in the study of meaning systems, because the content of pretense is potentially idiosyncratic and relatively arbitrary. In order to begin and maintain social pretend play, children must make explicit communications that establish the play elements and their meanings (Garvey & Berndt, 1977). We therefore expected that examination of children's disagreements during pretend play would be an efficient method for gaining information about their thinking—their ideas about their immediate world of pretend play, and possibility about what they view to be "real" outside of play as well.

The strategy of examining disagreements is also a way to consider the social use of themes in play. Disagreements are critical moments which threaten the social continuity of play. Children must maximally call upon and activate the resources at their command. In disagreements we might see what themes offer as a resource or constraint in the social construction of play.

A second aspect of the sampling method is the analysis of the play of unacquainted children, whose lack of previous familiarity provides further cause of explicitness in communications about play elements. As described in greater detail below, play episodes used in this analysis are those occurring in the first of 12 play-group sessions among previously unacquainted children.

The notion of "dramatism" proposed by Kenneth Burke (1969) was chosen to guide the analysis of thematic components because it proposes not only the components of dramatic themes—agent (actor or role), scene, act, purpose, and agency—but also that these elements are necessarily interrelated. Burke points out that language, as symbolic act, has dramatic implications. An act necessarily has a scene, an actor, and so forth. Transposing this scheme onto the elements of children's fantasy dramas allowed us to examine how children might refer to and use these implied relations between elements in fantasy play, and how these may or may not act as thematic constraints on their play. This necessity can be seen as more than only a propositional logic, but as also including a predicational logic. That is, when the nature of an act is specified, an appropriate scene can also be specified. Since in social pretend play children construct their dramas together, a diagramming of the elements being offered by different children promised to convey not only the content of themes, but also their social usage.

This article outlnes the method of analysis and presents two examples of its application in order to consider its usefulness for understanding children's pretend play interactions.

METHODS

The play episodes considered here are from videotaped laboratory play of two groups previously unacquainted 5-year-old children from Cambridge, Massachusetts. When they volunteered for the study, the parents and children were told that this was a study about how children play and make friends with each other. The groups were composed of six children each, three girls and three boys, who came to the university for 12 1-hour sessions held after school during a 3-week period. The 20 ft × 25 ft playroom was equipped with various toys, board games, art and construction supplies, and a 3 ft × 6 ft sand play table. An adult supervisor was always present, usually staying in a small kitchen attached to the playroom and intervening in the children's play as little as possible.

The segments considered in this study are all extended fantasy play episodes in the first half-hour of play of the two play groups. The first day was chosen to minimize the presence of shared understandings based on acquaintanceship and to see how children would handle the problem of establishing joint play when the need to reach consensus was greatest.

The first step in analysis was to locate disagreements. These were identified when any of the following occurred: two or more attempts were made by a child to persuade another child to change his or her ongoing behavior, regardless of the persuadee's response; explicit noncompliance to a request; use of "no," "you can't," or other negatives in reference to another child's behaviors or statements.

The second step in analysis was to code each utterance in the transcript (whether in a disagreement or not) in terms of the dramatic elements introduced (either by reference or enactment) and the relation of these to previously mentioned elements. The relation of an element to previously introduced elements was coded as either no relation, or as one or more of the following: consistent with elements previously introduced by the speaker, consistent within contradiction with elements previously introduced by another child; in contradiction with elements previously introduced by the speaker; in contradiction with elements previously introduced by another child.[2] Reliability of the element coding was calculated among pairs in a group of four coders over fantasy play episodes totaling 85 lines of transcript. The average intercoder agreement for the identification of element types was 66.5 percent where disagreements include present/absent disagreements, and 77.7 percent where only element type is considered.

The following example illustrates the method of coding. This episode occurs just after the children have entered the playroom.

Example 1.
On entering the playroom, Ronda tries out the telephone, then the cash register; then Polly tries the phone, Ronda then says to Polly:

1.	R>P:	Pretend this was a restaurant, O.K.?
2.	P:	OK.
3.	R>P:	OK, and I'll be the waiter.

Melinda approaches them; she has been wandering around the room looking at various games. Ronda walks around the snack table as if not sure of her next move, then goes up to Melinda, who is watching Polly at the cash register:

4.	R>M:	Excuse me, sit right ... (grabs Melinda by shoulders).
5.	M:	(resists)
6.	R>M:	OK, what would you like for lunch?
7.	M:	(no response)
8.	R>M:	You're at the restaurant and you've always got to eat there. You can't just stand around.
9.	M:	(looks around)
10.	R>M:	OK, what would you like?
11.	M:	Cou- could I get it myself? I wanna get it myself.

They both bend down and look at some toy dishes on the shelf.

12.   R>M: Here's the coffee and stuff. I'm gonna play
                   Barbie doll.
                   (she goes to the small table nearby)
13.   M>RP: Is there real stuff in here? (looks at
                   coffee cup with liquid sealed in the sides
14.   R: (ignores)

Lines 4-12 are coded as a "disagreement" episode because Ronda made two or more attempts to persuade Melinda to play customer (lines 4,6,8,10), as well as using a negative reference to Melinda's current behavior (line 8).

In this episode, the following elements are coded:

Speaker	Element	Line
R	Scene 1 = restaurant	1
R	Character 1 = waiter	3
R	Behavior 1 = seating of customer	4
R	Character 2 = customer (implied through reciprocal)	4
R	Behavior 2 = order taking	6
R	Behavior 3 = eating	8
R	Behavior 4 = not standing around	8
M	Behavior 5= self-serve	11
R	Behavior 6 = show coffee	12
R	Object 1 = coffee	12
R	Scene 2 = play Barbie doll	12

THEMES EXPLAINED BY CHILDREN

For the two groups, 48.7 minutes out of the 52 transcribed contained social pretend play, and there were 34 disagreement episodes. The core arguments—the most fully developed arguments—of each episode were examined. Several types of statments were found: 1) first and most frequent, rule-like statements, rephrasable in the form, "Do/do not do this because ...." (16/34 cases); 2) statements of personal preference such as "I wanna get it myself," and "I do not need any," (5/34); 3) use of normative language ("should," "have to") without offering a reason (4/34); 4) offering a contrasting proposition without explaining a link to former elements (4/34); 5) reference to social norms such as sharing and taking turns (4/34); and miscellaneous (1/34).

Brenneis and Lein (1977), Eisenberg and Garvey (1981), and Walton and Sedlack (1982) have found similar types of statements in more extended studies of children's disputes; and Much and

Shweder (1978) have categorized the kinds of rules implicitly referred to in such episodes. These authors' interests, however, while varying, have not concerned so much the specific thematic content of disagreement episodes and its role in the ongoing social interaction.

Examining the thematic content of these core arguments, we found that in the first type above, which were half of all cases, children stated a necessary relationship between two or more dramatic elements (a "rule"). Some examples of rule-like statements are these: "You're at the restaurant, you've always got to eat there, you can't just stand around." These statements spell out a rule about which behaviors are appropriate or inappropriate in a restaurant scene. "I haven't buyed anything yet" during an argument about when and how to exchange money implies a rule governing the appropriate sequence of behaviors in making a purchase—selecting the goods and then paying. "You can't come in here 'cause this is where we make the stuff" said by the waitress to customer in the restaurant implies a rule precluding customers (certain kinds of agents) from certain spaces (parts of scene). In some cases the operative relationship between elements is expressed within the utterance itself, as in the first and third examples above; in others, it is implicit, referring to prior or planned action—[I don't pay now because] "I haven't buyed anything yet." Eisenberg and Garvey (1981) have pointed out that statements such as these are explanations, which fulfill norms of polite social procedure following public opposition. Similarly, Brenneis Lein (1977) found "reasoned arguments to be one category of response in a sociolinguistic study of children's dispute settlement.

These cases in which rules involving relationships between elements are spelled out by children appear to be potential clues to children's constructions of reality. Before asserting that they are, it is necessary to determine whether these are only pretend rules that children propose for the current play or statements that reflect more generally shared cultural knowledge derived from common real-life situations. In pretense we would expect to find many rule-like statements describing elements of a fantasy world because such statements are necessary in order for children to establish and maintain play (cf. Garvey & Berndt, 1977). In this study, however, the rule-like statements that children made during disagreements described rules that adult culture members (the coders) could agree were "real." We know that customers cannot go into the food preparation area in restaurants, and so forth. In other words, while children may agree on many arbitrary and nonrealistic rules in play, these children resorted to real-life rules as a social strategy during disagreements.

Turning to the other response types found, in which children did not spell out rules explicitly, some appear to refer to a relationship of necessity between elements, even though the logic is not spelled out in an utterance. A number of the personal preference statements (e.g., "I wanna get it myself," "I do not need any") took place during role enactments, and it is possible that they were role-appropriate behaviors calling upon an appropriate act/actor relation even though this is not spelled out as a rule in the utterance. Others leave the relationship unspecified. Types 3 and 4 imply relations of necessity without naming both elements outright. Type 5 refers to social procedural rules (e.g., sharing, taking turns) that transcend specific subject matter and thus do not directly inform us about thematic structures. But type 1—and often type 2—statements refer to, or heavily imply, necessary relations between thematic elements, and we can infer a great deal about children's interpretations of cultural realities from these.[3]

Turning from these core arguments to the episodes as a whole, most thematic elements that children offered were not explained, and the researcher's interpretation of them must rely on their meaning as commonly understood by adult culture members. The coding of these elements using Burke's (1969) terms allows a diagramming of the structure of a thematic domain. For example, in the restaurant episode above, Ronda offers a total of nine elements, including acts, characters, and scenic objects, all mutually consistent. Thus she has elaborated this scene in several dimensions for us.

SOCIAL USE OF THEMES

Moving beyond these core statements of disagreements and looking at the relations of thematic elements offered by different children over longer sequences of pretend play, we find that rhythmic patterns of disagreeing and agreeing appear to emerge. These patterns are perhaps one aspect of the social agenda of play that Schwartzman (1976, 1978, 1982) has described in which pretend play is an opportunity for social moves, providing metaphoric commentary on real-life social relations. In our own analysis, with its narrower focus within fantasy episodes only, the relations between thematic elements seem to be ways in which metaphor operates. At this point the social and thematic agendas of play intertwine.

These important patterns of disagreeing and agreeing are not fully evident if we use only the overt linguistic criteria of disagreement in our original definition for disagreements. Through the thematic coding a new kind of disagreement was discerned that was fully embedded in thematic meanings. These "thematically embedded" disagreements were not detected by the original coding of disagreements because those criteria depended purposely on more explicit signs of disagreement not related to theme. At this point we were also primed to search for thematically embedded ways of agreeing, ways to repair social disruption through theme.

An example of thematically embedded disagreement is the following. In Example 1, after a few persuasion attempts, Ronda presents an argument (line 8) that sets out relationships between the scene and two behaviors, which invalidates Melinda's current standing-around behavior. Melinda's eventual response (line 11) is a thematically embedded disagreement. Her question, "Could I get it myself?" is thematically consistent with the scene and role proposed for her by Ronda—a restaurant customer. But it is inconsistent with the manner of service intended by Ronda. Melinda wants self-service! Ronda replies to her with another thematically embedded disagreement. While her showing the coffee is consistent with Melinda's request, in the same turn she announces she will "play Barbie doll," a new theme incompatible with restaurant.

Neither the social meaning nor communicative complexity of Melinda's move in "Could I get it myself?" are revealed if her statement is seen only as a request and apart from its dramatistic implications. By behaving consistently with two of Ronda's elements (scene and customer) but inconsistently with another (mode of service) she engages in partial noncooperation. Ronda's reply is likewise mixed. She first complies with the theme but then departs from it. Here the inherent relations between dramatic elements are the substance of a social exchange ending in separation.

If children do not use some of the explicit markers of disagreement that we used as our own criteria to identify them, and use thematically embedded disagreements instead, there are several social implications. On the one hand, their perception by other children as disagreements depends on the shared knowledge of the meanings of the elements and increases the chance of misunderstanding. At the same time, the avoidance of more blatant markers and reliance on theme may be a more subtle way to disagree and may be more amenable either to repairs or to achieving intended social manipulations.

An example of this occurs later in the restaurant episode. Ronda makes a thematic repair to a thematic disagreement that has temporarily halted joint play. During a disagreement with Melinda, this time about waiter and cashier roles, Ronda announces she is going to paint and "be a artist person." Although this is also thematically inconsistent with the restaurant scene, she later successfully repairs this break by saying, "and this art store is right next to the restaurant."

Example 2 shows clearly the alternation of disagreeing and agreeing. Because the disagreement structure is clearly marked linguistically and the dramatic schemata is weaker, the thematic elements appear to play a service role here. Still, the dramatistic implications of the elements are the matter in which the debate is manifested.

1. B: Pretend there's dragons bustin' this [the hill].
2. N: No sir, he can't come out, I'm burying him!

3. B: Ok, pretend when they're all buried; they broke out;
         they tried to break out and they could.
4. N: 'Cause it was dry hard sand.
5. B: It was dry sand, and it was soft.
6. N: And it, no, it was like cement.
7. B: I know, but they still broke out.
8. N: No sir.
9. B: I know but . . . which ones do ya want to break out?
10. N: Um . . . that one, that . . . there's some ones.

The issue at hand is Brian's desire for a "busting out" action, and Ned's objection to it. Brian modifies his proposal for action to "when they're all buried, they tried to (break out) and could" (line 3) to agree with Ned, to which Ned returns by supplying a consistent and complementary scenic element for this action, linked explicitly by cause (line 4). Brian objects now by a partial disagreement, adjusting the scenic element (line 5), to which Ned replies with a stronger disagreement, "No, it was like cement" (line 6). Brian follows with a strong insistence on his original proposal for action (line 7), reinstituting overt disagreement that is countered in kind by Ned—"No sir" (line 8). At this potential standoff Brian combines thematic and social conventions for a useful move. "Which ones do you want to break out?" is a request allowing Ned the privilege of choosing, thereby alloting him social status. The dramatistic substance for this move involves dividing of the action between two sets of actors.

DISCUSSION

The side-by-side analysis of themes and disagreements highlights an intertwining of thematic and social agendas in these and other episodes. The use of Burke's (1969) dramatistic terminology draws our attention to inherent relations between thematic elements, which allows a multidimensional diagramming of the structure of thematic domains and scripts. In addition, identifying the relations between play theme elements informs us about the social relationships of the children who propose them.

We found that children often made explicit statements during disagreements about the relations of two or more elements, and all these "rules" were ones that adult culture members could agree were "real." They were not simply fantastical creations of the play in progress. Apparently, even during pretend play, children try to justify their individual position during disagreements by referring to knowledge that they believe has preestablished consensual validity. Examining children's disagreements during play is thus likely to be a good means to obtain information on their thinking about the world and their view of common knowledge. The method could perhaps be especially useful in areas in which children's experience and understandings may be different from that of adult observers and for which interpretation might otherwise be difficult.

Finally, the method provokes some thoughts about freedom and constraint in children's fantasy play. Although children are free in fantasy play to select a theme, once it is chosen they must work within certain thematic constraints. As the children co-construct fantasy, theme is the matter pushed and pulled and shaped, like clay, by the participants. But it is not infinitely malleable. The process seems similar to music. In the first several bars of a piece, stylistic conventions are referred to and established that guide, to a large extent, the further development of the piece and determine the meaning of particular sounds within the piece. In pretend play, such constraints include the cultural schemata and scripts of theme, which, like the cultural conventions of social and communicative procedures, help to determine the nature of social interactions.

Notes

1. Research for this study was supported by NSF grant no. BNS-78-09119 and NIMH grant no. 5 RO 1 MH 34723 to David Lubin and David Forbes. We wish to thank Patrice Miller, Dorothy Danaher, Steven Hite, Barry Paul, Louise Ross, and Frank Sherwood for their assistance, and Karen Watson-Gegeo for helpful comments on an earlier draft of this paper.

2. A coding manual may be obtained by writing to the authors at 513 Larsen Hall, Harvard Graduate School of Education, Cambridge, MA. 02138.

3. An additional study initiated by Victoria Kelly examines types 1, 3, and 5 as references to social norms; it is reported in Kelly, V.E. (1983).

REFERENCES

Bateson, G. (1956). The message "this is play." In B. Schaffner (Ed.), *Group processes: transactions of the second conference* (pp. 145-246). New York: Macy Foundation.

Brenneis, D., & Lein, L. (1977). "You fruithead": A sociolinguistic approach to children's dispute settlement. In S. Ervin-Trip & C. Mitchell-Kernan (Eds.), *Child discourse* (pp. 49-65). New York: Academic Press.

Brenner, J., & Mueller, E. (1982). Shared meaning in boy toddlers' peer relations. *Child Development, 53,* 380-391.

Burke, K. (1969). *A grammar of motives.* Berkeley, CA: University of California Press. (Original work published 1945).

Eisenberg, A.R., & Garvey, C. (1981). Children's use of verbal strategies in resolving conflicts. *Discourse Processes, 4,* 149-170.

Fein, G.G. (1981). Pretend play in childhood: An integrative review. *Child Development, 52,* 1095-1118.

Franklin, M.B. (1983). Play as the creation of imaginary situations: The role of language. In S. Wapner and B. Wapner (Eds.), *Towards a holistic developmental psychology* (pp. 197-220). Hillsdale, NJ: Erlbaum.

Garvey, C., & Berndt, R. (1977). The organization of pretend play. *Catalog of Selected Documents in Psychology, 7,* Ms. no. 1589.

Goffman, E. (1974). *Frame analysis: An essay on the organization of experience.* New York: Harper and Row.

Kelly, V.E. (1983). *Assessing children's knowledge of social norms: An observational method.* Unpublished qualifying paper, Harvard Graduate School of Education, Cambridge, MA.

LeVine, R.A. (1982). *Culture, behavior, and personality* (2nd ed.). New York: Aldine.

Much, N.C., & Shweder, R.A. (1978). Speaking of rules: The analysis of culture in breach. *New Directions for Child Development, 2,* 19-39.

Nelson, K., & Gruendel, J.M. (1979). At morning it's lunchtime: A scriptal view of children's dialogues. *Discourse Processes, 2,* 73-94.

Schwartzman, H.B. (1976). Children's play: A sideways glance at make-believe. In D.F. Lancy & B.A. Tindall (Eds.), *The anthropological study of play: Problems and prospects* (pp. 198-205). New York: Leisure Press.

Schwartzman, H.B. (1978). *Transformations: The anthropology of children's play.* New York: Plenum.

Schwartzman, H.B. (1982). Play and metaphor. In J. Loy (Ed.), *The paradoxes of play* (pp. 25-33). New York: Leisure Press.

Sutton-Smith, B. (1979). Epilogue: Play as performance. In B. Sutton-Smith (Ed.), *Play and learning* (pp. 294-321). New York: Gardner Press.

Walton, M.D., & Sedlack, A.J. (1982). Making amends: A grammar-based analysis of children's social interaction. *Merrill-Palmer Quarterly, 28,* 389-412.

MERE CHILD'S PLAY

Brian Vandenberg
University of Missouri, St. Louis

"Child's play" is a phrase that refers to something easy or of little consequence. It also reflects cultural values about children and play that
have had a subtle influence on the way psychologists have studied
the topic of children's play. What follows is a sketch of some of the
ways these values are manifest in research on children's play and
suggestions for how we might change our approach.

PLAY AS HANDMAIDEN

Psychologists have spent a good deal of time discussing, debating,
and researching the question: "What are the adaptive benefits of
play?" This question springs, in part, from the nature of the activity
itself. Play has no concrete payoffs; that is, there is no obvious
improvement in the ecological status of the player. In fact, playing
seems to expose the young to hazards that are quite unnecessary.

Many have suggested that the biological payoff of play is that it
broadens the individual's range of potential behaviors, enhancing the
possibility of survival in an ever-changing environment. Some, refin-
ing this further, suggest that play provides the behavioral flexibility
essential for insightful problem solving (Bruner, 1972).

Identifying the adaptive benefits of play and linking it to insightful
problem solving are legitimate, scientific approaches to a puzzling
phenomena. These approaches also are characteristic of our cultural values. We as Americans are a pragmatic people and solve
problems for financial gain. The notion of a pay off or a bottom line,
derived from the financial balance sheet, also pervades our science.
A behavior has to show a profit—that is, an adaptive net gain—or the
environment, like the financial market place, will drive it out. Frivolity
has a short half-life in this world view. The playing child snared in this
cultural-scientific net becomes a rather grim youth who bravely
endures play in order to become a more accomplished puzzle solver.

As befits our values, the problem solving, and not the play, gains importance in his line of research. This bias was evidenced in a recent symposium in which I participated, entitled "Is play a causal agent in development?" (Vandenberg, 1980a). This title is revealing. It would seem rather odd to question whether cognition is a causal agent in development. It is odd because cognition is not an important aspect *in* development; it is an important aspect *of* development. Our failure to frame the question in a similar way with regard to play reveals that we view play as mereley a handmaiden to more central features of development, such as problem solving.

The methods employed in the research on this question are also instructive. The children are usually given a play experience followed by a test, and their test performance is compared to a nonplay group. The children's play is solitary, and they are tested individually. The problems and play materials are selected by the experimenter, usually for reasons that have little to do with the children's lives (e.g., because they can be reliably scored or because they were used with chimpanzees; c.f Vandenberg, 1980b). The view of the child implied in this paradigm is of an isolated player, tested by an adult who administers decontextualized tests in order to assess the productivity of the child's play. The ecology of this testing situation seems rather severe, but it is not just an anomalous situation that results from the constraints of experimental design; it actually closely approximates the classroom, where individual performance on tasks presented by the teacher is graded, and cooperating with peers is seen as cheating.

The question about the adaptive features of play, the attempts to find the payoff of play in problem-solving skills, and the asocial, decontextualized testing environment all have strong ties to important values of the culture. While this research gives us important clues about the mystery of children's play, we must realize the limitations of this approach. When viewed through the looking glass of our adult cultural values, our understanding of children's play is distorted. To overcome these limitations, we need to realize that our values are manifest in our research. With this in mind, while not attempting to present an exhaustive review of all questions about children's play that have been addressed by psychologists, I would like to review questions that relate to issues with which I am most familiar. However, an analysis of these questions could reveal the potential limitations of investigations in other areas as well.

In addition to identifying the adaptive benefits of play, another important question that has attracted attention is whether play can stimulate creativity (c.f. Vandenberg, 1980b). There are a number of similarities of this research with the problem-solving research I just mentioned, only this time play is the handmaiden to creativity. But why creativity?

Our culture is infatuated with creativity, and for good reason, since creativity in the form of technological innovation creates wealth. We are becoming painfully aware of this fact as other nations, most notably Japan, have begun to challenge our technological dominance. An increasing number of reports in the media have covered the potential damaging consequences of allowing the pace of our technological innovations to fall behind another country's. For example, there recently has been a series in the *Wall Street Journal* entitled "Technology Duel," and an issue of *Newsweek* was devoted to "The Japanese Threat." The metaphors used (e.g., a "duel," a "threat") point out how fearful we are of losing our technological edge. Here is a sampling of what is being said:

Japanese technology has not only come of age: it is leapfrogging into a new one. Even as competitors in the West reel from Japanese domination of established industries like autos, steel and television sets, Tokyo is preparing an unprecedented high-tech challenge in the fields of the future. The stakes are enormous. Technology will set the economic agenda in the developed countries for the remainder of this century and beyond. Unless U.S. and European firms rally to the challenge, the prosperity and the jobs that flow from this new industrial revolution will almost certainly go to the Asian giant . . . . "The technological battle with the Japanese is really an industrial equivalent to the East-West arms race." (Newsweek, August 9, 1984, p. 48)

So, our interest in linking children's play with creativity has been spawned in an atmosphere of concern about developing a skill that is highly valued for our societal well-being. In a sense, children's play is a potentially valuable natural resource that can be used to develop creative individuals who will be the source of technological innovation so necessary for our economic survival. I am not implying that researchers are consciously responding to a national call to produce creative workers for the front lines of our duel with Japan. What I am saying is that the questions asked and the way they are researched are influenced by the cultural-political-economic context, and frequently we are unaware of the link between this context and our research.

A third question that has been pursued rather vigorously is if and how fantasy play can be used to enhance the development of social and cognitive skills (Rubin et al., 1983). As was the case with the last two questions, play is subsidiary to other, more culturally valued attributes. Fantasy is used to develop skills that will be of some use to the individual—skills that will have some concrete payoff in the culture.

Fantasy is used in a similar way in the adult world. One of the major uses of fantasy in our culture is in advertising. Through advertisement, companies attempt to convince the buying public of the need to purchase their product. Great sums of money are spent in creating believable fantasies about a product—of convincing the public that "Coke is the real thing." Our economy hinges upon the success of companies in convincing the public to spend their money in ever-increasing amounts. Thus, fantasy for profit is a common—and important—way of considering fantasy.

CHILD PRIORITY APPROACH

In all three questions discussed above, our understanding of children's play has been distorted by imposing adult values on their play. This is probably inevitable. However, I think this tendency has been accentuated as a result of the success of Piaget, who has, in subtle ways, sanctioned this as an appropriate way to investigate topics in human development. In Piaget's theory, ontological priority is given to adult forms of cognition, and the task is to chart how children acquire these mature thought structures. Such an approach, while fruitful, also blinds us to important clues that suggest alternative meanings.

For example, it is a common observation that children in their play will mimic adults; this is evidenced in their playing house, school, and other well-known games. Various authors have suggested that this reveals the preparatory functions of play—the individuals practice the roles, rules, and skills that will be necessary in adulthood (Rubin et al., 1983). However, the emotional state that accompanies these activities contradicts this interpretation. The children's play is charged with a tense excitement. This is not the type of emotional valence we would expect to accompany a practice session. I think an alternative way of looking at such activities is to view it as children playing with "hope." They are constructing a basis for hope that changes their lives. We adults do the same thing. Our hopes for the future are fantasies—mental fabrications of future possibilites that give our current life meaning, and a tense excitement. The importance of hopeful fantasies is underscored by recent research that indicates that when an individual loses hope—that is, a compelling, meaningful fantasy about their future—death is not far behind. For us symbol-using, future-looking creatures, fantasy play is the very stuff of life.

Perhaps the only major difference between adult and children's hope is that children's fantasies are public. Can you imagine how we would feel if our adult hopes and dreams were public? Most of us would be embarrassed. A number of theorists have suggested that the development of cognitive skills and inner speech enables children to internalize their fantasy play, which enables them to engage in more mature forms of fantasy. I think this explanation might be somewhat self-serving for us adults. The question is, what are the motivations that push fantasy inward? The cognitive skills provide the means but not the impetus. The impetus, I think, comes from our embarrassment. The cognitive skills that allow for the internalization of fantasy also allow for the internalization of an external audience. We develop the capacity to evaluate our behavior from the perspective of this imaginary audience, and hence, also acquire the capacity for embarrassment. We become more aware and less bold.

This exchange of self-knowledge for embarrassment is an important aspect of development that has been overlooked as a result of our overvaluing adulthood and rationality and our depreciating childhood and fantasy. I suspect that we are missing other important insights as well. Perhaps we could improve our understanding by reversing the ontological priority: to use children's play as the master template and search for their buried, distorted manifestations in adult activities; to believe that children boldly state what we adults only dare whisper.

I think one can see more clearly how this approach might be useful by returning to the question of the role of children's fantasy that I touched on earlier. Rather than ask how fantasy can aid in the development of adult valued skills, we could ask how children's myths illuminate important adult needs.

This past Christmas, I had a long discussion with a mother whose young daughter was in the throes of the Christmas excitement. Her daughter was anxiously awaiting Santa's arrival, was concerned if she had been naughty or nice this past year, and was planning what she would do with all the gifts she was expecting. Her mother also told me that her daughter had begun to ask those telling questions that signaled that this might be her last enchanted Christmas: "How does Santa get down the chimney with his bag? What if a house doesn't have a chimney?"

Her mother and I both lamented the loss of innocence that seems to accompany the growth of the intellect. This, of course, is a very common view of children's fantasy shared by Piaget, Freud, and many others: fantasy is a rather interesting but developmentally idiosyncratic phenomena that is undermined by the development of more sophisticated, rational thought (Rubin et al., 1983).

This explanation of children's fantasy follows from the perspective that gives ontological priority to adults. But if we take the child-priority perspective, where the Santa Claus myth is paradigmatic, we are led to the belief that myths are fundamental energizers of action and meaning for humans. This perspective asks: "What are the myths that energize adulthood?"

Religion is one myth system that serves as a wellspring for human meaning. There are political and economic myths as well; "Better dead than Red" exemplifies, in a rather extreme fashion, the effects of these types of myths. Science is another myth system that has had a pervasive effect on contemporary thought. This myth, having become universally accepted as reality is harder to see. Science's emphasis on logic has led to the belief that through reasoning we can fathom reality. We can see this myth in operation in the usual explanation of children, through improvement in their reasoning powers, outgrow their naive fantasies, and by the power of logical thought, come to intuit reality.

The child-priority approach, however, indicates that the Santa Claus myth is replaced by adult myths deemed by culture to represent reality. In this case, it is the mythical belief in rationality that leads to the myth that adults have no myths. We have come full circle. By taking the child-priority approach to myths, we have come to understand the adult myths that have led us to dismiss the importance of children's myths.

Sketched above are some of the ways that our investigation of children's play has been influenced by cultural values. These values pervade all phases of our work, from the way we frame questions to where and how we look for answers. They are also embedded in our belief that adult behaviors have more developmental stature than childhood forms. While we have generated some useful hypotheses and have gained some important insights, our understanding of childen's play is rather constricted. The playing child that emerges from this worldview is an awkward, joyless creature. This distortion of children and their play might also be a measure of the distortion of our understanding of ourselves; for in our research on children's play we are seeing the reflected vision of ourselves. Perhaps by giving children's play its ontological due, we can begin to gain some insight into the confusing world of adulthood.

REFERENCES

Bruner, J.S. (1972). Nature and uses of immaturity. *American Psychologist, 27, 687-708.*

Rubin, K.H., Fein, G.G., & Vandenberg, B. (1983). Play. In P.H. Mussen (Ed.), *Handbook of child psychology: Social development* (pp. 693-774). New York: John Wiley.

Vandenberg, B. (1980a, September). *Play: A causal agent in problem solving?* Paper presented at the meeting of the American Psychological Association, Montreal, Canada.

Vandenberg, B. (1980b). Play, problem-solving and creativity. In K.R. Rubin (Ed.), *New directions for child development: Children's play* No. 9. (pp. 49-68). San Francisco: Jossey Bass.

4

PLAY IN LITERATURE

INTRODUCTION

Garry E. Chick

Language has the unique quality of being both a potential medium for play and a means for describing play. Literature, as one form of language organization, additionally provides the opportunity to observe language play that is representative of a particular time and place. Through the analysis of literature, we can learn not only about the ability of an author to use language playfully, or to describe play, but we can also discover the author's conception of playfulness or play in a singular cultural context.

In regard to one form of literature, Huizinga (1955) has suggested that, "All poetry is born of play," a relationship that is amply demonstrated in two of the papers in this section. The following papers also establish that different poetic genres—here the sonnet and the hymn—provide varied formats for play, as do other literary forms, such as parody and the novel. Literature, in its many forms, thus provides a remarkably fertile area for play research.

The papers in this chapter demonstrate a variety of ways in which play and literature are related. Literature may be about play, there may be play of or play in literature, or literature may be both work and play at once. Perhaps other relationships exist as well, but surely these selections reflect the growing interest in, and the potential of, literature for the study of play.

Nardo analyzes representative examples of two poetic forms—a hymn by Donne and a sonnet by Milton—and finds that, while both authors may have played in the writing of the poems, the former calls for a playful response from the reader while the latter does not. Nardo suggests that the first poem characterizes the quality of play in literature while the second represents the ontological quality of the play of literature.

While poetry would seem to lend itself most easily to play with the sounds and meanings of words, Manley indicates that parody, here in the form of 19th century British fairy tales, has two rather different goals, those of making both serious and humorous comments on its target at the same time. In their use of comedy in order to criticize, Manley suggests that parodists are simultaneously working and playing.

Differing substantially from the other authors in this section, Riley analyzes the role played by a recreational activity—running—in two recent novels, instead of examining the playful aspects of a literary form. In *The World According to Garp* and *Dubin's Lives,* running provides the protagonists not with a means of escape or flight, a common theme in American novels, but with a means of self-confrontation.

In an Elizabethan sonnet sequence, Benson finds that ludic elements, such as word play and the use of various literary devices, furnish clues to significant aspects of the sonnet and illustrate how the sonneteer plays with language. Play qualities include the mastering of self-imposed obstacles in communication, competition with other practitioners of the genre, and encoding messages that would be understood one way by uninitiated readers and another by young poets of the courtly circle.

REFERENCE

Huizinga, J. (1955). *Homo ludens: A study of the play element in culture.* Boston: Beacon.

THE PLAY OF AND THE PLAY IN LITERATURE

Anna K. Nardo
Louisiana State University

The assertion that all literary texts are play has for centuries generated discussion among poets, cultural historians, psychoanalysts, and philosophers. Although aestheticians may properly classify works of art as play, the common-sense judgment of readers frequently conflicts with this classification. The example of two contemporary English novels illustrates this conflict. Samuel Richardson's *Clarissa* (1748), a psychological study of a pure heroine victimized by tyrannical parents and raped by a scoundrel, seems far from playful. But Laurence Sterne's *The Life and Opinions of Tristram Shandy* (1760-67) is among the most playful works ever written: its meandering narrator gets so entangled in the events leading to his conception and birth that the promised subject of the novel, his life and opinions, is completely forgotten. Aestheticians who see all literature as ludic would classify both of these novels as play, but readers rightly feel that *Clarissa* is deadly earnest while *Tristram Shandy* is sheer play.

Faced with this conflict between the classifications of aestheticians and the common-sense judgments of readers, the practical critic needs a way to reconcile theories of art with the practice of interpreting playful texts. This essay attempts to reconcile theory and practice by surveying some representative theories of literary play and testing them on two poetic examples. Although all literature may be classified ontologically as play, these poems demonstrate how the practical critic may use play theory to discriminate those texts that self-consciously frame themselves as play and call for playful responses from their readers from those texts that do not.

Defining play as a state free from the constraints of subjective or objective necessity, the 19-century poet Friedrich Schiller (1795) argues that play harmonizes man's fundamental impulses—the outward-turning impulse of sense and the inward-turning impulse of reason. This equipoise produces "Beauty," the aim of all art, including literature. For, if the object of sense is life and the object of reason is form, then the object of play, which harmonizes sense and reason, matter and spirit, is living form or Beauty. So, Schiller (1795) concludes, "Man shall only play *only play* with Beauty, and he shall play *only with Beauty*" (p. 80).

Less philosophical and more historical than Schiller, 20th-century cultural historian Johan Huizinga (1955) argues that "All poetry is born of play; the sacred play of worship, the festive play of courtship, the martial play of the contest, the disputatious play of braggadocio, mockery, and invective, the nimble play of wit and readiness" (p. 129). Other social forms that Huzinga (1955) believes originated in play—forms such as religion, science, law, war, and politics—become less playful as they become more organized, but poetry, he asserts, is always played.

Although he is a psychoanalyst, not a historian, D.W. Winnicott (1971) agrees that all culture, including literature, begins in play; however, he locates the point of origin not in man's cultural past, but in the earliest exchanges between mother and child. Once merged with the source of nurture, the child inevitably faces separation, a painful experience that reveals to him the gulf between in-here and out-there. In play, however, he may fill up the space of separation with a blanket, a stuffed monkey, or other objects so invested with part of himself that they become neither wholly external, like the world beyond his control, nor wholly internal, like hallucinations. As the child grows and learns to locate himself in an alien world, this in-between "play space" expands to embrace the adult play of culture, including literature with its rich resources of fantasy and wish fulfillment. Winnicott's theory of literature's origin in the playful equipoise between objective and subjective realities is a type of psychoanalytic version of Schiller's aesthetic philosophy of the origin of Beauty in the play that harmonizes sense and reason, life and form, matter and spirit.

A more radical proponent of the play theory of literature than either Schiller, Huizinga, or Winnicott is the contemporary French philosopher Jacques Derrida (1970), who agrees that all culture is played, but denies that we determine the play. Since he believes that there are no absolute centers—neither subjects like authors or readers, nor objects like texts that have fixed significations—then all literature is a free play. Authors and readers are themselves merely the results of the free play of human constituting factors, as is language, so the texts authors produce are written not by integral selves, but by the free play of language as it has been played in previous texts. Derrida's extreme antihumanist position raises a fundamental question of belief — whether or not selves exist. Because practical critics generally assume that authors and readers have selves that can determine the nature of their play with texts, they find Derrida's theory unproductive for what is usually called literary interpretation. Instead, Derrida's followers engage in free play with the text that makes no claim to truth.

If, as these four representative theorists assert, literature is in origin and essence a form of play, then who are the primary players— the author while writing the text, or the audience while reading it? Authors have frequently acknowledged the play spirit present in the act of creating. While building a fictive world, the author engages in make-believe, the "as if" quality so common to play (Freud, 1907; Auden, 1976). While crafting his language, whether poetry or prose, into a form to mirror his idea, he engages in a kind of competitive interchange between his medium—sounds, syntax, figures of speech, conventions, genres—and his idea (Untermeyer, 1938). The result of his imaginative, manipulative, even agonistic play is a text, an invitation for a reader to share his play.

The reader who accepts the invitation may engage the text agonistically, pitting his interpretive skills against the author's use of sounds, syntax, figures of speech, conventions, genres, and other elements of the literary medium. The reader may also willingly suspend his disbelief to share the author's make-believe, participating in the "as if" quality of the world of art (Coleridge, 1817). The mode of being in this world—neither actual phenomenon nor delusion—has the peculiar equipoise between objective and subjective reality noted, from different perspectives, by both Schiller and Winnicott. A number of theorists have tried to describe, if not define, this in-between status that art shares with play. Gregory Bateson (1972) muses that the ballerina dancing *Swan Lake* both is and is not a swan. Eugen Fink (1968) marvels that, although we play in the real world, play creates "an enigmatic realm that is not nothing, and yet is nothing real" (p. 23). And Hans-Georg Gadamer (1975) argues that the illusions of art help man recognize himself in his cultural world and thereby return him more fully to reality, by means of illusion. So, when the reader shares the author's play, the text becomes a playground with its own mode of being—somewhere between real and not real.

From this perspective all literature may be classified as play, but those who have read widely know that in practice this theoretical conclusion simply feels wrong. Some texts are notably more playful than others. Although both make their readers laugh, John Barth's short-story "Lost in the Funhouse" (1968) plays with the techniques of short-story writing and with audience expectations about stories of adolescent initiation, while John Kennedy Toole's novel *Confeder-*

acy of Dunces (1980) simply tells a hilarious story of a philosophical fat man and his misadventures among a bizarre cast of New Orleanean caricatures. One is funny because it is playful, and the other is satiric and comic, but not particularly playful.

Perhaps one reason for this discrepancy between the ontological status of literature as play and readers' judgments of works as sometimes playful sometimes not lies in the evolution of literary forms. Literature, as Huizinga, Winnicott, and others claim, may have originated in play, but in becoming an organized cultural form it developed structures, rules, and codes that apply in a realm of its own—the aesthetic domain. Although the aesthetic may have its roots in play, it often conceals or transcends those roots, creating an experience that we would not normally describe as play. No one I know would spontaneously call Fyodor Dostoyevsky's *Crime and Punishment* (1964) play. Nor does the presence of humor guarantee that a work is playful. The genre of comedy has evolved from its beginning in horseplay into a separate cultural form.

Unfortunately, theorists concerned with the origins and ontological status of literature have often blurred these distinctions, bringing the practical critic of playful texts to an apparent impasse. This impasse is, however, only apparent, not actual, because of the essential nature of play. It is a context, a frame, or a stance players adopt toward a source, almost any source—such as an object when toying with a pencil, a person when teasing a friend, a role when acting Macbeth, or an activity when playing war (Bateson, 1972; Goffman, 1974; Schwartzman, 1978). One may even play in the aesthetic domain with literature itself, and authors do it all the time. Since literature has evolved into an organized cultural form with its own structures, conventions, and codes, an author may adopt the play stance toward these structures, as John Barth does in "Lost in the Funhouse." Authors often play with literary conventions that they expect their audiences to recognize, thereby consciously beckoning readers to become playmates, to join in a romp with the very stuff of literature. In nonplayful literature these structures, conventions, and codes, albeit originating in the play that is all art, have become instrumental means whereby effects are generated in readers, not objects of the author's self-conscious play.

Authors may also project from the text a ludic self that calls for a playful response from readers. In nonplayful literature the voice projected from the text, whether a persona or the author's own voice, is generally that of a single (albeit complex) self, seeking definable (albeit complex) communication of an idea, an emotion, an experience to the reader. In playful texts, however, the voice projected from the text may be tricky, placing itself in the radically ambiguous play frame that Bateson (1972) discovered while watching otters at play. The playful nips of the otters were bites, but not real bites; they were bites defining themselves as nonbites. Not unlike Bateson's otters, the self behind the voice of playful texts may define himself paradoxically with a glint in his eye—perhaps displaying the literary equivalent of the chimpanzee's play face. A comparison of two 17th-century English religious lyrics may help verify these abstractions.

John Milton, after a promising start as a young poet, interrupted his poetic career to serve the revolutionary cause in Oliver Cromwell's government. By 1652, however, after years of service, he had arrived at mid-life only to be struck blind. As a record of anger and frustration, but ultimate submission to God's will, he composed the following sonet:

> When I consider how my light is spent,
>   Ere half my days, in this dark world and wide,
>   And that one Talent which is death to hide,
>   Lodg'd with me useless, though my Soul more bent
> To serve therewith my Maker, and present
>   My true account, lest he returning chide;
>   "Doth God exact day-labor, light denied,"
>   I fondly ask; But patience to prevent
> That murmur, soon replies, "God doth not need
>   Either man's work or his own gifts; who best
> Bear his mild yoke, they serve him best; his State
> Is Kingly. Thousands at his bidding speed
>   And post o'er Land and Ocean without rest:
>   They also serve who only stand and wait (Milton, 1673).

Although no one can be privy to the mind of a long-dead poet, Milton probably played while writing this serious poem. As a sonnet, it required masterful skill with language to fulfill its rigid requirements of meter and rhyme. Yet within this form Milton manipulates its conventions to match his meaning, transcends the sonnet's brevity with allusions, and makes words serve double functions. He artfully ends the thought of the octave in the middle of line eight to suggest the intervention of "patience to prevent" his almost blasphemous murmurings, which rumble through the first seven lines, from totally controlling the sonnet's first movement. He subtly weaves into the texture of what appears to be spontaneous thought allusions to the parable of the talents and to the distinctions that arcane angelology draws between messenger angels, who "post o'er Land and Ocean," and contemplative angels, "who only stand and wait" before God's radiance. And he ends the sonnet with a pun on "wait," meaning both to attend idly and to serve actively—a quibble that encapsulates the speaker's hard-won realization that passive waiting is active service.

Whether or not this technical virtuosity resulted from Milton's play when he wrote the sonnet, the voice projected by the poem is not playful. It does not call attention to its use of literary conventions to invite the reader to pit his interpretive skills against the poet's cleverness. Rather, Milton uses literary structures and codes to create a miniature drama of a blind man on a spiritual pilgrimage to light, and through sonnet form, allusions, and puns he summons the reader to identify with the poetic voice and journey with him out of spiritual blindness toward submission before God's throne.

Like Milton, John Donne faced mid-life with anxiety, which he tried to allay by submission to God. Probably in 1623 after a serious illness, he recorded one such attempt at submission in "A Hymn to God the Father":

I
Wilt thou forgive that sin where I begun,
   Which was my sin, though it were done before?
Wilt thou forgive that sin, through which I run,
   And do run still: though still I do deplore?
     When thou hast done, thou hast not done,
      For I have more.

II
Wilt thou forgive that sin which I have won
   Others to sin? and, made my sin their door?
Wilt thou forgive that sin which I did shun
   A year, or two: but wallowed in, a score?
     When thou hast done, thou hast not done,
      For I have more.

III
I have a sin of fear, that when I have spun
   My last thread, I shall perish on the shore;
But swear by thy self, that at my death thy son
   Shall shine as he shines now, and heretofore;
     And, having done that, thou hast done,
      I fear no more (Donne, 1633).

As a hymn, a religious lyric set to music, this poem tested Donne's composing skills as the sonnet form did Milton's. Its stanzaic pattern, repetitive questions, and refrain, which puns on the speaker's name, suggest that the act of writing the hymn may also have been play for Donne. More importantly, however, the voice singing this hymn, unlike the well-defined voice projected from Milton's sonnet, is ambiguous and playful indeed.

Donne's catalogue of sins, his reiterated prayers for forgiveness, and his longing to bask in the radiance of the Son of God characterize him as a rueful penitent working out his salvation in fear and trembling. Yet, behind the penitent dances the irrepressible, slippery sinner who seems almost gleeful at dredging up sin after sin to exhaust even God's patience. The refrain sounds like the boast of a playful child running from his father, to whom the hymn is explicitly addressed. Teasing "God the Father" to chase and catch him, the impish speaker taunts, "When thou hast done [finished], thou hast not done [the man], / For I have more." Here the pun on Donne's name contrasts markedly to Milton's pun on *wait* in the sonnet on his blindness. Whereas Milton's climactic pun compresses the poem's dramatic tension into one word, thereby moving the reader to share the speaker's experience of frustration and submission, Donne's name pun characterizes the speaker, who both seeks and runs away from grace abounding, as a ludic self, playing catch-me-if-you-can with God.

Likewise, the voice projected from the hymn plays something like hide-and-seek with the reader. On at least one level, Donne's hymn is not a solemn musical offering to God, but a game for the reader to test his ability to get the joke. Will he recognize *done* as *Donne*, and maybe even *more* as *More*—a pun on the family name of Donne's deceased wife, whom he may have loved idolatrously? The refrain may imply that God cannot have done (finished) and have Donne (the man) so long as Donne has more sins and his passion for Anne More. Instead of increasing the reader's identification with the speaker, as does Milton's pun, Donne's wit both distances and attracts the reader, making him a playmate, even a competitor who is challenged not only to get the joke, but to find the hiding speaker. Is he a sincere penitent terrified that his sins abound more than grace, and that he "shall perish on the shore" at his death? Or is he a tease whose insatiable needs demand repeated assurances of love, and who while pleading to God for these assurances always has an eye on the reader whom he also wants to impress with his flashy wit? The voice of this poem is an artful dodger who almost dares the reader to pin him down.

These two representative examples suggest that—although both authors may have played while writing these poems, and readers may imaginatively share the authors' self-dramatization in the poems—the hymn self-consciously frames itself as play and calls for a playful response from its reader, while the sonnet does not. Furthermore, these examples generate two related questions that may help the practical critic of playful texts who is stymied by aestheticians' classification of all literature as play: What kind of voice does the text project—the voice of a single self who wants to communicate a definable (if complex) idea, emotion, or experience to the reader, or the voice of an ambiguous, ludic self who wants to play with the reader (Lanham, 1976)? What kind of response does the voice call for from the reader—understanding of the communicated idea and empathy with the emotion or experience, or countermoves as in a game, solutions as in a puzzle, or a tense anticipation of the next play, a tension that precludes complete empathy (Ong, 1975)?

Answering these questions reveals that, because of the origin of literature in play and its ontological status as play, works like *Clarissa, The Confederacy of Dunces,* and Milton's sonnet on his blindness represent the play *of* literature; whereas, because they project the voice of a ludic self inviting the reader to come out and play, works like *Tristram Shandy,* "Lost in the Funhouse," and Donne's hymn represent the play *in* literature.

REFERENCES

Auden, W.H. (1976). Freedom and necessity in poetry: My lead mine. In J.S. Bruner, A. Jolly, & K. Sylva (Eds.), *Play: Its role in development and evolution* (pp. 584-585). New York: Basic Books.

Barth, J. (1968). Lost in the funhouse. In *Lost in the funhouse: Fiction for print, tape, live voice.* Garden City, NY: Doubleday.

Bateson, G. (1972). *Steps to an ecology of mind.* New York: Ballantine Books.

Coleridge, S.T. (1951). Biographia Literaria. In E. Schneider (Ed.), *Samuel Taylor Coleridge: Selected poetry and prose.* New York: Rinehart. (Original work published 1817)

Derrida, J. (1970). Structure, sign, and play in the discourses of the human sciences. In R. Macksey & E. Donato (Eds.), *The structuralist controversy: The language of criticism and the sciences of man* (pp. 247-265). Baltimore, MD: The Johns Hopkins Press.

Donne, J. (1971). A hymn to God the Father. In A.J. Smith (Ed.), *John Donne: The complete English poems.* New York: Penguin Books. (Original work published 1633)

Dostoyevsky, F. (1964). *Crime and punishment* (G. Gibian, Ed.; J. Coulson, Trans.). New York: W.W. Norton. (Original work published 1867)

Fink, E. (1968). The oasis of happiness: Toward an ontology of play (U. & T. Saine, Trans.). *Yale French Studies: Game, Play, Literature, 41,* 19-30.

Freud, S. (1959). Creative writers and day-dreaming. In J. Strachey (Ed. and Trans.), *The standard edition of the complete psychological works of Sigmund Freud* (Vol. 9), pp. 143-153. London: Hogarth Press. (Original work published 1907)

Gadamer, H. (1975) *Truth and method* (G. Barden & J. Cumming, Trans.). New York: Seabury Press. (Original work published 1960)

Goffman, E. (1974). *Frame analysis: An essay on the organization of experience.* New York: Harper & Row.

Huizinga, J. (1955). *Homo ludens: A study of the play element in culture* (R.F.C. Hull, Trans.). Boston, MA: Beacon Press. (Original work published 1949)

Lanham, R.A. (1976). *The motives of eloquence: Literary rhetoric in the Renaissance.* New Haven, CT: Yale University Press.

Milton, J. (1957). Sonnet 19. In M.Y. Hughes (Ed.)., *John Milton: Complete poems and major prose.* Indianapolis, IN: Odyssey Press. (Original work published 1673)

Ong, W.J. (1975). The writer's audience is always a fiction. *Publications of the Modern Language Association, 90,* 9-21.

Richardson, S. (1932). *Clarissa* (Vols. 1-4) (W.L. Phelps, Ed.). London: J.M. Dent. (Original work published 1748)

Schiller, F. (1954). *On the aesthetic education of man* (R. Snell, Ed. and Trans.). London: Routledge & Kegan Paul. (Original work published 1795)

Schwartzman, H.B. (1978). *Transformations: The anthropology of children's play.* New York: Plenum Press.

Sterne, L. (1980). *Tristram Shandy* (H. Anderson, Ed.). New York: W.W. Norton. (Original work published 1760-67)

Toole, J.K. (1980). *A confederacy of dunces.* Baton Rouge, LA: Louisiana State University Press.

Untermeyer, L. (1938). *Play in poetry.* New York: Harcourt, Brace and Company.

Winnicott, D.W. (1971). *Playing and reality.* New York: Basic Books.

PARODY: SIMULTANEOUS WORK AND PLAY

K.E.B. Manley
University of Northern Colorado[1]

A number of scholars who have recently examined the nature of play point out the problems involved in the assumption that the definition of play includes a dichotomy between work and play. For example, Stevens (1980) discusses the origins of the problem in Huizinga's classic definition of play and summarizes the subsequent discussions of scholars who have questioned various elements of that definition. Csikszentmihaly (1981) questions whether play can be considered outside the world of ordinary reality and suggests that it is in fact part of ordinary reality. If work is considered part of ordinary reality, then consideration of play in the same category naturally blurs the line between them. Further, in an introduction to several articles on work and play, H. Schwartzman (1978) indicates that western ideas about work make it difficult for us to see that work can be playful and play can be experienced as work. Schwartzman (1978) comments that play can exist *at* work and that there is play *in* work; there is also work *at* play and work *in* play. Similarly, in a discussion of the centuries-old Mesoamerican ballgame, Humphrey (1981) states: "In conclusion, it becomes immediately obvious that the Mesoamerican ballgame functioned on many levels which completely elude that very hazy (and I would suggest non-existent) line between work, play, life, and cosmology" (p. 147). I argue that literary parody is an activity that is at once serious and playful and thus is simultaneously play and work.

Literary parody exists alongside several forms that are close to it: burlesque, travesty, and satire. Thrall and Hibbard (1960) indicate that burlesque usually has a literary form as its target and characteristically uses exaggeration for comic effect. Travesty, however, simply presents a serious subject frivolously. They define parody as a form that is usually directed at a specific work or author and that either ridicules in a nonsensical fashion or criticizes by brilliant treatment. Dane (1980) differentiates parody and satire by pointing out that parody refers to words while satire refers to things; in other words, parody refers to the sign itself and satire to the contents of the sign. A further definition of parody appears in a lengthy study of parody as criticism of fiction. This study defines literacy parody as "the critical refunctioning of preformed literary material with comic effect" (Rose 1979, p. 30). The comic effect results from the establishment of a discrepancy between texts, and, unlike satire, parody includes its target in its own structure. The target need not be limited to a literary form, but may include style or conventions; and parody is ambivalent because it is both critical and sympathetic toward its target.

A number of characteristics link parody with play. For example, if the dichotomy between work and play exists, and play is a metalanguage commenting on and criticizing the world of work (Turner, 1973), one can argue that parody is play, for it also comments upon and criticizes a world that might be considered work (i.e., the world of fiction). Parody, in other words, is metafiction (Rose, 1979). If fiction is not a part of the world of work, however, parody can still be considered play, for play exists that is about play (Adams, 1980).

If the dichotomy between work and play does not exist, parody even more closely resembles play; like play that is also work, it has two goals (Rose, 1979). One can see the two goals for play in the example of rock climbing discussed by Csikszentimhaly (1981), who states that an activity may be playful or serious depending on the perspective of the viewer. Harris (1981) elaborates on this point by suggesting that players' perspectives may shift from goal to goal in rapid succession. This idea of shifting goals is also supported by Stevens' (1980) discussion of paradigmatic shifts from levels of structure to levels of experience. Though the parodist, like the player, faces a two-goal situation, the parodist does not shift from goal to goal because parody includes its target in its structure. Parody requires the parodist to be both playful and serious at the same time.

In a very recent definition of play, H. Schwartzman (1982) states that we should see play as "a process of creative and spontaneous metaphor construction and identity communication" rather than as "an orderly, rule-governed, competitive and identity-absorbing system" (p. 25). Though one might argue about the spontaneity involved, parody certainly includes metaphor construction, and the process is certainly creative. The metaphor construction in parody occurs because parody makes an implicit comparison between the text in which the parody is embodied and a style, form, or convention that is outside that text. In Gilbert and Sullivan's *Pirates of Penzance* (1880), for example, the major-general compares his behavior to that of a true "model of a modern major-general" (p. 155). The text (parody) refers us to something outside the text. Parody, then, involves creative metaphor construction. This characteristic is also a characteristic of play.

In summary, we can characterize parody as play because we can understand parody as both serious and playful comment on literature. We can also see parody as play because it comments on an aspect of the world of work. If we assume literature to be play, parody can still qualify as play, since play about play exists. Like some other forms of play, parody has twin goals. But unlike the players in mountain climbing or football, the parodist does not temporarily forget one goal while concentrating on the other . Parody, like play, also constructs metaphor. Because parody makes serious comment on its target as well as treating that target with humor, a consideration of parody as play expands the definition of the nature of play. Since it is at once serious and playful, parody is an example of simultaneous play and work.

The examples that I use to illustrate the twin goals of parody and its nature as simultaneous work and play come from British literary fairy tales of the 19th century. The authors of these tales use parody both to entertain and to criticize the traditional tales. Their twin goals are to encourage their audience to read with enjoyment and to discourage that audience from taking the magic in the tales too seriously. In order to accomplish those goals they manipulate the names in and conventions of traditional tales. The result is humor as well as serious comment on the traditional tales; in parodying the style or conventions of traditional fairy tales, the authors are involved in both play and work.

Though parody is an important example of play in literature, it is not the only literary form that can be playful. Nardo (1980) suggests that George Herbert's collection of lyrical poems entitled *The Temple* is at once serious and playful and also suggests that Herbert was aware of two audiences. Similarly, J. Schwartzman (1980) argues that fiction "as a communicational mode shares paradoxical aspects with play" (p. 39) and discusses the paradoxical and playful nature of post-modern fiction.

Awareness of two audiences is an element in parody as well as in Herbert's lyrical poetry. The double audience indicates a double attitude and twin goals. In the case of parody the double attitude is that parodists both mock and admire the target (Rose, 1979). For British 19th-century imitators of traditional fairy tales, the twin goals were to entertain and to criticize, and the two audiences were the children for whom the tales were intended and the parents who perhaps read the tales to the children; or, if they did not do so, at least determined whether the tales were suitable.

Traditional fairy tales, known to folklorists as *märchen*, attracted 19th-century British authors for several reasons. The number of translations of traditional *märchen* into English was one factor in their attractiveness, for compared with the two previous centuries, translations increased markedly in the 19th century. The Arabian Nights Tales had been translated in 1708, and Perrault's rather literary fairy tales had been translated in 1729, but they did not achieve the popularity of Edgar Taylor's 1823 translation of the Grimms' *Kinder- und Hausmärchen.* He followed that volume with a second in 1826, and these two volumes were the beginning of a steady stream of translations from various sources (Kotzin, 1972). By the middle of the century, British authors were well supplied with translations of traditional tales.

Another reason for the increased interest in traditional *märchen* was their gradual acceptance as good children's literature. Though in the early part of the century the traditional tales were generally still opposed as children's fare, as early as 1802 Charles Lamb had spoken out against that opposition. Attitudes slowly changed to favor the traditional tales, and by the time Taylor translated the Grimms' tales, a number of voices were speaking in the tales' favor. By the late 1830s and the 1840s, most people considered *märchen* good children's literature (Kotzin, 1972).

The improved climate for traditional *märchen* and the availability of translations from various sources were joined by an awareness of a lack of British traditional *märchen*, and all these factors encouraged British authors to try writing their own *märchen.* A fourth encouraging factor was a new awareness, through translations, that authors in other countries were writing literary *märchen.* Two examples are Ludwig Tieck's *Der blonde Eckbert,* written in 1797 but little known in Britain until 1813, and Hans Christian Andersen's collection, translated into English in 1846. From the late 1830s on, probably strongly encouraged by publishers, British authors turned out a number of literary *märchen.* Some examples are *The King of the Golden River, The Hope of the Katzekopfs, The Rose and the Ring,* and *Water Babies* (Kotzin, 1972).

The authors of these literary *märchen* exploited the didacticism inherent in the traditional *märchen,* but they were uneasy about the latter's use of magic. The Victorians were concerned that their children receive an honest view of the world—be educated as well as entertained—through what they read. The result was a double attitude toward traditional *märchen* that resulted in instances of parody. The literary imitators both admired and criticized their models—were both playful and serious in their imitations. Their parody, then, was work in the sense that it seriously discouraged Victorian children's belief in magic, but it was play because the authors manipulated the conventions of traditional *märchen* for comic effect.

Often, parody of traditional *märchen* occurs in the use of names. Such parody appears in *The Rose and the Ring* (Thackeray, 1855) and *The Light Princess* (MacDonald, 1867). In the former, Fairy

Blackstick is a good fairy whose name *Blackstick* obviously refers to the wand fairies are supposed to carry. The title *The Light Princess* refers to a heroine who has neither bodily weight nor the capacity to be serious. The epithet in the latter name allows the narrator to increase the humor and the parody of the way traditional fairy-tale princesses were supposed to behave by punning on the word *gravity*. In Francis Paget's *The Hope of the Katzekopfs* (1844), the good fairy's name is *Lady Abracadabra*. Like Thackeray's *Blackstick,* it is a name intended to reduce the seriousness of the magical agent. A final example occurs in Dickens' *The Magic Fishbone* (1868). The name of the prince in the story is *Ceratinpersonio*. All these names introduce a humor that is nonexistent in the traditional models; traditional *märchen* take magic seriously. The authors of literary *märchen,* however, could not allow children to take magic seriously and thus "played with" names. At the same time, these authors were criticizing the straightforward use of magic in the traditional *märchen*. These authors "play" when setting up a comparison between the traditional fairy godmother and a fairy named *Blackstick,* but they "work" in criticizing the belief in magic that the traditional fairy godmother embodies.

Some authors work and play with traditional *märchen* by parodying accepted characteristics of the genre. In *The Magic Fishbone,* for example, the fairy godmother behaves toward the king as if she were both a mother and a spoiled child; first she scolds him for asking questions and then has a temper tantrum, stamping her foot on the ground and saying, "I am sick of your grownup reasons" (Dickens, 1868 p. 166). Like Thackeray in *The Rose and the Ring,* the author does not want his young readers (or the parental ones, for that matter) to take the convention of the fairy godmother seriously. Dickens' setting also indicates a distrust of the traditional *märchen,* and again that distrust appears through humor. Though the main characters are a princess and her father, the king receives a salary, and there is never enough money; quarter-days, which are paydays, never come soon enough. In treating the king like an ordinary clerk, Dickens reduces his importance and, by implication, the position of any monarch who appears in traditional *märchen*. He creates a situation that is at once humorous and serious. In addition, Dickens uses the prince, the previously-mentioned Certainpersonio, as a reward for the princess's good behavior rather than vice versa. And instead of being engaged in doing brave deeds, as princes in the traditional *märchen* are, he is "sitting by himself, eating barley-sugar, and waiting to be ninety" (Dickens, 1868, p. 177). Again, the author sets up a metaphorical situation and makes his prince a comical figure compared with the traditional prince; at the same time, however, his goal is to criticize the traditional model.

In *The Rose and the Ring,* Thackeray's names are not only humorous in themselves, but through them Thackeray makes humorous comment on the serious courtly settings of the traditional *marchen.* The governess in *The Rose and the Ring,* for example, is *Mrs. Gruffanuff;* a great warrior who serves one of the princesses is *Count Hogginarmo;* the captain of the guard at one court is *Hedzoff;* and one of the kingdoms in the story is *Crim Tartary.* The humor here not only criticizes the characters in traditional *märchen,* but also the traditional *märchen* settings. Thackeray seems to be saying that a royal court at which magical events take place is no court at all.

Andrew Lang's *Prince Prigio* (1889) provides a further example of parody of accepted characteristics of traditional *märchen;* in this tale it is the oldest rather than the youngest son who succeeds in slaying the dragon, and the oldest takes on this task only after persuading his father to sent the youngest out first. After all, as he says, "It is always the eldest son who goes out first and comes to grief on these occasions, and it is always the third son that succeeds" (Lang, 1889, p. 19). In another of Lang's tales, *Prince Ricardo* (1893), the author provides a similar twist by having Princess Jaqueline, whom the prince previously rescued, become the rescuer herself; she saves Ricardo from a giant. Again, simultaneous play and work are involved here. The princess-as-rescuer situation is comic because it violates the audience's expectations of traditional *märchen;* at the same time, the comedy provides a critique of an accepted *märchen* convention.

The parody involved in many 19th-century British authors' imitations of traditional *märchen* often involves names and accepted conventions of the traditional models. It is a result of an awareness of two audiences: parents and children. The awareness of two audiences meant that the authors had two goals, one playful and one serious. Though there are other forms of play in which two goals exist, in those forms the player appears to suspend, temporarily, one goal in favor of the other. Parody is unlike these forms of play because it sets up metaphorical relationships and contains its target within its structure.

Parodists are at once serious and playful because they use comedy in order to criticize. Because it is an activity that is at once playful and serious—is simultaneously play and work—parody expands the definition of play.

Note

1. I wish to thank the Dean of Arts and Sciences, the faculty of the English Department, and the higher administration of the University of Northern Colorado for the released time that made revision of this paper possible.

REFERENCES

Adams, C.R. (1980). Distinctive features of play and games: A folk model from Southern Africa. In H.B. Schwartzman (Ed.)., *Play and culture* (pp. 150-162). West Point, NY: Leisure Press.

Csikszentmihaly, M. (1981). Some paradoxes in the definition of play. In A.T. Cheska (Ed.), *Play as context* (pp. 14-26). West Point, NY: Leisure Press.

Dane, J.A. (1980). Parody and satire: A theoretical model. *Genre, 13,* 145-159.

Dickens, C. (1959). *The magic fishbone.* London: J.M. Dent. (Originally published 1868)

Gilbert, W.S. (1936). The pirates of Penzance. In *The complete plays of Gilbert and Sullivan* (pp. 141-181). New York; Modern Library. (Original work published 1880)

Harris, J.C. (1981). Beyond Huizinga: Relationships between play and culture. In A.T. Cheska (Ed.)., *Play as context* (pp. 26-36). West Point, NY: Leisure Press.

Humphrey, R.L. (1981). Play as life: Suggestions for a cognitive study of the Mesoamerican ballgame. In A.T. Cheska (Ed.), *Play as context* (pp. 134-149). West Point, N.Y.: Leisure Press.

Kotzin, M.C. (1972). *Dickens and the fairy tale.* Bowling Green, Ohio: Bowling Green University Popular Press.

Lang, A. (1889). *Prince Prigio.* Bristol: J.W. Arrowsmith.

Lang, A. (1893). *Prince Ricardo of Pantouflia.* Bristol: J.W. Arrowsmith.

MacDonald, G. (1867). The light princess. In G. MacDonald, *Dealings with the fairies* (p. 1-99). London: A. Strahan.

Nardo, A.K. (1980). Play, literature, and the poetry of George Herbert. In H.B. Schwartzman (Ed.), *Play and Culture* (pp. 30-38). West Point, NY: Leisure Press.

Paget, F. (1968) *The hope of the Katzekopfs.* New York: Johnson Reprint Corporation. (Original work published 1844)

Rose, M.A. (1979). *Parody/metafiction:* London: Croom Helm.

Schwartzman, H.B. (1978). Introduction to chapter IV. In M.A. Salter (Ed.), *Play: Anthropological perspectives* (pp. 185-187). West Point, NY: Leisure Press.

Schwartzman, H.B. (1982). Play and metaphor. In J.W. Loy (Ed.), *The Paradoxes of play* (pp. 25-33). West Point, NY: Leisure Press.

Schwartzman, J. (1980). Paradox, play, and post-modern fiction. In H.B. Schwartzman (Ed.), *Play and culture* (pp. 38-48). West Point, NY: Leisure Press.

Stevens, P., Jr. (1980). Play and work: A false dichotomy? In H.B. Schwartzman (Ed.), *Play and culture* (pp. 316-324). West Point, NY: Leisure Press.

Thackery, W.M. (1959). *The rose and the ring.* London: J.M. Dent. (Original work published 1855)

Thrall, W.F. & Hibbard, A. (1960). *A handbook to literature* (rev. ed.). New York: Odyssey Press.

Turner, V. (1973). Foreword. In F.E. Manning, *Black clubs in Bermuda* (pp. xv-xx). Ithaca, NY: Cornell University Press.

RECREATIONAL RUNNING IN *THE WORLD ACCORDING TO GARP* AND *DUBIN'S LIVES*

Kathryn Riley
Louisiana State University

Throughout American fiction, the hero in flight has darted in and out of the literary landscape with all the frequency of an archetype. In 19th-century fiction, for example, we find Natty Bumppo making excur-sessions into the wilderness and Huck Finn planning to "light out for the territory." Likewise, the 20th century has given us Ralph Ellison's *Invisible Man,* with the protagonist's terrorized flight through the "border area," and the cross-country saga of Jack Kerouac's *On the Road.*

As these examples suggest, flight has traditionally been a pre-rogative of the American protagonist, even though he has sometimes sung the song of the open road in a resolutely minor key. Indeed, crit-ics have identified this obsession with flight as one of the touchstones of American fiction. For example, Fiedler (1966) comments that the protagonists in many classic American novels "turn from society to nature or nightmare out of a desperate need to avoid the facts of woo-ing, marriage, and child-bearing" (p. 25). Tanner (1971) also finds that "a central concern for the hero of many recent American novels is this: can he find a freedom which is not a jelly, and can he establish an identity which is not a prison?" (p. 19).

In many ways, though, the protagonists of contemporary Ameri-can fiction are more domesticated than their earlier counterparts like Natty and Huck. Correspondingly, several contemporary American writers have adapted the act of "lighting out" to the more mundane "territory" occupied by their heroes. This paper examines two recent novels—*The World According to Garp* by John Irving (1976) and *Dubin's Lives* by Bernard Malamud (1977)—in which open-ended flight has been transformed into a more domestic pasttime: recre-ational running. The discussion of the role played by recreational running in these novels considers the following points: a general comparison of traditional, open-ended flight and recreational running; and an analysis of the major similarities and differences between the two types of movement. These points are summarized briefly in this section and then, in the subsequent sections, applied in while bearing superficial resemblances to its open-ended counterpart, differs qualitatively from that earlier activity. In particular, the analysis shows that running functions in each novel as a metaphor for a cycle of behavior that the protagonist must break in order to resolve his personal and professional conflicts.

COMPARISON OF FLIGHT AND RUNNING

A general comparison of traditional, open-ended flight and recreational running reveals several points of similarity and difference between the two types of movement. These points are summarized briefly in this section and then, in the subsequent sections, applied in more detail to the novels under discussion.

One similarity between flight and running is that both are predominantly solitary activities: the emphasis is on the hero's movement through space alone. Second, both flight and running are purifying activities: they require self-discipline and self-reliance, both physical and spiritual endurance. Third, both activities have heroic or romantic overtones, a quality that is closely related to the first two points of similarity. That is, both flight and running set the protagonist apart (either permanently, as in the first case, or temporarily, as in the second) from other members of his society. Further, both activities entail setting a personal goal and then fulfilling it—accomplishments that again place the protagonist on a different level from other members of this society.

Beyond these similarities, however, the two forms of movement diverge in several significant ways. First, the nature of flight typically is linear and open-ended. The protagonist is often more concerned with leaving than with arriving; his escape from society (what he is running from) often takes precedence over his destination (what he is running to). In fact, it is not unusual for American writers to close their novels with the protagonist taking flight, thus leaving his ultimate destination unknown. Recreational running, on the other hand, is circular and closed. The scope of the two activities is secondary with respect to this point. Even a marathon, although perhaps the most extended form of recreational running, still begins and ends at fixed points.

Second, flight is frequently an indefinite activity, with no clear limitations on the time and space over which it may range. In contrast, a runner usually sets finite spatial and temporal goals. Third, these differences in the natures of flight and running are closely related to a difference in the purpose of each activity. Open-ended flight traditionally is a means for the protagonist to permanently escape society. Running, on the other hand, is a means of temporarily escaping, while still remaining a part of, society. Put another way, flight is an antisocial activity, whereas running is a socially sanctioned one.

These differences between flight and running are presented schematically in Figures 1 and 2. As Figure 1 shows, flight in the American novel is traditionally a linear, open-ended activity in which the protagonist moves away from society and toward an unknown point.

Figure 1. Schematic representation of flight in the traditional American novel.

In contrast, running is part of a recursive cycle that both T.S. Garp and William Dubin follow at several points throughout their stories. Each protagonist experiences pressures created by social forces — in particular, demands placed on them by marriage and family and by the writing profession. Running allows them a temporary escape from these personal and professional problems, but also entails an eventual return to society and its pressures. This cyclical pattern is illustrated in Figure 2.

To summarize, recreational running both resembles and differs from open-ended flight. The next two sections discuss in more detail how these similarities and differences manifest themselves in *The World According to Garp* and *Dubin's Lives*.

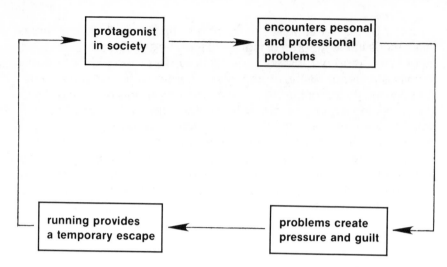

Figure 2. Schematic representation of running in *The World According to Garp* and *Dubin's Lives*.

THE REWARDS OF RUNNING FOR GARP AND DUBIN

Running in *The World According to Garp* and *Dubin's Lives* bears several points of resemblance to its traditional counterpart, open-ended flight. First, both Garp and Dubin are attracted to the solitary nature of running. From an early age, for example, Garp rejects games involving balls (and, by extension, teams) because, as he puts it, "The ball stands between the athlete and his exercise .... And when one further removes one's body from the contest by an extension device—such as a racket, a bat, or a stick—all purity of movement, strength, and focus is lost" (p. 51). Interestingly, Garp's other main sport, wrestling, has several points in common with running. While wrestling is performed against an opponent, and is therefore not a solitary sport, a wrestler does separate himself from his team in order to perform; a wrestler also relies on his "purity of movement, strength, and focus" rather than on an "extension device." Garp turns to both running and wrestling at the Steering Academy, his prep school, and continues both sports throughout his adult life. Furthermore, with rare exceptions, Garp's running is a solitary activity.

In a similar way, Dubin makes a point not only of running alone, but also of avoiding encounters with others while he is out on his runs. At one point he goes so far as to hide behind a tree until a neighbor of his passes by (p. 13). Dubin consistently chooses times and places for his running that will help him avoid contact with others. He takes his exercise at the crack of dawn—"if a car appeared this early in the morning, neither jogger nor driver dared look at each other" (p. 132) — and in the dead of winter along lonely country paths, "the one man in town visible on the snow-rutted roads" (p. 158).

For both Garp and Dubin, then, running offers a welcome chance for extended solitude. This preference is congruent with the fact that both men write for a living, a vocation that also reflects their inclination toward solitary activity. In fact, explicit comparisons between running and writing are brought out in both novels. For example, we are told that "At the end of a mile, Garp felt he was just getting started. ('A novelist, even then—though I didn't know it,' Garp would write, years later)" (p. 62). For Dubin, similarly, both exercise and writing constitute an "imposition on the poor self" (p. 123).

In addition to being attracted to the solitude offered by running, both men look to it as a means of purifying the self through discipline and exertion. As mentioned earlier, Garp defines the essence of sport in terms of the "purity of movement, strength, and focus" that it requires. Along the same lines, Irving notes that "sports did not feel like recreation to Garp. Nothing felt like recreation to Garp. From the beginning, he appeared to believe that there was something strenuous to achieve . . . . Even before young Garp knew he was going to be a writer, or knew what he wanted to be, it appears he did nothing 'for fun'" pp. 51-52). This quest for purification, begun early in Garp's life, is also part of his approach as an adult.

Dubin espouses the same stoic philosophy about his exercise: "Dubin assailed winter by daily testing himself: running through its icy womb to demonstrate he was not afraid of the dead season" (p. 132); he further looks upon running as a "self-inflicted cure" (p. 133). Clearly, both Garp and Dubin regard their running as a means of purifying and strengthening both the body and the soul.

We also find that both men derive a certain heroic or romantic sense of fulfillment from their running, again recalling earlier American protagonists' associations with open-ended flight. Garp, for example, uses his running to become a kind of suburban Lone Ranger—he chases down speeding cars in his neighborhood and chastises their drivers for endangering the children on his block:

He had properly bullied every fast driver in the neighborhood. The streets around Garp's house were cut in squares, bordered every block by stop signs; Garp could usually catch up to a car, on foot, provided that the car obeyed the stop signs . . . .

Most drivers were impressed with Garp, and even if they swore about him later, they were polite and apologetic to his face, assuring him that they would not speed in the neighborhood again. It was clear to them that Garp was in good physical shape. (p. 181)

At one point when Garp is running in the park near his home, he experiences the "one real-life drama" of his 5 years of marriage; he apprehends a man who has sexually assaulted a 10-year-old girl. For several months afterward, he assumes the title of hero, "the one who nabbed the molester in the park" (pp. 141-146). Not surprisingly, this sudden celebrity tempts him to pursue heroic endeavors full time: "And sometimes someone would ask, 'And what is it you *do* Mister Garp?'

"The following silence would pain Garp, as he stood thinking that it was probably best to say that he *ran*—for a living. He cruised the parks, a molester-nabber by profession. He hung around phone booths, like that man in the cape—waiting for disasters. Any of this would make more sense to them than what he really did.

"I write," Garp would finally admit. Disapointment —even suspicion—all over their once-admiring faces" (p. 147).

Along less dramatic lines, Garp is also propositioned by a neighbor, Mrs. Ralph, whom he meets while chasing down her car. (pp. 181-182).

Such heroic and romantic aspirations appear in Dubin as well. He prides himself on his ability to defy rough roads and dangerous weather: "He ran in rain, slush, in end-of-December fog—to show weather, winter staring at him as he went by, the quality of Dubin's self, his premise, the thought he ran by" (p. 132). And Dubin first meets Fanny, the woman who will become his mistress, while he is out running. Malamud's comment on this incident points explicitly to Dubin's chivalric fantasies: "Ah, Dubin, you meet a pretty girl on the road and are braced to hop on a horse in pursuit of youth" (p. 8).

The passages discussed in this section illustrate that both Garp and Dubin look to their running for several of the same types of fulfilment that American protagonists have traditionally associated with flight. Recreational running offers them a chance for solitude, a means of purification, and a sense of heroism and romanticism.

THE COMPLICATIONS OF RUNNING FOR GARP AND DUBIN

This section examines two related points: how the differences between flight and running manifest themselves in *The World According to Garp* and *Dubin's Lives,* and what complications arise when Garp and Dubin attempt to use running as a means of flight. In particular, the distinctive features of running—the fact that it is circular, closed, and temporary—contribute to Garp's and Dubin's ability to use running only as a partial escape from their professional and personal anxieties.

Both Garp and Dubin experience a good deal of professional frustration, either from writer's block or from an inability to produce quality work. Predictably, both men turn to running as an outlet for this frustration. For example, we are told that the quality of Garp's daily existence "was controlled by how good a day he's had writing, and how good a run he'd had. If the writing went poorly, he took it out on himself with a long, hard run" (pp. 175-176). Likewise, Dubin finds that exercise is a way to counteract the stasis of writer's block: "he sat regularly at his desk, promising himself he would stay with it if something good evolved; but day after day very little did—an aimless page or two; so he went—after three prescribed working hours—for a routine walk in any weather . . . . a man had to conjure up some relief from nothing much achieved" (p. 123).

The problem for both writers, however, arises from the temporary, circular nature of running. Rather than offering them a permanent escape, running merely returns both men to the scene of the crime: the writing desk. For Garp and Dubin, achievement through running is at best a weak substitute for achievement through writing, less a reward for accomplishment than punishment for the lack of it.

Garp and Dubin also attempt to escape through their running from personal conflicts such as familial and romantic problems. One striking example of such an attempt occurs while Garp and his family are recuperating from the car accident in which Garp's son Walt has been killed. Blaming his wife Helen for Walt's death, Garp leaves his family every day for a long, solitary period of exercise. His activities are limited by his broken jaw, but the urge to run is still strong: "He tried running on the beach but he had to give it up; it jarred his jaw and jangled his tongue against his teeth. But he walked for miles along the sand" (p. 275).

Dubin displays similar behavior following a disappointing week in Venice with his mistress Fanny. Upon return, he submits himself to a strenuous regime of exercise: "Nothing like a little 'agitation' . . . . to escape misery. He ran from his gross belly, from Fanny in all her guises, naked to not quite . . . . He ran from heartbreak revived, his dreary discipline, loyal wife, depression afflicting him. Sometimes his legs went faster than his body cared to go."

"What a miserable price to pay for unpleasure!" (p. 125).

However, as with their attempts to run from their writing problems, both Garp and Dubin gain only a momentary reprieve by running from their marital problems. The temporary, circular nature of running leads them back to their families and marriages and to the conflicts that have arisen in them.

Another set of complications arises in these novels when the heroic aspirations that Garp and Dubin bring to running are subverted by larger, uncontrollable forces. At numerous points in Irving's novel, Garp literally runs into forces that remind him — and us — of the limitations of heroism. Consider, for example, his apprehension of the sexual assailant in the park, the act that brings him the temporary title of hero. Some time later, Garp discovers that the assailant has been released due to insufficient evidence. Although Garp feels himself "tremble with violence," he is nonetheless helpless in the face of this injustice (p. 147). Consider also the "vigilance," as Garp calls it, with which he patrols his neighborhood. The futility of his efforts is tragically underscored when Walt is killed while riding in Garp's own car. Still later, while out running near his mother's refuge for women, Garp is nearly killed by a car driven by a fanatical feminist. And, as a final irony, Garp jogs to the scene of his assassination, the wrestling room at the school where he is coaching.

Dubin's heroic efforts—which, as mentioned, often lead him to a fearless confrontation with nature—are also severely undercut at times. A representative episode of this type takes place during the long, hard winter of discontent between Dubin and his wife Kitty. One morning, Dubin foolishly tries to take his exercise during an intense blizzard and loses his way on the country roads. Dubin is confronted at this point with a frightening vision of his own death: "He saw himself buried amid trees in snow up to his neck. Embarrassing to die so close to the road: like drowning in a bathtub . . . . "The Woods were growing dark . . . . Suppose it snowed until nightfall and throughout the night until morning—Dubin frozen stiff, snowman. Death's scarecrow" (p. 152). On the verge of freezing, Dubin is finally rescued by Kitty.

The incidents outlined in this section point clearly to significant differences between flight and the recreational running in Irving and Malamud's novels. Rather than serving as an escape route, running brings both Garp and Dubin back to the personal and professional difficulties that these men must resolve. Rather than providing them with a romantic or heroic sense of freedom and control, running pushes them toward the stark realization of their own limitations. In short, running serves less as a path to transcendence than as a path to self-confrontation.

THEMATIC IMPLICATIONS

The preceding discussion demonstrates that recreational running is both a continuation of and a departure from flight, the traditional prerogative of the American protagonist. By having Garp and Dubin run, both Irving and Malamud endow their protagonists with qualities that recall the classic American protagonist: namely, a concern with solitary movement through space, with purification through self-discipline, and with romantic and heroic aspirations.

Thus Garp and Dubin bring certain ideals and expectations to their running. Both men, however, are also confronted repeatedly with the limitations of these ideals, largely due to the circular, temporary nature of running. Again recalling the image of a cycle, their running is often triggered by their professional or marital problems and provides only a temporary reprieve before leading each man back to the source of conflict.

Seen in light of other elements of these novels, such patterns suggest that running may be a metaphor for Garp and Dubin's need to reconcile their aspirations and their limitations. For Garp, this reconciliation involves acknowledging that constant vigilance is impossible. In *The World According to Garp*, the inescapable presence of pain and death—a presence captured in that novel by the image of the "Under Toad"—is ultimately immune to the type of surveillance that Garp tries to maintain over his family and neighborhood. Nor is such unrelenting vigilance even desirable, for it would entail living in constant fear. For Dubin, reconciliation involves choosing between the youthful freedom offered by his mistress Fanny and the flawed but enduring love offered by his wife Kitty. And both men must work at reconciling themselves to the demands and frustrations of their vocation, writing.

The activity of running in *The World According to Garp* and *Dubin's Lives* therefore reveals the vicious cycle in which each of the protagonists is caught. They have essentially two alternatives in trying to break this cycle: either escaping permanently—that is, turning their running into open-ended flight—or, as both men choose instead, breaking the cycle through a leap of faith that involves acknowledging the imperfections in themselves and the world they live in. Thus running dramatizes in these novels the temptation to "light out," the illusory quality of that possibility, and the need to come to terms with a modern "territory" that is often confusing but also profoundly promising.

REFERENCES

Fiedler, L.A. (1966). *Love and death in the American novel* (rev. ed.). New York: Stein and Day.

Irving, J. (1976). *The world according to Garp*. New York: E.P. Dutton.

Malamud, B. (1977). *Dubin's lives*. New York: Farrar, Straus, and Giroux.

Tanner, T. (1971). *City of words: American fiction 1950-1970*. New York: Harper and Row.

PLAY THEORY AND AN ELIZABETHAN SONNET SEQUENCE

Nancy A. Benson
Mercy College

Perspectives of play and game have proven virtually indispensable for some of those who study Medieval and Renaissance literature. Not only can major figures be read with fresh discernment, as Anna K. Nardo (1980, 1982) has shown, but the use of ludic theory as an analytic tool can also throw new light on works previously neglected or misunderstood. A case in point is the Elizabethan poet Samuel Daniel, who has been all but eclipsed by more illustrious contemporaries including William Shakespeare, Sir Philip Sidney, and Edmund Spenser. Among Daniel's more interesting work is his sonnet sequence *Delia*, in which Daniel takes up the genre that seems to have functioned as a test of poetic mettle for the practitioners of his day. Unfortunately, *Delia* has too often been misread as lackluster, sentimental or "Platonic" verse (Pearson, 1966). I think that Daniel invites a more sophisticated reading when certain play modes in *Delia* are recognized, modes that illuminate significant aspects of the genre and the period.

First, what are the identifying characteristics of the genre? The traditional sonnet (or "little song") adheres to a 14-line pattern with approximately 10 syllables per line in iambic rhythm and follows one of two complicated rhyme schemes. Typically, it laments an unrequited love for an idealized lady and draws upon an ample but specialized stock of metaphors, epithets, allusions, verse ornaments, and tropes derived in large measure from Petrarch's lyrics to Laura in the 14th century. These poetic materials enable the sonneteer to strike certain poses that become stylized into a ritual performance. Thus, he invokes mythological figures such as Sisyphus and Prometheus as analogues for his plight; he compares the lady's hair to golden wires and her complexion to roses and lilies; he weeps an ocean of tears; he suffers from sleeplessness; her glances wound him like arrows; and so on (John, 1964). Furthermore, it was the vogue to produce these sonnets in sequences or series of 50 to 150 and more, held together by some suggestion of plot, autobiographical reference, or seasonal analogue.

In the 1590s, a sudden upsurge of sonnet-sequence publication took place, led off by Spenser's *Amoretti* and Sidney's *Astrophel and Stella*, joined by a lengthy list of lesser-known examples including *Delia*, and capped in the next decade, somewhat after the vogue had passed, by the sonnets of Shakespeare himself. Before or in lieu of actual publication, Elizabethan sonnets were probably circulated in manuscript form among the members of court—a coterie well versed in the established sonnet conventions (Spriet, 1968).

Hence it is clear that the sonnet sequence presents a text and context of considerable social and linguistic complexity. It also fulfills certain criteria of play and game as identified by Huizinga (1955), Caillois (1961), and Bateson (1972). The sonnet embraces both rigorously observed rules and patterned imitation (agon and mimicry) in a special kind of make-believe. It is set off by precise boundaries in time and space; its structured appearance on the page is a frame clearly signalling its artifice and creating an expectation for a rarefied type of experience that transcends the everyday. With these freely chosen stringencies operating in the composing process and affecting the reader's participation in the poem, the sonneteer both follows and stretches the rules to project his own personal style and compete for poetic renown. His challenge is to present not just pleasing sameness but also delightful difference to a discriminating audience or community or players, for the life of the Renaissance courtier itself can best be understood in terms of play and game (Stevens, 1961; Lanham, 1976).

Thus the sonnet provides a special balance of necessity and freedom, of accepted imperatives and chosen alternatives, which becomes the means of demonstrating the poet's own powers. One is reminded of basic theory stemming from Karl Groos (1901) that pleasure in overcoming self-imposed difficulties and the exhibition of prowess are essential features of play, and that play gives satisfaction in the "joy of being a cause" and the concomitant feeling of power. The sonnet is symbolic play transforming reality through the materials of language, image, and thought. Like all poets, the sonneteer must play with and against the rules of language itself in order to subordinate them to poetry (Beaujour, 1971). Inevitably he also engages in competition with past masters of the genre (in this case, Petrarch and his French imitators) as well as his contemporaries. He may also play off his own version of the genre against the received norms. In sum, Elizabethan sonnet sequences fit Huizinga's (1955) identification of one ludic activity as "a contest for the best representation of something" (p. 13). For late 16th-century poets in England, the challenge was to produce the most agreeable native version of the Petrarchan model.

Samuel Daniel meets these ludic challenges in three ways: by exploring his own poetic strengths to the exclusion of other possibilities, by playfully manipulating and even inverting aspects of Petrarchan rhetoric, and by coding within his sequence a message that would be read one way by the uninitiated and another by his target audience — the young poets of the courtly circle. For there is much evidence that the poems address themselves, through their ostensible praise of a lady, to the more essential issue of poetic immortality. And in his skillful impersonation of the traditional lover-poet, this aspiring literary competitor can also present his own credentials.

In a first version of the sonnets printed surreptitiously in 1591, the speaker launches his poems with an ostentatious address to the verse itself, "Go wailing verse," a deliberate echo of one of Petrarch's (1949) *Rime,* "Ite rime dolente" (p. 347). In his sonnet, Daniel calls attention to the imitative qualities and functions the verses bear while he bestows his own stamp of individuality. As "wailing verse," his sonnets convey the proper tone of love-sick complaint, though Daniel's (1969) speaker wears his rue with a difference:

> Go wailing verse, the infants of my love,
> Minerva-like, brought forth without a Mother,
> Present the image of the cares I prove,
> Witness your Father's grief exceeds all other.[1]

Petrarch is not the only sonnet master taken on in these lines, for Daniel's mentor, Sidney, had presented himself in the opening sonnet of Astrophel and Stella as "great with child to speak and helpless in my throes" (Sidney, 1969, p. 163). Della's lover is, in contrast, not "helpless," but possessed of a sense of fruition. There is a competitive element of assurance and self-assertiveness here in the speaker's identification with Jove, who in Greek myth androgynously gave birth to Minerva, the goddess who sprang fully armed from his brain. The metaphor of these self-generated, complaining progeny is ingeniously developed in the next two quatrains. Denied the role of "mother," the lady is nonetheless made guilty of neglect: she has "starved" these "infants" because of her "sleeping pity." The exhortation to the verse continues:

> Sigh out a story of her cruel deeds,
> With interrupted accents of despair;
> A monument that whosoever reads,
> May justly praise and blame my loveless fair.
> Say her disdain hath dried up my blood,
> And starved you, in succours still denying;
> Press to her eyes, importune me some good,
> Waken her sleeping pity with your crying.

Significantly, the poet anticipates an audience ("whosoever reads") that will reach well beyond the lady herself. It has been integral to the genre that the illusion of confidences about a private emotion be delivered in a thoroughly public mode. Moreover, the rhetoric of pleading allows as much for the presentation of self as for the solicitation of favors. The word "monument" carries the root meaning of admonishment but more obviously conveys the sense of visible memorial or record. And if the monument will stand for Delia, it will stand for the poet-lover as well. The poems will record a balance of praise and blame deserved by the lady, as have sonnets throughout history.

In regard to form, Daniel shows here his love of classical symmetry and proportion in the parallel grammatical constructions that carry the flow of the verse through the four divisions of the poem. Like other games, a poem provides an enclosure and highly ordered structures that contrast sharply with the randomness of phenomena outside the playground. Each of the poem's divisions begins with an imperative verb, including the final couplet:

Knock at that hard heart, beg till you have moved her;
And tell th' unkind, how dearly I have loved her.

This sonnet creates resolution and closure not only by the concluding couplet itself but also by its echoes of the sounds ending lines 2 and 4 ("Mother" and "other"). Daniel favors this three-quatrain-and-couplet construction introduced to England by the Earl of Surrey rather than the alternative Italian form of octave and sestet. The English form provides a sense of individual semantic and linguistic units carefully fitted into a whole, and Daniel's polished execution of this pattern may well have influenced Shakespeare's choice of the form for most of his own sonnets.

Despite the traditional rhetoric of "Go wailing verse," the "disdain" and "cruel deeds" of the "loveless fair," one senses that the lady is not really the dominant figure in these pieces, an impression that is to be strongly corroborated as the sequence progresses. One would expect, for example, that the allusion in this first sonnet to Minerva, the chaste goddess of wisdom, would operate in reference to the lady; instead, it is reserved for the poetry. It is the verse that is associated with purity, power, and beauty. And though the poet may represent himself as a victim, he is not a passive sufferer as is the typical Petrarchan lover. Rather, this sonnet evinces a self-conscious reflexiveness, signalling to the adept that poetry itself is the subject of the poem. Within the 50 sonnets of the standard version of *Delia*, there is a self-referential element in 22 of them, almost half. In *Delia*, the lady becomes a mere backdrop for the histrionic poet, for Delia possesses even less a personality than do most other sonnet heroines. Much of the matter treated in Elizabethan sonnets in general, and particularly in Daniel's, seems to be there for the sake of the manner.

This first sonnet has given notice that the forensic theme of judgment will be a strong element in the series, and thus the pleader's prevailing strategy seems to be to make the best case for himself as poet-lover. John Stevens (1961) has made a useful distinction between the lover-as-poet and the poet-as-lover. The lover-as-poet uses words to advance himself in the game of love, whereas the poet-as-lover enters the game of love for the sake of his performance as poet. I see Daniel as using the rhetoric of love in precisely the latter way. Similarly, Kenneth Burke (1969) has isolated the concept of "pure persuasion" as opposed to persuasion for the purpose of acquiring material advantage. Although Burke does not explicitly call it play, the self-pleasing principle is clearly ludic and applicable to *Delia*: "Pure persuasion involves the saying of something not for the extra-verbal advantage to be got by the saying, but because it *likes the feel* of a summons. It would be nonplused if the summons were answered" (p. 68, italics mine).

The succeeding sonnet deploys and transmutes the dominant metaphor of its predecessor by recasting the "wailing infants" into "offspring" that are "fatal anthems." Even more expressly than its sister sonnet, this one designates an audience: the young court versifiers would appreciate the ritualized significance of what was played and could read the subtext. The rigors dramatized in the poem can apply to a poetic enterprise as well as to a romantic one:

> If so it hap this offspring of my care,
> These fatal anthems, sad and mournful Songs,
> Come to their view, who like afflicted are;
> Let them yet sigh their own, and moan my wrongs.
>   But untouched hearts, with unaffected eye,
> Approach not to behold so great distress:
> Clear-sighted you, soon note what is awry,
> While blinded ones my errors never guess.
>   You blinded souls whom youths and errors lead,
> You outcast Eaglets, dazzled with your sun:
> Ah you, and none but you my sorrows read,
> You best can judge the wrongs that she hath done.
>   That she hath done, the motive of my pain,
>   Who whilst I love, doth kill me with disdain.

The metaphor of the neglected children is here transferred to the ingroup itself, so close is the relation understood between poets and their verse, as a variation of the progeny conceit is introduced in the image of "outcast eaglets." The ironically expressed requirement for the shared poetic experience is that only those similarly "blinded" can "read" and "judge" properly.

An all but obligatory gesture in the sonneteer's game of pretense includes avowals of the sincerity of his love and disclaimers of mere rhetorical displays in the service of fame. So Daniel makes his bid for inclusion among distinguished company as an early sonnet (4) insists, as did Petrarch and certain of his followers, that no ambition is involved:

> These plaintive verse, the Posts of my desire,
> Which haste for succour to her slow regard:
> Bear not report of any slender fire,
> Forging a grief to win a fame's reward.
> Nor are my passions limned for outward hue,
> For that no colors can depaint my sorrows:
> Delia herself, and all the world may view
> Best in my face, how cares hath tilled deep sorrows.
> No Bays I seek to deck my mourning brow,
> O clear-eyed Rector of the holy Hill:
> My humble accents crave the Olive bow,
> Of her mild pity and relenting will.
> These lines I use t'unburden mine own heart;
> My love affects no fame, not steems of art.

The "bays" or laurel branch sacred to Apollo, the prize traditionally sought by poets, is ostentatiously rejected for the "olive bow," the "humble" and noncompetitive symbol of peace and "relenting will." But Sidney has indicated in his *Defence of Poesy* of 1595 how such poetic statements are to be read: "Now, for the poet, he affirmeth nothing and therefore never lieth" (Sidney, 1969, p. 136)—a clear affirmation of the play principle.

Since imitation is integral to the sonnet, but like other essentials must be denied or disguised, Daniel insists on the uniqueness of his passion, and there is a competitive thrust in several of the sonnets as he disparages the tactics of rival poets. Perhaps Spenser is the chief target in Sonnet 46:

> Let others sing of Knights and Paladins,
> In aged accents, and untimely words;
> Paint shadows in imaginary lines,
> Which well the reach of their high wits records;
> But I must sing of thee and those fair eyes,
> Authentic shall my verse in time to come,
> When yet th'unborn shall say, 'Lo where she lies',
> Whose beauty made him speak that else was dumb.

The remarkable word usage here is the adjective-turned-verb "authentic." The meaning seems to be that the poet's verse will prove

Delia's actual existence and the truth about her attributes to future generations. But the syntax also links "authentic" with "verse" so that the poetry too is rendered genuine and truthful. The verse-as-monument theme reasserts itself in "Lo where she lies," a formula primarily found in epitaphs and elegies, and is reiterated in the third quatrain's powerful utterance, in which Daniel shows a mastery of his medium that any poet might envy:

> These are the arks, the trophies I erect,
> That fortify thy name against old age;
> And these thy sacred virtues must protect,
> Against the Dark and time's consuming rage.

In a tradition largely devoted to classical imagery, the term "arks" carries Biblical significance not common in sonnets. One remembers two types of arks in the Old Testament: the refuge Noah built against the flood and the chest enclosing the two tablets of stone containing the Ten Commandments—thus, the Ark of the Covenant. Both types appear to be conflated as the poet pledges a heroic defense of the lady's name, not against slander, as in the courtly love tradition, but against the far more formidable foe of mortality itself. The truth is that in bestowing immortality upon the name of Delia, Daniel can prevent the death of his own name. One of the striking features of this sonnet sequence is the prominence of the "eternizing" or "monumentalizing" conceit over other standard sonnet themes. Eight of the sonnets, or 16 percent, emphasize this poetic function. When one adds to this number the three additional sonnets (31-33) dealing with transience and the inevitability of decay, the role of poetry in the defense against death becomes even stronger.

Nor does this kind of seriousness preclude play, as Otto Rank (1975) and Ernest Becker (1973) have shown. In his *Art and Artist*, Rank identifies the creative urge with the effort to eternalize personality. His section on "Games and Destiny" traces the origin of games (as does Huizinga) to cultic festivals that featured mythic representations of the victory of the deity over the powers of darkness and death. Becker (1973) sees all cultural fabrications as "denials of death," and shows how they share with play the means of sovereignty over a natural reality of danger and vulnerability.

Though the poet overtly impersonates the modest, unassuming suppliant, the covert message is about poetic achievement and renown. In a self-referential sonnet (30), the speaker anticipates the loss of Delia's beauty to "tyrant Time's desire," then in a strategic shift to the past tense, specifically dedicates his verse as a preserving and restoring force:

Go you, my verse, go tell her what she was;
For what she was she best shall find in you.
   Your fiery heat lets not her glory pass
   But Phoenix-like shall make her live anew.

A subtle but significant deviation from the standard Petrarchan ideology has occurred. Whereas the lady has traditionally been the tyrant, Daniel makes Time usurp her role so that her hegemony is limited indeed. The phoenix image, usually applied to the poet, is similarly transposed so that it is the lady who will be reborn out of the ashes of her once-flaming beauty by virtue of the "fiery heat" of the poems in their unextinguishable perpetuity. Thus, the poet has replaced the Petrachan lady as the source of *ethos* (it is *his* faith that is exemplary), and the lady replaces the poet as the source of *pathos* (it is *her* beauty that is doomed to fade). This seems to be Daniel's most original contribution to the genre and another indication of his ludic impulse. Significantly, through Daniel's playful inversion of the strengths of the poet and the lady, it is the poet who comes out well ahead.

The next five sonnets (31-35), at the very heart of the sequence, comprise a mini-series that capitalizes on the immortalizing theme. The unity and importance of these sonnets for Daniel's purposes are further emphasized by a "chain" effect, a stylistic device popularized by Daniel, in which the last line of one sonnet is repeated as the first line of the next. The provinces of poetry and play obviously overlap here also: the exaggeration of order and the repetition of items in a pattern that would not normally occur are play elements identified by Ellis (1973). And one could easily relate the chain device to the round dances and circle games of folk cultures. Repetition and circularity also seem connected to the control, transformation, and even trancendence of time achieved in play. For playtime is privileged temporal space carved out of ordinary reality and having the effect of arresting or modifying the linear flow of time. It is "charmed" time, and one of the most potent techniques of the charm or spell historically has been repetition.

Daniel's verse often achieves an incantatory quality in its measured cadence and high incidence of sonorous vowels. His most famous sonnet (45) is an apostrophe to sleep:

   Care-charmer sleep, son of the Sable night,
Brother to death in silent darkness born:
Relieve my languish and restore the light,
With dark forgetting of my cares return.

This exploitation of the phonic possibilities of language recalls Roland Barthes' (1967) identification of "opaque" as opposed to "transparent" style, a concern with verbal surface rather than with linguistic content. This is language calling attention to itself as language, a concept clearly compatible with play theory.

In making his own pastiche of conventional Petrarchan strategies, choosing some and rejecting others to fit his own proficiencies, Daniel plays the sonnet game with grace and ingenuity. Although Delia is portrayed through hyperbolic play and in mock-serious categories long emptied of credible feeling from the point of view of the real world, she is a necessary invention. Daniel follows his models by restructuring reality into a separate world that meets Eugen Fink's (1971) description of play: "an enigmatic world that is not nothing and yet is nothing real" (p. 21). In an early sonnet of the series (6), which begins with stock phrases ("Fair is my love and cruel as she's fair") and seems at first merely a rehearsal of typical tropes and *topoi*, a revealing turn near the end of the poem explains Delia's role:

> Chastity and Beauty, which were deadly foes,
> Live reconciled friends within her brow:
> And had she pity to conjoin with those,
> Then who had heard the plaints I utter now.
>> O had she not been fair and thus unkind,
>> My Muse had slept, and none had known my mind.

If the poet's performance is stereotyped, so is the lady's. She is under an inherent obligation imposed by the genre: since "fair," therefore "unkind." But the penalties the lady seems to be imposing are really the means of scoring in the sonnet game since through her "cruelty" the poet can win acclaim. Delia is the creative principle that has to be embodied in a fictive figure so that Daniel can carry off his imposture and demonstrate his mastery of the genre.

Another playful indication that Daniel's concern is literary rather than erotic is the name he has chosen for his lady: *Delia* is an anagram of *ideal* (Shawcross, 1974). Devotion to Delia may be seen as representing devotion to poetry, the most demanding and capricious of mistresses. The sequence invites reading by the initiated as a kind of allegory of the poetic life. A common definition of allegory as one thing related and another understood is close to Bateson's (1972) two peculiarities of play: first, "the messages or signals exchanged . . . are in a certain sense untrue or not meant"; and second, "that which is denoted by these signals is nonexistent" (p. 183). Daniel seems to celebrate the ideal of poetry and the poet's own powers as one passion masquerades for another in a "metalinguistic" game (Bateson, 1972, p. 178). For this, too, there is a precedent: Petrarch's *Laura* herself had been associated with the *laurel* of poetic fame.[2] In claims for the lady's immortality, Daniel asserts his own and that of all poets who play this game to win. (Incidentally, by understanding what

Daniel's sonnets and others are about, one can perhaps look at Shakespeare's sonnets with a more sophisticated eye, thereby avoiding fruitless efforts to place the "fair young man" and the "dark lady" among actual persons in Shakespeare's life history.)

Through the perspectives of play and game, one sees sonnet making as a trial of wits, a test of skills, a performance in a public arena, an impersonation that calls on a repertory of gestures and utterances. It is a strategy that pits a player against self-imposed obstacles, against his own creative source, and against other players past and present. It is framed interaction between poet and reader that manipulates the latter's expectation and surprise, essential components of the pleasures of literature.

Thus, knowledge of play theory helps the literary critic choose appropriate criteria by which a literary artifact is to be judged. It encourages a close reading of the text and research into antecedent and contemporary texts for analysis of the interplay between them. Play theory combines well with other approaches to literature, for it is congenial with formalist, post-structuralist, phenomenological, and even psychoanalytic schools of criticism. Finally, it affirms the aesthetic autonomy of poetry, which Suzanne K. Langer (1953) has described as the creation of "illusory events" developing in a "virtual world" peculiar to the poem (pp. 216-219). The operative word here is "virtual," and what is created is "pure semblance." Poetry perceived as play means, among other things, that it is an end in itself, an adventure, a means of power and transcendence. Much yet remains to be done, however, in exploring the shared territory of play and aesthetics, of play forms and art forms. In the spirit of Schiller and Huizinga, such inquiry should proceed apace.

Notes

1. The authoritative edition is the Scolar Press facsimile (Daniel 1969). Spelling has been modernized for this paper, but capitalization and punctuation have been retained. All quotations are from this edition, and sonnet numbers are indicated in the absence of pagination.

2. See Petrarch's (1949, Familiari II, p. xxxiii) disclaimer that Laura is a mere symbol for his ambition.

REFERENCES

Barthes, R. (1967). Science vs. literature. *Times Literary Supplement, 56,* 897-898.

Bateson, G. (1972). *Steps to an ecology of mind.* New York: Ballentine.

Beaujour, M. (1971). The game of poetics. In J. Ehrmann (Ed.). *Game, play, literature* (pp. 58-67). Boston: Beacon.

Becker, E. (1973). *The denial of death.* New York: Free Press, Macmillan.

Burke, K. (1969). *A rhetoric of motives.* Berkeley: University of California Press.

Caillois, R. (1961). *Man, play and games* (M. Barash, Trans.). New York: Free Press of Glencoe.

Daniel, S. (1969). *Delia with the complaint of Rosamond.* London: Scolar Press.

Ellis, M.J. (1973). *Why people play.* Englewood Cliffs: Prentice-Hall.

Fink, E. (1971). The oasis of happiness: Toward an ontology of play. In J. Ehrmann (Ed.), *Game, play, literature* (pp. 19-30). Boston: Beacon.

Groos, K. (1901). *The play of man* (E. Baldwin, Trans.). New York: Appleton.

Huizinga, J. (1955). *Homo ludens: A study of the play element in culture.* Boston: Beacon.

John, C.L. (1964). *The Elizabethan sonnet sequences.* New York: Russell & Russell. (Original work published 1938)

Langer, S.K. (1953). *Feeling and form.* New York: Scribner's.

Lonham, R.A. (1976). *The motives of eloquence: Literary rhetoric in the Renaissance.* New Haven: Yale University Press.

Nardo, A.K. (1980). Play, literature and the poetry of George Herbert. In H. B. Schwartzman (Ed.), *Play and culture* (pp. 30-48). West Point, N.Y.: Leisure Press.

Nardo, A. K. (1982). The poetry of John Donne's liminal play. In J. Loy (Ed.), *The paradoxes of play* (pp. 34-41). West Point, N.Y.: Leisure Press.

Pearson, E.L. (1966). *Elizabethan love conventions.* New York: Barnes & Noble.

Petrarch, Francesca. (1949). *Songs and sonnets.* (T. Mommsen, Trans.) New York: Putnam.

Rank, O. (1975). *Art and artist: Creative urge and personality development.* (C.F. Atkinson, Trans.). New York: Agathon.

Shawcross, J.T. (1974). The poet as orator: One phase of his judicial pose. In T.O. Sloan & R.B. Waddington (Eds.), *The rhetoric of Renaissance poetry from Wyatt to Milton* (pp. 5-36). Berkeley: University of California Press.

Sidney, P. (1969). *Selected prose and poetry.* R. Kimbrough (Ed.), New York: Holt, Rinehart & Winston.

Spriet, P. (1968). *Samuel Daniel: Sa vie: son oeuvre* [Samuel Daniel: His life; his work]. Paris: Didier.

Stevens, J. (1961). *Music and poetry in the early Tudor court.* London: Methuen.

5

PLAY IN CELEBRATION AND RITUAL

INTRODUCTION

Kendall Blanchard

In keeping with the theme of the 1983 TAASP meetings ("Reunion du Mardi Gras"), many presentations addressed the issues of celebration and ritual. The papers in this section are two of these. In both cases, the central theme is ritual, obvious in festival but not so obvious in a hot bath, but important as a perspective in both contexts. Also, in both of the events described there is a mood of playfulness, but a playfulness that seems to occur within a prescribed pattern that is not completely consistent with Huizinga's (1950) suggestion that play is "a free activity standing quite consciously 'outside' ordinary life" (p. 13). On the other hand, it illustrates Norbeck's (1971) contention that human play is unique among animal play behaviors because "it is molded by culture" (p. 48) and that it is an important form of social communication.

The Miracle paper provides a clear demonstration of the way in which an "ordinary" event (i.e., a hot bath) has more than ordinary ritual implications. It is suggested that the commercial hot bath allows one the opportunity to experience voluntarily the classic states of the ritual process: separation, liminality, and reincorporation. At that level, the bath is not unlike other events that are more explicitly ritualistic. On the other hand, its recreational and therapeutic qualities make the bath a distinctive experience with its own ideology.

Gradante has described the colorful San Pedro festival in the small Andean town of La Plata, focusing on the role of the "mask." It is suggested that the principal function of the mask is not its concealing of personal identity nor its facilitation of licentious behavior frequently associated with festival. Rather, the mask is a message about the wearer and the cultural value system in which he or she participates.

Both papers make it clear that the way one plays, the way one chooses to use leisure time, is a statement about culture. In this sense, both are reiterations of the importance of play and play studies.

REFERENCES

Huizinga, J. (1950). *Homo ludens: A study of the play element in culture.* Boston: Beacon Press.

Norbeck, E. (1971, December). Man at play. *Natural History Magazine* (special supplement): 48-53.

VOLUNTARY RITUAL AS RECREATIONAL THERAPY: A STUDY OF THE BATHS AT HOT SPRINGS, ARKANSAS

Andrew W. Miracle, Jr.
Texas Christian University

There is no consensus among anthropologists on the precise nature and definition of ritual. For example, there has been no resolution of the debate between Radcliffe-Brown and Malinowski in the 1930s over the relationship between ritual and anxiety. (See, for example, Homans, 1972; Malinowski, 1972; and Radcliffe-Brown, 1972.) Is ritual stress relieving or stress producing? Other issues also remain unresolved and usually are ignored by those reporting on ritual. Is ritual necessarily religious or may secular ceremonies be considered ritual? Is ritual always a social phenomenon or may the isolated idiosyncratic behaviors of individuals also constitute ritual?

Perhaps no single work has refocused these questions in recent times more than the collection of papers prepared for the Wenner-Gren Foundation symposium in Burg Wartenstein, Austria, and subsequently produced in a volume edited by Sally F. Moore and Barbara G. Myerhoff (1977) entitled *Secular Ritual*. What is significant about the collection of papers is that there is seemingly little agreement among the 14 contributors. For example, Gluckman and Gluckman (1977) abjure the use of the term "secular ritual," preferring to speak of ceremonies and ceremonious behaviours in secular contexts. Jack Goody (1977) questions the use of the term "ritual" altogether. Goody believes that when the term is applied as widely as some have done to any formalized behavior, the term is a hindrance to analysis rather than a conceptual aid. Moreover, since the editors made a conscious decision to consider only collective ceremonial forms of behavior, the symposium side-stepped the issue of individual ritual behavior and its neurophysiological significance (Moore and Myerhoff, 1977).

What follows is a description of a single event that I argue is ritual. That is, this event meets most of the criteria usually established by traditional definitions of ritual: it is explained by mythology; it involves attributes of the sacred; it evinces the three stages of ritual identified by van Gennep (i.e., separation, liminality, and reincorporation); it involves the use of symbols; it is structured; it is stereotyped and repetitive; and it elicits neurophysiological effects similar to those associated with many other ritual formats.

However, this event would not be considered ritual by some scholars for two reasons. First, the participants do not perceive it as a religious event. That is, the event does not address and move the spirit world (cf., Gluckman and Gluckman, 1977, p. 242). Second, participation is voluntary—totally voluntary. The individual participant determines the time and place of the event after deciding to participate.

The illustrative ritual is taking a hot mineral bath in a commercial bathhouse in Hot Springs, Arkansas. After describing the event, I return to a consideration of these points and address additional theoretical and methodological issues.

THE BATHS AT HOT SPRINGS

There is a rich history and mythology surrounding the hot springs of Arkansas as recorded in many popular publications that are available locally. It is said that the Indians discovered the springs and named the area The Valley of the Vapors. They revered the place as sacred ground, where warriors could lay aside their arms to bathe in peace. Many believe that DeSoto visited Hot Springs around 1541.

Supposedly the Indians believed that the water from the 47 springs were warmed by the breath of the Great Spirit. Today, however, it is usually explained that water is heated by contact with hot rock within the earth. It emerges as springs at the base of Hot Springs Mountain. The pools made from the springs are crystal clear with only a blue-green algae growing in them.

The presence of radioactivity in the water has been thought to have salutary effects. For over a century, the baths have been reported to give relief to the following conditions: gout or rheumatism, after the acute or inflammatory stage; neuralgia, when dependent upon gout, rheumatism, malaria, or metallic poisoning; the early stages of chronic Brights' disease; catarrhal conditions of the gall bladder; certain forms of disease of the pelvic organs and sterility in women; chronic malaria; alcoholism and drug addictions; many skin diseases; and in some cases, cardiovascular disease with increased tension in the blood vessels.

Particular springs were said to cure specific ailments and have distinct properties. Egg Spring could boil an egg. Mud Hole Spring had a muddy bottom. Rocks around Big Iron Spring were encrusted with iron oxide deposits. "Arsenic Spring" is a mystery because analysis reveals no arsenic. However, Kidney and Liver Springs were said to heal the respective portions of the body for which they were named. Hundreds dangled their feet in Corn Hole Spring to relieve corns, bunions, and other foot ailments.

Advertisements still claim "9 out of 10 people reported to have received hoped-for health benefits." The baths promised to reduce tension and to "prolong active life for the older ages."

The first bathhouses opened in 1830 with one wooden tub in which one could bathe three times for a dollar. In 1919, the price of a single bath at one of 21 bathhouses ranged between 55¢ and 80¢, except at the Pythian Bathhouse for "colored" folks, which was 40¢. Today, only six baths are open for business. Prices range from $4.90 to $7.25 for a single bath. Massages are $6.30 to $9.00, and a whirlpool at any of the facilities is an additional $1.50.

Four baths are still open on Bathhouse Row: the Superior, the Health Services, the Buckstaff, and the Lamar. In addition, the Arlington and the Majestic Hotels also operate baths.

Like Hot Springs itself, little seems to have changed at the baths in the past 60 years except prices. The tubs, rocking chairs, Tiffany windows, and some of the people appear to have been here since well before the "crash of '29."

BATHING AT THE BUCKSTAFF

In 1982, two friends and I went to bathe at the Buckstaff, one of the houses on Bathhouse Row. We entered the lobby lined with rattan rockers, paid the fees at the front desk, and placed all valuables into a deposit box. I was given the key to my box as well as a key to a clothes locker. These keys were attached to elastic bands to be worn like bracelets around the wrist. Then I was given a ticket indicating the services purchased. Males and females are strictly segregated, except in the lobby, with the men's bath on the first floor and the women's on the second.

Having paid $14.00 for a bath, whirlpool, and a massage, I entered the men's locker room. An elderly Caucasian attendant in a white uniform showed me to my assigned locker. I undressed, wrapped a white sheet around my body, and looking like a bedraggled Roman, trundled off to the bathing room.

Opening the door to the bathing room released a warm, moist . rush of air that comfortably enveloped my body. I was greeted by my assigned attendant, who was black and about 25 to 30 years old, as were all the attendants inside the bathing area. The bathing attendants wore white towels wrapped around their waists and rubber sandals on their feet.

All of the dozen or so guests wore two elastic bracelets with keys dangling from them. The bathers' ages ranged from approximately 25 to 85 years. Regulars seemed to be elderly, and the younger men there for the first time.

Upon entering the bathing room my friends and I were separated by the attendants. I was not to see them again until my bath had been completed.

My attendant was friendly and helpful, leading me courteously from station to station within the bath. He introduced himself as Bobby and asked my name. I replied, "Andy."

"All right, Mr. Andy," he said, "come right this way."

The overall impression of the bathhouse was medicinal. The attendants behaved like nurses; the facilities themselves were hospital-like in their Spartan cleanliness.

The first stop was the sitz bath. Bobby explained that this was good for hemorrhoids and problems of the genitalia. "You don't look like you need this," he said. I accepted his advice and followed him to the whirlpool.

There I saw large porcelain-lined tubs that were equipped with single-jet whirlpools. These tubs were methodically scrubbed after each use. Bobby adjusted the water temperature to about 105 degrees and helped me into the high-sided tub. I was given a couple of small cups of water to drink. The whirlpool proved to be a relaxing beginning to my morning at the bath.

After the whirlpool, Bobby led me to a steam closet, the size of an outhouse. With the door closed, the steam issuing from a floor vent soon heated the small space. Bobby told me to count to 120 and then come out.

Next I was ushered to a sheet-covered table and told to lie down. Bobby asked if I had any particular pains. Informed that I had a sore shoulder and stiff knees and elbows, Bobby wrapped hot towels around my joints and placed another one under my shoulder. I was instructed to keep my knees together and my arms by my sides. Then Bobby wrapped the sheet around me so that only my face was unswaddled.

The cocoon treatment was marvelous. I relaxed into a sweaty protoplasm. The sweat, instead of providing a cooling effect through evaporation, was heated by the towels and sheet. The result was a steam bath for a mummy.

Drowsiness overcame me, even though I had awakened only two hours earlier from a good night's sleep. The sensation was not unlike that which one experiences from meditation or from soaking too long in a hot bath. Bobby checked on me periodically, finally rousing me after about 15 to 20 minutes. He led me first to a shower and then to the cooling room.

The cooling room contained about a dozen lounges. Several other toga-clad guests were resting, waiting to be called into the massage room. Signs instructed guests not to smoke or talk. Some were ignoring the latter prohibition, discussing the sumptuous meals and quantities of alcohol they had consumed the previous night.

Business was brisk, requiring a 15-minute wait for the massage. I found I needed that time to cool off. I was still sweating when I was called across the hall for my massage. Following the massage I was instructed to return to the locker room. I dressed and exited into the lobby where I was soon rejoined by my companions.

Interviews with other patrons at other bathhouses confirmed that my experience at the Buckstaff was similar to that of others. For example, one woman described her "mysterious experience at The Baths" as follows: "We chatted in hushed tones (more in deference to the atmosphere than to the posted quiet signs) about what brought us to Hot Springs. None admit coming for cures. Some were vacationing but many were in town to attend professional conferences. Those who had previously experienced the mineral baths, described them glowingly as 'wonderful,' 'heavenly,' or 'the most relaxing experience I've ever had.'

"When I entered the bathing area, I became drowsy, drugged by the sensuality of the bathhouse atmosphere, its heat and steam. Weak-kneed, I had to be helped from the deep tub after soaking for 25 minutes. I was draped in a sheet to retain the heat and then led to a row of cots. A hot towel was placed behind my neck and a towel dipped in ice water placed around my face; I was left to float in a woozy world suspended between earth and the clouds. The sensation was pleasurable. Afterwards I felt rejuvenated."

CONCLUSION

The three stages of the bathing ritual are easily demarcated. In the locker room one is separated in time and space from the normal realm of life. This is done through the segregation of the sexes, removal of clothing, and putting on a plain white sheet and key bracelets as the uniform of the day. Finally, one is separated from one's companions.

Liminality begins with entry into the bathing room. The Caucasion clerks and attendants on the outside are replaced by young Blacks who seemingly represent an athletic ideal. A stylized form of interaction pertains, with the attendants using formal titles of address and the patrons using familiar ones. All movements within the bathing area are directed by the attendants, and the instructions are the same for everyone. The language symbolizes former times, as do the furnishings and general ambiance of the bathhouse. There is both sensory deprivation and sensory overload, with the effect of an altered state of consciousness at least a possibility.

Reincorporation begins in the cooling room, but is not completed until one returns to the locker room, dresses, and then rejoins one's companions in the lobby.

The bathing event described is ritual; it conforms to familiar definitions of ritual. For example, consider that of Myerhoff (1977): "Ritual is an act or actions intentionally conducted by a group of people employing one or more symbols in a repetitive, formal, precise, highly stylized fashion" (p. 199). In addition, the event considered here has a concomitant mythology, it affects the psyche and physiology, and it produces true believers.

This example illustrates the need to move beyond the categorization of ritual into religious and secular—a systematization that is firmly grounded in the dualistic Durkheimian distinction of sacred and profane. There are problems in attempting to define the sacred (or the mystical). The sacred may be different for different participants. Moreover, the sacred may vary even for the same participant at similar but separate events. For example, an individual may have a mystical experience at Mass one Sunday, but not have the same or similar experience at the following Sunday's Mass.

The example considered above also illustrates the need to move beyond the methodological distinctions of studying observable behavior as events or studying the meaning attributed to those behaviors. The difficulty stems from theoretical confusion. The notion that ritual is an observable event conflicts with the notion that ritual has effects on the individual (e.g., psychological or physiological), and that these two are somehow mediated by symbols.

Analyzing behavior is difficult enough. Reaching consensus regarding the meaning of symbols and symbolic behavior is virtually impossible. This is especially so since ritual is usually held to be multivocal. How does one know when all meanings have been detected? How does one then determine primacy among those meanings? The problem is that out of the forest of symbols one can never know if one's hierarchy of symbols yielded by analysis is equivalent to the hierarchy as perceived by individual participants. Neither can one know if the effect of a symbol is approximate for all participants, even those of the same class.

How can this theoretical and methodological impasse in the study of ritual be resolved? One possible solution is to search for empirical associations between behavior and the corresponding neurophysiological changes precipitated within individual participants, and then examine the selection and understanding of symbols. Contemporary technological advances increasingly are providing the means to accomplish this, even if only in a rudimentary fashion as yet. However, such a solution would also necessitate the construction of a unified frame for analyzing behavior. In the case of ritual this would mean articulating the connections between the manifest behavior of the individual and the significance of that behavior in terms of the individual's neurophysiological and cognitive systems.

Murray Leaf (1979) has provided an accounting of the historical and theoretical bases of such a unified frame. A unified frame also has been recognized in the work of some structuralists. Leach (1976) has stated, "Cultural devices, however complex, must always be built on biological foundations" (p. 47). Eliot Chapple has been providing us with examples of such a unified theoretical frame since 1942. However, the most recent and specific example is the work of D'Aquili, Laughlin, McManus, et al. entitled *The Spectrum of Ritual, A Biogenetic Structural Analysis* (1979).

Finally, let us consider briefly typologies of ritual. If categorical labels are to be attached to ritual, they should be descriptive ones, indicating a particular arena of life in which ritual has been applied. It is in this sense that I have offered this example that I have labeled a "voluntary" ritual. However, the same ritual could have been labeled recreational or therapeutic with equal validity. None of these labels would change the experience of the event. The utility of such labels is heuristic.

In this sense, what I am suggesting is what Victor Turner has done with respect to liminal and liminoid. The experiences are functionally equivalent (Turner, 1977) although the labels allow one to understand better the varieties of occurrence. Clearly the ritual experience in Hot Springs fits the parameters suggested by Turner's model for ritual in a post-tribal society.

Turner's model provides an understanding of the general types of ritual common in Western industrialized societies. One might hypothesize that these voluntary rituals, which in Turner's terms produce liminoid experiences, represent an adaptation within heterogeneous societies that have weakly shared common ritual formats. Such a hypothesis assumes certain universal functions of ritual behavior for the organism. While these functions cannot be articulated fully, it may be that *Homo sapiens* need some as yet undetermined minimal amount of ritual behavior to assist in the control of anxiety, to promote paradigmatic shifts, or to focus individual energies through selective attention and cue utilization.

REFERENCES

Chapple, E.D., & Coon, C.S. (1942). *Principles of anthropology.* New York: H. Holt & Company.

D'Aquili, E.G., McLaughlin, C.D. Jr. McManus, J. with Burns, T., et al. (1979). *The spectrum of ritual: A biogenetic structural analysis.* New York: Columbia University Press.

Gluckman, M. & Gluckman, M. (1977) On drama, and games and athletic contests. In S.F. Moore & B. Myerhoff (Eds), *Secular ritual* (pp. 227-243). Assen: Van Gorcum.

Goody, J. (1977). Against "ritual": Loosely structured thoughts on a loosely defined topic. In S.F. Moore & B. Myerhoff (Eds.), *Secular ritual* (pp. 25-35). Assen: Van Gorcum.

Homans, G. (1972). Anxiety and ritual: The theories of Malinowski and Radcliffe-Brown. In W.A. Lessa & E.Z. Vogt (Eds.), *Reader in comparative religion: An anthropological approach* (3rd ed.), (pp. 83-88). New York: Harper & Row. (Reprinted from *American Anthropologist,* 1941), *43,* 164-172).

Leach, E. (1976). *Culture and communication: The logic by which symbols are connected.* Cambridge University Press.

Leaf, M.J. (1979). *Man, mind and science: A history of anthropology.* New York: Columbia University Press.

Malinowski, B. (1972). The role of magic and religion. In W.A. Lessa & E.Z. Vogt (Eds.), *Reader in comparative religion: An anthropological approach* (3rd ed.), (pp. 63-72). New York: Harper & Row. (Excerpted from B. Malinowski [1931]. Culture. In E.R.A. Seligman & A. Johnson [Eds.], *Encyclopedia of Social Sciences, 4,* 6734-642. New York: Macmillan.)

Moore, S.F., & Myerhoff (1977). *Secular ritual.* Assen: Van Gorcum.

Myerhoff, B. (1977). We don't wrap herring in a printed page: Fusion, fictions and continuity in a secular ritual. In S.F. Moore & B.G. Myerhoff (Eds.) *Secular ritual* (pp. 199-224). Assen: Van Gorcum.

Radcliffe-Brown, A.R. (1972). Taboo. In W. A. Lessa & E.Z. Vogt (Eds.) *Reader in comparative religion: An anthropological approach* (3rd ed.) (pp. 72-83). New York: Harper and Row. (Reprinted from A.R. Radcliffe-Brown.) (1939). *Taboo.* Cambridge: Cambridge University Press.)

Turner, V. (1977). Variations on a theme of liminality. In S.F. Moore & B. G. Myerhoff (Eds.), *Secular ritual* (pp. 36-52). Assen: Van Gorcum.

THE MESSAGE IN THE MASK: COSTUMING IN THE FESTIVAL CONTEXT

William J. Gradante
Fort Worth, Texas

For years, folklorists, anthropologists, historians, theologians, and many others have attempted to understand and explain just what it is that happens to the nature of human experience during the kind of cultural event known as "carnival" or "festival." From the plethora of literature that has been written on the subject, we may infer that there may be more than just one "explanation" or "interpretation." The intent of this essay is to interpret the Saint Peter festival behavior observed over the course of several years in a small town nestled in the southern Colombian Andes. Though it is clear that a multitude of additional aspects must be taken into account in any full-scale examination of festival behavior, the primary focus of this essay is limited to the single, though multifaceted phenomenon of costuming and masking.

The principal questions addressed include the following: What is a mask? What can a mask do, and how and why does it work? Who wears a mask? Most importantly, to what ends is costuming and masking behavior utilized by participants in the Feast of Saint Peter? Both historical and contemporary perspectives are employed in the examination of the role of costuming and masking as essential elements in the establishment of the festival frame of play.

The mask may be considered to be any item or items of material culture that serve to achieve a socio-psychological transformation in the wearer and viewer through the culturally significant alteration of the wearer's appearance. This may include facial masks, full-body costumes, or various combinations of the two. But just what kind of power is inherent in the mask or costume? In a 1972 study of Nova Scotia island mumming, Richard Bauman (1972) notes that: "bel-snickling represented a performance occasion for those who were

172

not usually performers: the one event of the year in which those who ordinarily did not feel they had the talent or were otherwise too self-conscious to perform had an opportunity to do so, protected by the anonymity of their disguises" (p. 235). Later, in a 1978 article coauthored with Roger Abrahams, Bauman adds that carnival is "a time when the rude and sporty segment of the community holds the stage and the rest of the community is compelled to acknowledge their presence...[O]nly the very sporty are attracted to playing carnival; the participation of sensible people, if at all, will be through observing without joining" (Abrahams & Bauman, 1978, p. 203).

The problem we have here is one considered by Marianne Mesnil in her 1976 article entitled "The Masked Festival: Disguise or Affirmation?" My question is: Does it have to be one or the other? In my own fieldwork I have discovered that while one man is too embarrassed to participate in the revelry without the "protection" of a costume, his neighbor is, quite frankly, embarrassed by the very idea of having to wear some silly costume in the first place! All men are not equal, and thus they choose to participate in highly individualized ways. Because the subject of this essay is the masking behaviors and the masquers themselves as participants in what we term the festival's "fool-making" process, a brief exploration of the history of the fool as a socio-cultural entity is both relevant and enlightening.

Since the days of antiquity, members of the ruling classes all over the world have employed human "freaks" of various sorts to provide "comic relief" for themselves and their courtiers. These "freaks" have ranged from the pygmy and midget to the physically deformed and the mentally deficient. But as Willeford (1969) points out, by "the time of Elizabeth I a distinction came to be expressed between the 'natural' and the 'artificial' fool, the latter being the person who 'professionally counterfeits folly'" (p. 10).

Whatever his ostensible "abnormality" it is the fool's characteristic "otherness" that has distinguished him throughout history. During the Middle Ages and the Renaissance the traditional "motley" garb and scepter-like bauble of the fool became established as his trademarks, the opposite or "mirror image" of the monarch. But as Tietze-Conrat (1957) observes: "The moral contained in Schuppio's device 'Mirror of the monarch' is that every prince should have either a historian or a jester at court, for what a Chancellor refuses to say and a Court Chaplain may not say, a jester and a historian will. The latter tells what has happened, a jester what is happening now. Thus the fool is a necessity and a blessing" (p. 70). Because of the fool's purported feeble-mindedness, whether it be real or feigned, "his famous privilege and power of 'speaking the truth,' even when his master could not do it, was based on the convention that, for the jester, everything, including the most sacred matters, was mere play" (Willeford, 1969, p. 97).

The behavioral license and resultant special status of the court jester extends to his present-day counterpart, the festive masquer, who thus gains access to social privileges not customarily available. In his donning of a mask or costume within the socio-cultural frame of festival play, he at once assumes the identity and, ironically, the anonymity of the fool, his reward being a short-lived sojourn into the realm of fantasy. In the South American festival of our present study, even the individual who spends only a few hours in putting together a mask or costume succeeds at least in separating himself from the rank and file of unmasked festival participants by assuming the role of performer in the carnival's sphere of play. This will generally guarantee him a place in the Grand Parade, along with a few invitations to private parties to which he might not otherwise have been invited, as well as earn him a steady supply of free food and drink throughout the festival. Such costumes might consist of a false beard, a funny hat, a lady's wig, a cut-paper or papier-maché mask, or simply a made-up face and funny clothes.

The vast majority of individual costumes appearing in the Saint Peter festival tend to conform to the historical traditions of the European carnival and thus generally require a good deal of work. For example, the *Diablo* (Devil) costume is a common choice, although considerable latitude is evident in terms of color selection and design style. Most *Diablos* appear fully clothed in scarlet, with pointed tails, capes, short black whips, and topped off with papier-mache masks featuring horns, small beards, and hideous grins. Others abandon this more traditional representation, preferring black clothing or robes and more grotesque, beast-like headpieces. Similar variety is evident in the numerous animal costumes, the more common choices being wolves, alligators, and large birds.

Historically the formal study of the nature and function of festive play has elaborated and developed concepts such as the "reconciliations of opposites" and the playing out of the perennial struggle of "nature versus culture." The age-old figure of the "Wild Man"—half civilized and half beast—appears in our festival as the *Rey del Monte* (King of the Wilds), along with the Hobby Horse, in the present instance bearing the updated title of *El Gran Prix*. Another standard or "classical" carnival image that stands as an obvious example of this characteristic theme of "reversals" and "symbolic inversion" is that of the *Carrus Navalis*, the "ship on wheels," that has been linked mythologically with the amphibious vehicle of Saturn or Dionysius and etymologically with the term "carnival" itself.

The theme of the *Hombre al Reves* (The Upside Down or Reversed Man, see Figure 1) has been a recurrent one in the Saint Peter festivals of the past decade. Variations on this theme include *El Muerto Cargando el Vivo* (The Dead Man Carrying the Living Man, see Figure 2), *La Gorda y el Flaco* (The Fat Lady and the Skinny Man),

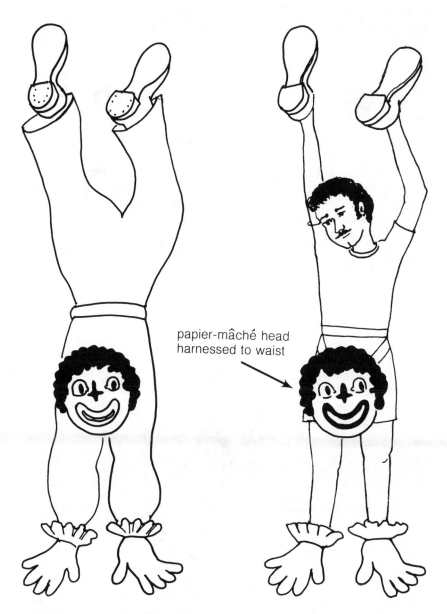

papier-mâché head
harnessed to waist

Figure 1. "El Hombre al Revés."

inversion" throughout history and throughout the world. That is, the emotional chaos and general disorder induced by means of the wholesale parody and burlesque of extant cultural norms paradoxically serve as "proof" of the ultimate validity of the status

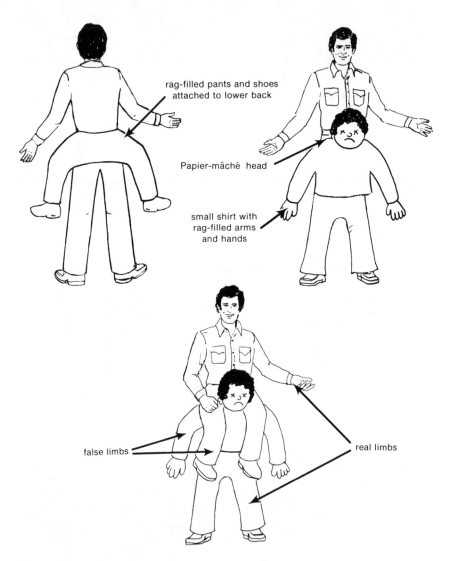

Figure 2. "El Muerto Cargando el Vivo."

and an interesting contemporary manifestation of the juxtaposition-ing of opposites, *Benetin Y Enias*, better known to North Americans as Mutt and Jeff.

While new interpretations of ancient carnivalesque images perennially reassert themselves in the Saint Peter festival, the supernatural creatures that live on in local legends and folk tales also provide inspiration for masquers. These include *El Mohan* (a long-haired, bearded, cigar-smoking, and infamously lecherous old river elf), *Los Matachines* (a pair of red-suited gnomes with enormous and hideously grotesque heads — in the local lexicon the name means "horrible faces"), and *El Tunjo de Oro* (a mischievous, childlike river elf wearing a golden mantle coveted by local fishermen).

The virtually universal carnival figure, the transvestite, is also amply represented in the Saint Peter celebrations. Though a number of young, unmarried men publicly exhibit their mothers' clothing each year, it is Tobito who has become a veritable festival legend by virtue of his annual transvestite antics. A poor, humble, and extremely timid carpenter in his early 40s, Tobito—along with his numerous feminine alter-egos, one of which happens to be a Catholic nun with the sacrilegious name of Sor Didez[1]—has become known as the principal carnival buffoon. Each year the local police stage a mock arrest and sentence Tobito to a year's probation during which he is forbidden to wear any disguises or create any public spectacles. It must be stressed that although his name has become synonymous with the concept of foolishness, Tobito is merely "playing the fool" for the sake of the festival and the comic delight of his friends and neighbors. He is not to be confused with any of several feeble-minded citizens, known simply as *bobos* (fools, village idiots), who subsist on menial labor and charity and participate in the festival without fully understanding its significance. That his contribution to the festivity is appreciated by his fellow citizens is attested to by the fact that weeks before the beginning of the festival, rumors con-cerning the nature of Tobito's latest outrageous costume have already begun to circulate, heightening the general ambiance of excitement and anticipation.

As a whole, the costumes described thus far reinforce the concept of man as the civilized, cultured being by publicly displaying the absurdity of the concepts of man as animal, man as the wild, uncivilized beast, man as the mythological, supernatural being—even "man" as "woman." These costuming and masking activities function, then, in a manner analogous to innumerable carnivalesque or saturnalian festivals and "rites of reversal" and "symbolic quo. In reference to the behavioral license of the court jester, Willeford (1969) explains that: "In tolerating such jokes the king partly affirms the royal power that the fool pretends to deny. Thus the office of the jester fulfills some of the same functions as the ritualized rebellion in which political subjects express actual and possible resentments against authority. The fact that the rebellion is allowed and even encouraged implies that the social institutions and the persons in power are strong enough to tolerate it; thus it serves the interests of authority and of social cohesion" (p. 155). A brief examination of the socio-political climate prevalent in the town at the time of our festival's emergence in its modern form is appropriate at this time.

During the 1950s the town of our study experienced the most violent socio-political turmoil since the wars of independence of the 1820s. On the national level the widespread violence and bloodshed of civil war was the order of the day. The terror of such a situation locally manifested itself in the form of a rekindling of ancient interfamilial enmities, the original causes of which, in many cases, still elude memory. The populace became politically polarized, and socio-political sanctions and their resultant animosities grew steadily more volatile.

As the feast of Saint Peter 1958 approached, the cultural vitality of the town was at its lowest ebb. It was at this crisis point that several of the town's most successful and highly respected citizens secretly met. This group, which included merchants, ranchers, planters, and doctors, and, among these, the heads of the most prominent families and political parties, decided that a reinterpretation of the traditionally family-oriented Saint Peter festival might help the townspeople to forget senseless old feelings of animosity and rekindle their sense of security and community.

They asked a young truck driver whose father had been brutally murdered in the course of the struggle to share his musical talents with them. Though none among them were musicians, they planned to appear in the streets as a band—a bad, and thus comical band— called "La Banda de Los Borrachos" (The Band of the Drunkards), hoping to serve as a catalyst for the emergence of a village-wide street festival. They began to rehearse secretly and constructed farcical musical instruments from reeds, gourds, and bamboo in order to lend credence to the ostensible reason for their chosen name—to protest the decadent state of the town band, whose members had grown more adept at drinking than at performing. Dressed in makeshift cloaks fashioned from old burlap coffee sacks, rope shoes, and Harlequinesque patched pants, they greeted the dawn of Saint Peter's Day with festive cacophony, singing humorous and often pornographic verses about their neighbors and each other. Whereas the court jester's behavioral license derived from his lowly position as "only a fool," that of "Los Borrachos" was due primarily to their anonymity. Their burlap—the fabric of only the humblest of the humble—covered their entire bodies, leaving only tiny holes for the eyes. Analogous to Christianity's archaic "fools for Christ," these latter-day "fools" exposed themselves to public ridicule in a desperate hope for a peaceful return to social order. The fool-making process (see Klapp 1949, pp. 159-160) complete, it only remained for the process to be reversed, which is precisely what happened when, late in the day, the exhausted revelers removed their hoods in order to accept proffered refreshments from their audience. The ultimate success of their experiment proved to be more than complete in that not only did the "musicians" receive unexpected applause for their performance, but the townspeople, upon witnessing the success of the cooperation between former adversaries, began to understand their purpose.

An additional and totally unforeseen result was that "La Banda de Los Borrachos" gradually developed into a permanent institution of social criticism and reform and, simultaneously, comic relief during the 25 subsequent festivals to date. The current "Borrachos," which include several sons and younger brothers of the original members, have no intention of abandoning their collective image of comic fools (or, in Klapp's [1949] terminology, "comic rogues"). However, over the years their costumes have come to consist of the traditional regional attire of rope shoes, ample white trousers, wide-brimmed straw hat, and scarlet neckerchief in combination with commercially printed T-shirts emblazoned with the name "La Banda de Los Borrachos" in large "drunken" letters.

It is interesting to compare the attire of the medieval court jester with that of the member of the Banda de Los Borrachos. Each wears clothing that functions to identify him as having a special status, one that awards him license in his personal behavior. In addition to his phallic bauble, the stereotypical headpiece of the jester features the cockscomb and ass's ears, appropriating the highly charged sexual symbolism traditionally attached to both the rooster and the ass in Western folk ideology. According to Willeford (1969): "The ass's ears and the cockscomb link the figures to animals famous for their sexuality as well as their silliness. The figures represent the intelligence of the phallus—a counterpart, on the level of instinct, to the reason of the head; or they represent reason drawn into the sphere of the instinctual element and overwhelmed by it" (p. 37).

In the following passage from Cleland's *Memoirs of a Woman of Pleasure* we see the ultimate manifestation of the symbolism of the fool's sexuality: "In keeping with the vulgar saying, 'A fool's bauble is a lady's play-fellow,' Fanny Hill's friend Louisa seduces an idiot, the sight of his genitals causing Fanny to remark, 'Nature had done so much for him in those parts, that she perhaps held herself acquitted in doing so little for his head'" (quoted in Willeford, 1969, p. 12).

Although the symbolism is not quite as explicit, the scarlet kerchief essential to the Borrachos' attire is not referred to as such (i.e., the *panuelo* [kerchief], but rather as *rabo de gallo* [the cock's tail]). In the local folk dance performed only during the festial of Saint Peter, the *rabo de gallo* is used by the male who, unfurling it, chases his female partner, chastising (snapping) her with it after she playfully steals his straw hat. Later in the dance the *sombrero* is returned in exchange for one end of the *rabo de gallo,* and the female coquettishly circles the kneeling male who holds the other end. The dance concludes with the male winding and unwinding the *rabo de gallo* around his partner's waist, ending with the pair waving it in the air.

As significant as the *rabo de gallo* is to the folk dances, possibly the most visually striking aspect of the Borrachos' costume is the apparent incongruity existing between the commercially printed T-shirt and the rest of the outfit, which is so consciously composed of the most typically old-fashioned elements. It must be remembered that it is precisely the jester's unique ability to "juggle" such incongruities that makes him successful as a comic. Like the skillful riddler who juxtaposes then wittily harmonizes seemingly contradictory concepts, the Borrachos' humor is based on the "fool's" disordering and manipulation of his audience's supposedly less "foolish" powers of reasoning.

Clearly, then, the nature of the costuming and masking practiced by the members of the Banda de Los Borrachos and the several other, more recently organized *murgas* (groups of ambulatory street singers) is profoundly distinct from that of the masquers described earlier. While for the latter masking behavior serves as a portal into the world of play as an end in itself, the former utilize the concept of masquerade to create a metacommunicative frame within the already established frame of play in order to afford themselves a highly exclusive platform for socio-political commentaries. Thus, cryptically speaking, there is more to play than simply play.

The most prominent difference between the medieval court jester and the member of the Banda de Los Borrachos is that while the jester is perpetually the fool and thus is permanently excused for his extraordinary behavior, today's unmasked Borrachos perform only once a year. Though their costumes tacitly proclaim their license and consequent immunity to punishment for their behavior, certain precautions must be taken nonetheless. As the source of the Borrachos' humor and social commentary is in the singing of satirical *coplas* (verses, couplets), it is of paramount importance that these verses be composed and performed with the utmost prudence and care. While the novice may resent the seemingly cumbersome limitations thus placed upon his creativity, the accomplished singer realizes that the artistic circumvention of such restrictions only makes the ultimate success of performing an effective *copla* that much sweeter.

The inherently improvisational musico-poetic device employed by the Borrachos in the creation of their unique brand of "musical comedy" is called the *coplas de rajaleña* (*rajaleña* couplets), colloquially termed simply *rajaleñas*. The Spanish term *rajaleña* refers literally to the splitting or chopping wood, but has a number of additional colloquial connotations as well. According to my principal informant, the most common metaphorical usage comes from the physical act of chopping wood—*sacarle chispas y astillas*—when one's efforts produce sparks and splinters. The better the performer of the *rajaleña,* the greater the quantity of "sparks and splinters" he produces; that is, the more poignent the public reaction he is capable of provoking. While the melodies to which the *rajaleñas* are sung are relatively simple and musically uninteresting, the texts themselves are delivered in the form of *coplas*, a Spanish verse form dating at least as far back as the 15th century. In the performance of the *coplas de rajaleña*, the singer/poet improviser has four rhymed octosyllabic lines in which to deliver his statement. While *coplas* have traditionally been used to relate historical events, express amorous intentions, or eulogize popular leaders, the vast majority of the *coplas de rajaleña* are comical and frequently rely on satire, colloquialism, and intricate word play in the communication of a message, whether it be an off-color joke or a biting criticism of local or national politics.

Americo Paredes (personal communication) has suggested an additional connotation to the term *rajaleña*: the practice of "criticizing or insulting without concern for the consequences." In view of the semantically potent nature of the social and often personal criticisms delivered in the medium of the *copla* during the festival, we are quickly reminded of the importance of the phenomenon of masquerade—and, significantly, masquerade as "only fools"—in its function of mitigating this potentially explosive situation. In addition, the Borrachos employ a mandatory formula for beginning any *copla* performance. All such initial *coplas* include a public request for permission, often in the name of the Banda de Los Borrachos and with apologies in advance. Two commonly heard examples are:

Permiso pido señores	I ask permission, gentlemen
Pa' cantar mi rajaleña	To sing my *rajaleña*
Con la Banda de los Borrachos	With the Band of Drunkards
La vieja murga plateña	The old street band of La Plata
Permiso pido señores	I ask permission, gentlemen
Para ponerme a cantar	That I may begin singing
Si alguna falta cometo	Should I become at all offensive
Me tendrán que perdonar	You'll have to excuse me

Corresponding ending formulas, utilized to close the metaphorical parentheses on the frame of play, include the following:

Ahora ya no canto más	Now I will stop singing
Y de todos me despido	And to all I bid goodbye
Solo ruego perdonar	I only beg forgiveness
Por si alguno se ha ofendido	If someone has been offended

Willeford (1969) states that: "The fool lives in a no-man's land in several senses, one of which is his connection with the area of consciousness into which hunches, intuitions, and interesting but not quite meaningful images and ideas emerge. He often seizes them before we are aware of them and plays with them trickily and jokingly, enjoying being ahead of us. This process is reflected in the structure of almost any clown routine. In it the clown is ahead of us in the sense that the points of his gags surprise us, even when he seems more stupid and less adapted to reality than we . . . And he is ahead of us, further, in that his routine requires a planning of artistic means and an anticipation of the audience's reactions. This quality of being ahead of us in time is part of what gives him his permanence. His special status as a fool deprives him of a dimension that we feel ourselves to have; yet the deliberate element of his show, when the fool is an actor, gives him another" (p. 70-71).

Some examples of his ability in the *coplero* (singer of *coplas*) to stay one step ahead of his listeners by means of his anticipation of the audience's reactions are presented below:

A la mujer de mi hermano	To the wife of my brother
yo se lo estaba metiendo . . .	I was putting (it) in . . .
El estantillo a la casa	The support beam of the house
Que se le estaba cayendo	As it was falling down
Anoche sone contigo	Last night I dreamed of you
Y se me derramo en la estera . . .	And it spilled out on the bedding
Una chuspita de plata . . .	A small bag of silver . . .
Usted, ¿Que pensaba que era?	What did you think I meant?

The *coplero*/fool breaks frame for an instant, just long enough to make his listeners wonder just who is the fool and who the nonfool. *Coplas* of social criticism are often set up by the *coplero* by first "playing the fool," and then jumping directly to the point. Such was the case when the following *copla* was sung in protest of the Festival Council's decision to ban free street dances in favor of closed dances with entrance fees:

Las coplas que aqui cantamos	The *coplas* that we sing here
Ni yo mismo las entiendo	Even I don't understand
Pero que sepa La Junta	But I hope the Festival Council
Lo que el pueblo esta sintiendo	Understands how the people feel

The following *copla* was directed at several former members of the Banda de Los Borrachos who, having recently met with financial success, felt they would be unnecessarily humbling themselves by associating with their former companions. They apparently believed that "playing the fool" was beneath men of their newly acquired status:

Por alli andan los rumores	The rumors have begun to fly
Que La Banda ya no agrada	That The Band performs no more
Pero no es que ya no toquen	It's not that they've stopped playing
Es que no hay vacas sagradas	It's that there are no more "sacred cows" ("stuffed shirts")

It took only these four lines to send the *vacas sagradas* scurrying home for their costumes before the townspeople realized who were the "real fools."

Throughout history the jester has been portrayed in literature as the counterpart of the royalty, as an aide, confidant, entertainer, and constant companion. The Banda de Los Borrachos follows this tradition by accompanying King Pericles Carnaval, his wife La Doña Anastacia (Lady Anastacia), and his mistress Luz Piranga. King Pericles, a slightly larger than life-size gourd effigy, annually leads a jubilant procession through the town astride a decrepit horse, signalling the commencement of the Saint Peter festival. On the final day of the celebration Lady Anastacia, a huge bottle lashed to a bamboo litter, is carried by the Borrachos from house to house in the collection of the *trago de Anastacia*, a potent mixture of various alcoholic beverages, honey, and fruit drinks (see Figure 3).

The Borrachos join the Creoles and Cajuns of rural Louisiana Mardi Gras celebrations and Bauman's La Have Island belsnicklers in this observance of the ancient tradition of house-to-house festival begging. Tietze-Conrat (1957) comments on the symbolic king-fool relationship: "The King, like Montezuma before him, gathered up these sub-humans and collected them together in his castle. He dressed them in most costly raiment. He had the portrait of the lowliest of the low hung in his rooms. Perhaps there is more to this kind of behavior than a rather malicious feeling of superiority . . . It is perversity which compels us. Perversity which titillates our senses. Good works atone for it . . . We are told in the Bible not to mock at fools. But we do, and then make amends in acts of charity" (p. 31). the

Borrachos perform before each house, asking that the occupants contribute either beverages to Lady Anastacia or money to buy some. In most cases, the Borrachos' antics earn both applause and a donation, often because the penurious are fearful of the kind of *coplas* that will be sung about them until their purse strings loosen.

By the end of the day the bottle will have been filled several times, yielding some 50 to 60 liters of murky brown liquid. The *trago de anastacia* is shared by all who care (or dare) to bring a cup, and the annual Testament of Pericles is read. The testament consists of a collection of humorous *coplas* recalling the "foolish" acts of some 50 or 60 of the town's more well-known citizens during the past year. All present share a healthy laugh, assure themselves that there will be no leftover *trago de Anastacia*, and stumble homeward as the last charred remains of King Pericles' gourd- and straw-stuffed clothing turn to ashes.

Figure 3. "La Doña Anastacia" (a large glass bottle mounted upon a bamboo litter and dressed in women's clothing).

CONCLUSION

From the jubilant entrance of King Pericles to the final drinking of the *trago de Anastacia*, we have observed the townspeople divided into two distinct parts—those in costume, in the thick of the festivity, and those on the sidewalk, in their workaday attire. By the time it is all over, many of the second group will have joined the first, experiencing the invigorating transformation from passive to active participant, from spectator to performer. But like all good things, the festival must come to an end, and all the *diablos*, dancers, transvestites, and Borrachos disappear into their white-washed stucco houses, only to reemerge as students, truck drivers, shopkeepers, and farmers. However, the festive experience inevitably seems to leave its indelible mark on one's personal perceptions of one's place in the universe, even if that universe extends no further than the towering circle of the Andes that surrounds and isolates the town. We can rest assured that no one will ever forget the year that "you were a rooster, I was a Borracho, and Tobito danced the merengue with the monsignor."

It would be inaccurate, in the case of our festival, to claim that only the very "sporty" or more rowdy elements of the population tend to be attracted to festival playing. Whether behind a mask, or as a member of a *murga*, a dance group, or a committee that conceives, designs, and constructs a float for the *barrio's* candidate for festival Queen, an individual encounters a nearly limitless variety of opportunities to collaborate in the creation of this event whose ultimate essence is play. While this playfulness may range from the totally frivolous to the quite serious verbal playing that characterizes the *copla* singing, each participant is capable of making a personal contribution to the overarching festival structure. Whether we capsulize the festival in Geertz's (1972) manner as a "story people tell themselves about themselves" (p. 26) or as a compilation of metacommunicative acts and events, the nature of festive play is hardly homogeneous. Each mask worn, float built, *copla* sung, and bottle emptied functions as a single tile imparting subtle nuance and shading or dramatic contrast to the grandiose mosaic portrait of the town and its culture that its inhabitants paint.

Note

1. Sor Didez is a play on words, meaning both "Sister Didez" (a nonsensical name) and "filth, squalor" (sordidez).

REFERENCES

Abrahams, R.D., & Bauman, R. (198), Ranges of festival behavior. In B.A. Babcock (Ed.), *The reversible world: Symbolic inversion in art and society* (p. 193-208). Ithaca, NY: Cornell University.

Bauman, R. (1972). Belsnickling in a Nova Scotia Island community. *Western Folklore, 31*(4), 229-243.

Geertz, C. (1972, winter). Deep play: Notes on the Balinese cockfight. *Daedalus,* 1-37.

Klapp, O.E. (1949). The fool as a social type. *American Journal of Sociology, 55,* 157-162.

Mesnil, M. (1976). The masked festival: Disguise or affirmation? *Cultures, 3*(2), 11-29.

Tietze-Conrat, E. (1957). *Dwarfs and jesters in art* (E. Osborn, Trans.). London: Phaidon Press. (Original pub. date not given)

Willeford, W. (1969). *The fool and his scepter: A study in clowns and jesters and their audience.* Evanston, IL: Northwestern University Press.

6

PLAY IN GAMES AND SPORTS

Introduction

Garry E. Chick

The study of games has a long history in anthropology, beginning with pioneers in the field such as Morgan and Tylor. The interest in games and sports evidenced in the early days of anthropology, however, has not been sustained, at least in the mainstream of the discipline. This can be demonstrated by looking at the contents of the journal of the American Anthropological Association, *American Anthropologist*. The cumulative index for the years 1888 to 1928 gives 23 references to games with 17 articles being devoted to game ethnography and one to gaming songs. During the period 1929 to 1938, the index includes 17 references to games, two of which are for gaming songs, but not a single article deals specifically with games. For 1939 to 1948 there are 10 references to games, with one article on games, but the period 1949 to 1958 has no references at all to games. Although the seminal article "Games in Culture" by Roberts, Arth, and Bush was published in the *American Anthropologist* in 1959, the journal contains no other references to games for the period 1959 to 1969. Since 1969, two articles on play have appeared, along with one relating combative sport and war, but the topic of games has otherwise been neglected.

It can be argued that the nature of the publications appearing in the *American Anthropologist* has changed from a primarily descriptive to a more theoretical or, at least, analytical orientation so that purely ethnographic accounts of games would be out of place in the journal. There are, as well, publications dealing with games that have appeared in other anthropological outlets. Nevertheless, the trend exhibited by the flagship journal of American anthropology strongly reflects a low level of interest in games in the discipline, as a whole.

Fortunately, the void in game studies left by anthropologists has been ably filled by researchers in other fields, notably physical education, recreation, sociology, and psychology. This multiplicity of fields of study is reflected in the membership of TAASP and in the orientations brought to bear on the study of games, as demonstrated by papers that appear in this section. The following papers utilize ethnographic, ethnohistorical, survey, and quasi-experimental methods, each of which permits a unique view of the topic under consideration and demonstrates the continuing value of research on games, both in their own right and in terms of their relationships to other aspects of culture.

Cheska reviews ethnohistorical evidence that indicates that the Eskimo adopted a number of Norse games, dances, and songs during a period of culture contact in Greenland during the period 1000 to 1500 A.D. the marked persistence of items of expressive culture has frequently been noted, and hence their analysis is a highly appropriate and useful tool understanding the dynamics of receptivity to and endurance of newly introduced cultural artifacts, either expressive or instrumental.

The remaining papers in this section each deal with a specific game, rather than a number of expressive forms. Chase operationalizes Csikszentmihalyi's now familiar concept of "flow" and applies it to arcade video game play. He finds that the flow experience is positively related to satisfaction with video game play, as well as with the frequency of play per week and the amount of time spent per play session. These results raise a number of significant questions concerning the nature of the flow experience and the structural characteristics of video games.

The game of Capture the Flag, as played by Boy Scouts, is the subject of a symbolic analysis by Mechling, who suggests that the game is a "perfect model of the male contest" as well as a means through which some boys experience power and prestige that are not normally accessible to them. Despite the overtly aggressive context of the game, Mechling finds that it permits the experience of fraternity among players. This game is also of interest because it provides the model for the current "Survival Game" wherein participants, usually adults, shoot each other with pellet guns firing packets of blood-colored dye. This fact makes Mechling's analysis all the more intriguing.

Park looks at change and continuity in the game of women's field hockey through an ethnographic presentation of the game, its play, and the formal organization of field hockey in the United States. Park describes how traditional values are both reinforced and modified to be more in line with contemporary values of women's sports.

Rees, Hammond, and Woodruff test the warning, voiced by some, that instrumental reasons may be replacing expressive reasons for participating in games and sports. In order to counter this trend, it has been argued, the control and organization of sports and games should be removed from coaches and officials and returned to the participants, thus enhancing intrinsic reasons for participation. Rees, Hammond, and Woodruff test this hypothesis by having church league basketball teams play half a season without referees and the other half with referees. In the former situation, players were responsible for calling fouls and settling disputes. Results indicate that the removal of referees did not diminish the instrumental nature of the competition, although there was some evidence of an expressive commitment by players to maintain game action.

In the final selection, Chick and Roberts show that both interest and skill in the strategic aspects of the game of eight ball pool vary directly with player expertise, although, at all levels of competence, players found the strategic part of the game to be less fun and to entail less concentration than the behaviors requiring physical skill. This suggests that the very nature of the game changes for players as they become more competent, with an ever greater amount of strategy required for successful performance. This qualitative change in the game may make it less suitable for the needs of some players.

These papers indicate that the interest in game research is strong and that such inquiry holds substantial promise for furthering understanding about games themselves and about the cultural context in which they are imbedded. Both the significance of the questions and the value of the answers found in these and similar studies reveal the egregious error in precluding such research from mainstream social science.

PLAYFUL EVIDENCE OF OLD AND NEW WORLD CONTACTS BETWEEN MEDIEVAL NORSEMEN AND GREENLAND ESKIMOS: A TENTATIVE HYPOTHESIS

Alyce Taylor Cheska
University of Illinois

History tells us that the Thule Eskimos[1] 2000 years ago started crossing Arctic America from Alaska to the north Atlantic islands such as Baffin and Ellsmere and arrived in Greenland about 1000 A.D.[2] The Vikings, on the other hand, started from Scandinavia, island-hopping across the North Atlantic about 700 A.D. and arriving in Greenland about the same time as the Eskimos. The proximity of these groups' respective migration and settlement patterns on Greenland's west coast posed the possibility of mutual cultural exchange, but this has not been conclusively determined. This researcher speculated that if common play artifacts appeared in both the Inuit and Norse Greenland sites of the medieval period, then the notion of cultural exchange would be strengthened. Further, if disproportionate amounts and/or change over time of Norse or Inuit play artifacts were identified in the other group's sites, an accompanying change in relationship might be surmised, such as friendly contacts deteriorating in later years. Finally, if games, songs, and dances recorded as practiced by the Greenland Inuit in the early 1700s A.D. (after two centuries of noncontact) bore a close resemblance to the medieval Norse activities, then such a prior exchange would be supported.

NORSEMAN TO GREENLAND

The Norse', or Vikings as these Scandinavians were called, discovery and settlement of Greenland was long in coming when compared with Iceland, which was settled in the 800s A.D. or earlier. Eric "the Red" Ericsson of Iceland was credited with Greenland's discovery in 982 A.D., which renowned Icelandic Author Are Torgilsson (1068-1148 A.D., quoted in Rink, 1084) later described: "The land called Greenland was discovered and peopled from Iceland. They (Erik the Red and his companions) found there in the eastern as well as the western tracts human dwellings, as well as fragments of (skin) boats and articles wrought of stone, giving evidence that the same race of people as those who inhabited Vinland, and whom the Greenlanders (viz., the settlers) called Skrellings, must have roamed about there" (p. 24).[3]

The two major Norse concentrations, the Eastern Settlement of 90 homesteads and the Western Settlement of 200 homesteads, and two monastic foundations with no more than 2000 to 3000 souls lay along the warmer southwest coast. Jenness (1955) placed the figure at 5000 persons. During the first two centuries of habitation the climate was still relatively warm and the settlers thrived. Their livestock fared rather well, but the long cold winters took their toll (Duason, 1941). Wood for constructing ocean-going ships was unavailable, thus boats were at a premium. At more northerly summer hunting and fishing grounds around Disko Island, some 180 miles north of the Arctic Circle, the colonists hunted seal, whales, and walrus, prepared congealed blubber, and collected driftwood. (These northern locations no doubt were where early Norse-Inuit contact took place.)

Items traded with the few European ships that came were walrus tusks, seal and bear skins in exchange for grain, wood, and iron (Kendrick, 1968). Unfortunately, by 1200 A.D. the weather became colder and many unfavorable changes affected the destiny of the Norsemen. An ill-timed decline of Norway's sea power practically eliminated sea trade with Greenland and virtually all the contacts with Europe (Ingstad, 1969). Other distresses in Europe — war, plague, famine, and pirateering—also contributed to the gradual abandonment of the Greenland colony starting in the late 1200s until the early 1700s A.D. Without essential European trade products, the Greenlanders were left to their own limited resources. In Europe rumors and reports about the plight of the Greenland Norsemen, their fall from Christianity, and adoption of native ways were reinforced by an infrequent visiting ship; one 80-year period passed between ships in the 1400s, and in the 1500s there was no word at all. By then, Greenland was a vague memory in Europe.

ESKIMOS TO GREENLAND

The early beginnings of the North American Eskimo or Inuit are hidden in antiquity.[4] However, most scholars agree that they originated in northern Asia (Jenness, 1940). The commonly accepted theory of the west to east flow of the Thule (Inuit) culture from the north coast of Alaska toward Greenland has been challenged by several scholars (Birket-Smith, 1936; Collins, 1943; Giddings, 1961; Jenness, 1940); one such proposition is that the proto-Thule may be an eastern extension of a central Arctic coast Birnirk culture or its contemporary (Taylor, 1963). Stewart (1983) has suggested an independent parallel development of proto-Thule peoples and the western Inuit culture. The reasons for the Thule extensive migration remain unknown, but two explanations are population pressure at home and hunting potentials. There is some evidence of Inuit habitation in Greenland circa 100 B.C. to 100 A.D., probably by the Dorset people (Rowley, 1940; Gad, 1971; Oswalt, 1977).

The Thule migration to Greenland took place sometime between the 10th century (McGhee, 1970; Taylor, 1963) and the 13th century (Stanford, 1973) by way of Ellsmere Island (Taylor, 1963; Schledermann, 1975, 1981). Mathiassen (quoted in Thalbitzer, 1941) summarized the southward movement of the Thule peoples about 900 A.D. along the western coast of Greenland, where they stayed between 1200 to 1300 A.D. near the area that today is called Thule. They then moved farther south (Upernivik), where their culture became slightly modified and was called Inugsuk. As the Thule migrated further south along Greenland's western coast line, they approached the Norse area of occupation. Thule migrations eventually circled the Greenland coast.

Evidence shows that the Norsemen and the Eskimos, through a strange sequence of events, both progressed to this geographic outpost of the world. At best this icebox of nature provided marginal adaptive opportunities for human existence, yet here two vitally different people occupied the same area at the same time. Two major questions arise: Was there mutual cultural exchange between these two peoples? If so, was this exchange supported by evidence of shared pastime activites?

EVIDENCE OF EXPRESSIVE CULTURAL EXCHANGES BETWEEN NORSEMEN AND MEDIEVAL NORSEMEN'S PASTIMES MEDIEVAL PERIOD (1000-1500 A.D.)

Five basic sources were examined to authenticate contact between the medieval Norsemen and the Thule Inuits in Greenland as evidenced by shared pastime activities: archaeological evidence of pastime artifacts in both Thule and Norsemen sites; historical reports by medieval contemporaries; literary and pictorial descriptions of play activities engaged in by both medieval Scandinavians and by the Thule people; descriptions of such activities by explorers, missionaries, ethnographers, and Inuit descendants in postmedieval Greenland; and folk legends of the Inuit and Scandinavian peoples.

Documentation verifies that contact did take place; the question now revolves around whether play activities were mutually exchanged. However, even if similar play activities were found, caution must be taken to account for their presence. Only specific activities practiced by Greenland Inuits that were also known to be present in Norse medieval culture strengthen the contact proposition. Thus, such games, dances, and songs knowingly engaged in by both peoples at that time period were used.

MEDIEVAL NORSEMEN'S PASTIMES

Games and dances in which medieval Norsemen were best known to participate include: boxing, buzz, chess, dancing (by men or women separately or in single-sex group, coed, in line, couple, or circle formation holding hands), dice, draughts (checkers), drumming (with dance and/or song), football (keep-away, goal), gymnastics (acrobatics on rope suspended tautly between house walls), hopping (body in prone position with weight on toes and hands while grasping short stick), hopping-stones *(Ganga Heljarbrui)*,[5] jacks, ice hockey, log (caber) toss, miniature (model) toys, pickup sticks, rounders (early baseball), "rowing to seal," skipping (over circling rope), snowballing, stone lifting, tobogganing (sliding), and wrestling (strength contests of hook, finger-hook, hand pull by handle, neck rope pull, waist rope pull) (Brunn, 1918; Gotlind, 1933; Lloyd, 1870; Wahlquist, 1980). Research of Arctic peoples has shown that all the above game and dance activities with the exception of the log (caber) toss have been associated with at least one Arctic Eskimo group's participation. This may show extensive diffusion of play activities from Europe to America as well as independent invention of play activities.

Two games, "hopping stones" ("Hel-bridges" or *Ganga Heljarbrui*) and "rowing to seal," are specifically listed by Oleson (1963) as played by Norsemen. Conflicting evidence by Gad (1971) maintained that "hopping stones" was of ancient Greenland Inuit origin. The game consisted of placing in a row a series of rough, differently sized and spaced stones over which each contestant sequentially hopped on one foot apparently as fast as possible without faltering— a test of strength and agility.

That participation in games was an integral part of the early Norsemen's life style is born out by a passage in the Saga of Fostraedra ("foster-brother saga") of 1200 A.D. in which a Greenlander challenged an Icelander, referring to his guest's stone-hopping ability compared to his own harpooning ability:

He who runs quickly on rocks
merrily boasts
that he the harpoon better
than we understand to swing.

Upon which the following conversation ensued,
"Thou missest too much of a grand pastime."
"Where from comest thou—which games are they now playing? What are they amusing themselves with there?" (Bruun, 1918, pp. 86, 88).

Bruun (1918) also recorded: "They [Greenland Norsemen] had few pleasures. When they visited each other, they either went by riding horses, by boat, or in the winter by slide [sled]. Now and then they amused themselves by jumping on one leg from stone to stone which were placed in a row. Such rows still exist several places in the Godthaabsfiord" (p. 406).

Archaeological evidence as well as literary evidence clearly showed that hopping-stones or *Ganga Heljarbrui* was played by the Greenland Norsemen. Thalbitzer (1924) has also identified many hopping-stone ruins at Inuit sites. In Eskimo legend of East Greenland the game is attributed to the "early" Norsemen. According to Thalbitzer (1924), the game probably was played by the Inuit into the 1800s, but today only rows of stones silently mark the past. Intriguingly, this game has not been found elsewhere in the Arctic Inuit cultures and stands in singular prominence as a Greenland pastime.

Little is known about the game "rowing to seal" aside from Oleson's (1963) reference. No information about how it was played has been located. The stones for the game apparently were placed in the shape of a boat, which suggests the same formation as the Norse rite of burying a "dead" boat by marking its shape with stones. It is conjectured that this religious ritual may have degenerated to a game of survival.

GREENLAND INUIT-NORSE CONTACT

Correlating the Greenland Inuit pastimes to Norse activities from 1000 to 1500 A.D. has demanded articulation of sources in archaeology, history, ethnography, literature, and legend. Paralleling this search is a secondary issue about the quality of the Norse-Inuit contact. Questions that come to mind are: Was the contact geographically limited? Was it short-lived or lasting? Was it friendly or hostile?

Did the quality of contact change over time? Could the contact have been indirect, thus negating the above concerns? Understanding the circumstances of possible "playful" exchange might help indicate the quality or atmosphere of exchange if any existed, which to date has not been clarified.

The view that friendly mutual exchange existed between the two peoples is tentatively supported by four arguments: the discovery of Norse material culture and trade items in Thule sites of that time period and before 1700 A.D.; medieval church graveyards with Norse this period; the basic nonhostile temperament of the modern Greenland Inuits; and evidence of Norse physiological characteristics in some Inuit descendants that early ethnographers reported.

The view that a hostile exchange existed is supported by: evidence showing destruction of the Norse Western and Eastern Settlements sometime between the late 1200s and 1500s A.D.; the disappearance of the Norsemen from Greenland during this time period and before 1700 A.D.; medieval church graveyard with Norse burials, including many children, indicating separated existence, even in the last desperate days; and both Eskimo and Norse legends refer to hostile relations.

Appealing as the evidence of personal Greenland Norse and Inuit contact is, an additional interpretation must be presented, that of indirect contact. By observation from a distance and subsequent imitation of Norse activities, the Inuits may have been indirectly influenced by the Greenland Norsemen. At deserted sites Inuits also may have found Norse objects that were carried back to the Inuit sites, accounting or the Norse artifacts found later in Inuit sites. This would explain in part the disporportionate larger number of Norse artifacts found in Inuit sites compared with Inuit artifacts found in Norse sites.[6] In the case of physical activities such as circle dance sequences and foot patterns, song rhythms, and possibly ballgames of soccer or ice hockey, the specificity and purpose of such actions may not be easily understood by only observation or by simply finding playing objects. Draughts (checkers) and chess would defy replication through only possessing gaming pieces; a person would have to have played the game or at least had an explanation.

Oleson (1963) infers a friendly exchange in his listing of 27 distinct culture items adopted by the Inuit people from the medieval Norsemen in Greenland. He stated: "All these [structures, installations, and games] supply us with proof that the Thule culture was preominately an Icelandic one, very distinctly set apart from the aboriginal cultures of America. There can be little doubt that their introduction into the Thule Culture stems from the Icelandic boothsitters[7] who met and intermixed with the ... Eskimos. They all date from the period of 1000 to 1500 A.D. (p. 55).

Bruun (1918), among others, records that there was not any mention of Eskimos in Norse writings until the 13th century, and then it was expressly stated that the "skraellings" lived to the north of the Norsemen. Rink (1875, 1877) recorded an Inuit legend that narrated that in the beginning, after their forefathers had come to the western settlement, they and the Norsemen lived—it is said—peacefully together; but subsequently disagreements arose. When Bruun in 1912 journeyed in the same area, he was informed that the "tradition of fights between the Eskimos and the Norsemen still prevail amongst the Eskimos of our day" (Bruun, 1918, p. 132). It was about 1370 A.D. that the Norse Western Settlement was destroyed by Eskimos. Brunn (1918) reported, "According to Iver Baardsen, who circa 1370 returned from Norway: 'Now the Skraellings have the whole western settlement, there are horses, goats, cattle and sheep, but everything is wild, and no people, Christian or heathen'" (p. 131). (In this context "heathen" refers to Norse non-Christians, some of whom may have returned to the worship of the old Norse pantheon.) The last Bishop of Greenland reported "that in the year 1379 the Skraellings 'had laid wast' the Greenlanders (Norsemen), killed 18 men and took two boys away in thraldom" (Brunn, 1918, p. 138). This was probably the first conflict between the Eskimos and the Eastern Settlement that finally was in ruins by 1500 A.D.

The Norse legends of the Eastern Settlement concluded that the understanding between Kablunaks (Norsemen) and the Greenlanders (Eskimos) was not of the best. However, they lived peacefully for a long time in the neighborhood of each other. But at last an Eskimo killed a Norseman who was taunting him, causing a bloody feud that ended with the complete destruction of the old Kablunaks (Bruun, 1918). These legends, "stories about the Ancient Kavilunait," recorded in Rink (1875), relate that the two peoples fell out of favor and that the Norsemen were killed by degrees, not through big battles between the members of the races, but by single attack and slaughter. This was the exact method used by the east coast Eskimos against each other until the 20th century.

According to Persson (1969) the last documentary information about the Norsemen, a marriage contract drawn up at Gardar, Greenland, was dated 1408 A.D. However, archaeological investigations (Norlund, 1930) showed that Greenland's contact with Europe occurred to about 1480 A.D. As the Thule Eskimos advanced southward from initial Norse contact in about 1200 A.D., they apparently did not mix with the Europeans. However, some racial intermarriage may have taken place later. For reasons only partially understood, the Thule people continued to spread throughout Greenland while the Norsemen disappeared by the 16th century (Rink, 1877). The ultimate fate of the Norsemen has remained unknown, but when ships from Europe once again reached the Greenland coast in the late 1500s, no living Norsemen were found.

It may be concluded that Inuit-Norse relations, which may have been friendly in early contacts, worsened over time as the distressed Norsemen's needs for the same resources as the Inuit accelerated. The lack of trade exchange with Europe must have forced the Norsemen to utilize their environment much as the Eskimos did in hunting and fishing.

Martin Forbisher rediscovered Greenland in 1576, and in 1578 he found Eskimos inhabiting Julianehaab, the former Norse settlement area. They had a few pieces of iron, bronze, buttons, and iron spearheads, showing contact with earlier Norse culture (Kendrick, 1968).

GREENLAND INUIT PASTIMES

In the year 1585, explorer John Davis landed in Greenland. He was greeted by a native with a kiss of the hand, a friendly European and not an Eskimo custom (Rink, 1877). His visit a year later confirmed that at that time the Eskimos knew or at least observed the game of football: "The Sunshine and the North Star [British boats sailing under John Davis for whom the Davis Straits is named], after following the ice to Iceland and sailing thence to Godthaab, where they played football and fought with the natives, finally departed for England on August 31" (Oleson, 1963, p. 157).

Davis' visits to Greenland are proof that between the late 1500s and the 1700s certain ships visited Greenland, primarily while searching for a northern passage through North America to India. It was also known that in the 1600s the Dutch carried on some trade with the west coast Inuit and that European vessels fished in Greenland waters. The introduction of European pastimes to the Inuit between the disappearance of the medieval Norsemen and the second wave of Norsemen after 1700 A.D. is more than a remote possibility. However, this has not been documented. With this precaution in mind, let's examine reports of several 20th century ethnographers and archaeologists regarding Greenland Inuit play activities and their association with Norse play activities.

The pristine postmedieval isolation of the east coast Ammassalik Inuit group due to the treacherous coastal cliffs, shore ice, and constant appearance of icebergs was stressed by Thalbitzer (1924). His description of hopping-stones indicated an expressive contact between the Eskimos and the medieval Norsemen:

> Another open-air game of skill especially characteristic of Greenland was *naanisartoq* 'skipping from stone to stone (sometimes boulders) placed in a row (across a plain).' Like the ball-games this was a game of contest requiring endurance and courage. In the Ammassat Fjord near Ammassalik, I saw on a ledge on the side of

the mountain above the camping ground, a row of a few big boulders where such games of contest were held in olden times; he who won the victory 'killed' *(toquppaait)* the others; the spectators cried: 'there at last he also won a victory over them as so often before *(piseeriniukannaaseet)*.' In West Greenland even as far north as Waigat (Disko Bay) such *naainsartoq* rows of stones are shown in many places, reminiscent of ancestral games of sport, and their presence has often been made a subject of comment in literature on the Eskimo, latest and more specifically described by M. Porsild. Giesecke described the game from the Disko Fjord in his journal for the year 1812. Nowadays Greenlanders sometimes ascribe these rows of stones to the days of the Norsemen. As far as is known, this game is not found out of Greenland. (Thalbitzer, 1924, p. 245)

Ballgames of football and ice hockey, both known as European games, were played by the Ammassalik as well as a game of whipping a ball around the settlement (Thalbitzer, 1914). Shinny, and its ancient form, "Knattleiker," (Mehl, 1948) was not found among medieval Norse pastimes in Europe, but was brought to Iceland from England and Ireland (Knudsen, 1906). These Greenlanders, the Eskimos, also played games with tops, buzzes, bull-roarers, and windwheels, called whirligigs. Thalbitzer (1941) also reported: "At an early age children are trained by games, especially trials of strength, wrestling and pulling with the arms to become strong . . . A favorite trial of strength consisted in lifting a great stone . . . The same sport is mentioned in the sagas about strong heroes, Kaashashuk and Kunuk for example" (p. 600).

These activities were praticed by the medieval Norsemen. The lifting of a great stone was often used in northern Europe as a test of maturity. If a youth could not lift the stone, he was not ready to assume the privileges of manhood.

Thalbitzer's (1924) observations of dance and song are significant to the contact theory of pastime activities. He reported that among the many singing dances from West Greenland known up to this century were dances with short song texts originating from Europe along with the beggar feast, or begging game, which occupied a special place. Earlier, Egede (1745/1818) noted Norse style song texts as he traveled among the natives in the early 1700s. In describing certain phallus dances, Thalbitzer (1924) remarked, "Besides the European dances, one sees at the Christmas season in several of the North Greenland colonies, a dance in which two masked persons take part, one of whom bears a huge phallus" (pp. 246-247). The use of an oversized phallus replica is a common accessory in Eskimo dances, and its uses at that season may infer the joining of the celebrative activities of the Inuit traditional Winter Solstice and Christmas (Birket-Smith, 1924). Thalbitzer (1924), remarking about the around dance, stated:

North of Disko Bay (70° N. latitude) I saw the old-fashioned *tiwaneq* combined with a round dance in which the dancers joined hands and circled from right to left. That dance form is perhaps still preserved there. The *tiwasoq* dancer stood in the center of the circle and led the singing, those in the circle joining the chorus. Compare our own European dancers of the Middle Ages. It is not improbable that the settlement of the Norsemen in South Greenland during the Middle Ages gave impetus to the custom which Europeans in Greenland called to 'balear,' (a term of Roman origin); however, it must be noted that the dancer in the center of the circle is in true Eskimo style. When the children of West Greenland play and sing *isitaaia*, the game is reminiscent of the old *tiwaneg* manner. (p. 249)

Egede (1741) described the round dance as follows: "The women, particularly the maidens, have likewise a game unto themselves, which is most like a dance, holding one another by the hand and together forming a circle; then they run about, backwards and forwards with each other, singing songs and making several motions and gyrations" (p. 96). Thalbitzer and Thuren (1911) considered this dance to be a survival from the dance of the Norsemen (p. 96).

When one notes that the common style for Inuit women's dancing is standing in one place with loosely bent knees moving the trunk, head, and arms to rhythm, seeing women with joined hands stepping in circle formation must have impressed Thalbitzer. The round dance was common in medieval Scandinavia (Nielsen, 1933).

Because of Thalbitzer's in-depth longitudinal study of Greenland Eskimos, he must be considered an important source concerning the contact theory. He confirmed that contact and expressive cultural exchange as shown in game, dance, and song took place between the Norsemen and the Eskimos during the medieval period. However, he remarked that the majority of the toys—such as dolls, tops, buzzes, bull-roarers, *ajajaq* ring and pin version, and the ball of these Eskimos were common to all Arctic Eskimos and that similarities of shinny and old knattleiker were probably due to chance (Thalbitzer, 1914). However, the many other commonly shared pastimes by Inuit and the medieval Norse, such as the circle dance patterns, folk songs, football games, ice hockey, stone lifting, and especially stone hopping, point strongly toward direct contact and expressive cultural exchange.

To Thalbitzer's evidence is added that of archaeologist Mathiassen. As part of the Danish systematic archaeological investigation of Greenland, Mathiassen was sent in 1929 to West Greenland, where he excavated the remains of medieval Eskimo settlements in Upernivik District on the island of Inugsuk, some 600 miles north of the early Norsemen's Western Settlement. He chose that area because both Norse and Eskimo ruins had been identified earlier, and he had examined a small rune stone dated in the late 13th century discovered on the island (Rink, 1877). Mathiassen became aware of a Greenland legend about the killing of Norsemen at Inugsuk, and the Eskimo fear of the Danes' vengeance was still being repeated into the 20th century. He uncovered over 5500 objects at different levels of Eskimo occupations from the earliest habitation in the 10th century to the 14th century.

Several pastime artifacts of pre-Norse contact period were found by Mathiassen, such as the ring and pin game pieces for *ajagag*; a ball of sealskin thought to have been used in an old Eskimo hand ball game (Birket-Smith, 1924); tops and wood pegs for spinning tops, a small buzz; a wind wheel (whirligig); over 100 traditional flat-faced dolls mostly of wood, but some of ivory and baleen; miniature (model) toys (replicas of weapons and utensils of adults such as harpoons, sleds, kayaks, snow knives, arrows, bowls, sleeping platforms).

In later excavation levels many Thule objects were found indicating contact with Norsemen: 30 wooden pieces for the game of draughts (checkers), 43 wood dolls among which were two representing Europeans, a man carved in a traditional style but with a top hat and a female carved with a dress outline (Inuit clothing for both male and female consisted of pants and hooded parka-style garments). Among the traditional miniature toys were also imitations of European objects such as guns, cross-bows, and boats with a keel. Mathiassen (1930), surprised to find products that had been borrowed from the Norsemen during this period so far north, summarized his work: "There are thus a fairly large number of culture elements in the Inugsuk Culture that with more or less certainty may be credited to influence from the medieval Norse cultures—besides some objects that must originate from direct trading connections with the Norsemen. . . . Consequently the Inugsuk Culture must be looked upon as a later phase of the Thule culture influenced by medieval Norse culture" (p. 300). Mathiassen (1930) stated further: "It is surprising to find such pronounced Norse influence in this old West Greenland culture; we do not know much about intercourse between Eskimos and Norsemen; not much is recorded about it in the writings that treat of the Norsemen in Greenland, and where such mention is made, it is mostly about hostilities between them. . . . It must be left to future investigations to show how far southward along the west coast Eskimos have lived while the Norsemen inhabited mostly southwesterly districts, at any rate not to any great extent, otherwise we would undoubtedly have heard more about them in the sagas" (p. 301).

Mathiassen's work established that there was expressive culture contact between the Thule peoples and the Norsemen in West Greenland between 1000 to 1300 A.D. that may well have been through friendly trade. However, it is feasible that the contact could have been indirect. Pastime artifacts found by Mathiassen at the later excavation levels could have been copied by observation or found at unoccupied sites. He also showed that the Norse culture exercised a certain influence on the Eskimo culture in that area, but one might question whether this influence was mutual. In other words, have traces from the Eskimo culture been found among Norsemen? In 1914, Thalbitzer concluded, "Hitherto there has been found practically no object of true Eskimo origin in the ruins of the Icelandic farms in south Greenland, or the reverse, namely Icelandic objects in the Eskimo ruins" (p. 696.) Among the few Eskimo-made objects found in Herjolfsnes and Gardar, southern Norse sites, were an oval baleen bowl and a snow knife handle of whale bone (Norlund, 1930). Both of the Thule specimens appeared to come from the north, thus testifying to the connection in the north and apparently little exchange in the south.

The combined evidence presented by Thalbitzer, Mathiassen, and Birket-Smith supports the contact proposition and suggests that an expressive cultural exchange in the form of games, dance, and song resulted. It also indicates that the directional flow was largely one way—from the Norse to the Inuit. In addition, Mathiassen has shown much of the borrowing occurred prior to the Inuit's major migration southward to the Norse settlements in the late 1200s, 1300s, and 1400s. It is entirely feasible that the friendly relations between persons of each group were enjoyed early in their contact, but disintegrated during the later phase. Amicability in the early northern contact stage is suggested by Thalbitzer and Mathiassen, and evidence of hostility in the later migratory stage is documented by Rink, Bruun, and Persson.

The second-wave colonization of Greenland began in 1721, spearheaded by the Norwegian Lutheran priest Hans Egede, who was searching for remnants of the earlier Norse colonists in order to renew their Christian faith. He settled near Godthaabfjord and established several new colonies along the southwest Greenland coast, essentially in the same area that the first Norsemen settled. Egede (1745/1818) in describing the natives around Julianehaab in the 1720s stated, "The people living there are rather beautiful and white." These fair-skinned Greenlanders contrasted markedly with the dark-skinned Eskimos he usually described and may have been descendants of the earlier Norsemen. Persson (1969) suggested that the descendants of the union of Icelanders and Eskimos could have lived isolated for centuries in this relatively inaccessible southern part of Greenland.

Egede (1745/1818) found the Greenland natives "playing, banqueting, and revelling, and engaging in drum songs" (p. 155). Among the playful activities that Egede observed that were also found in the medieval Norsemen's repertoire were: keep-away and football (two types of ball games), roulette, wrestling and strength contests, circle dancing, and songs. Ball playing, according to Egede, was their most common diversion, which they played two different ways. He explained: "They divide themselves into two parties; the first party throws the ball to each other; while those of the second party endeavour to get it from them, and so by turns. . . . The second manner is like our playing football. They mark out two barriers, at three or four hundred paces distance one from the other; then being divided into two parties, as before, they meet at the starting place, which is at the midway between the two barriers; and the ball being thrown upon the ground, they strive who first shall get at it, and kick it with the foot, each party towards their barrier. He that is the most nimble footed and getting the first to the barrier, has won the match" (pp. 162-163).

An Eskimo legend that ties the football game with earlier religious beliefs was also related by Egede (1745/1718): "Thus [they will tell you] the deceased play at football in Heaven, with the head of a morse [walrus], when it lightens, or the Northlight [aurora borealis] appears, which they fancy to be the souls of the deceased" (p. 163).

Egede (1745/1818) described roulette as a game of chance, stating: "They have a piece of wood pointed at one end, with a pin or peg in the midst, upon which it turns; when the boys are seated around, and everyone laid down what they play for, one of them turns the pointed piece of wood with his finger, that it wheels about like a mariner's compass; and when it has done, he that the point aims at, wins all that was laid down" (p. 162).

The customary games, dance, and singing engaged in as part of the natives' hospitality to visitors were frequently observed by Egede (1745/1818) and described thus: "When their acquaintance from abroad come to see them, they spend whole days and nights in singing and dancing; and as they love to pass for men of courage and valour, they will try forces together, in wrestling, struggling, and playing hook and crook, which is to grapple with the arms and fingers made crooked, and intangle like hooks. Whoever can pull the other from his place, thinks himself a man of worth and valour. The women's or rather the maiden's plays, consist in dancing around, holding one another by the hand, forming a circle, and singing of songs" (pp. 163-164).

It is of interest to note that the Greenland native wrestling style and the two kinds of ball games were participated in by Eastern Arctic Eskimos but not recorded for the Central and Western Eskimo as listed by ethnographers (Birket-Smith, 1929, 1936; Gulin, 1907; Glassford, 1976; Taylor, 1974; Thalbitzer, 1924; Turner, 1894). The migratory patterns of the Thule peoples over the Eastern Arctic could explain the diffusion of these pastimes. This observation is tentative, needing much more substantiation. However, it is within the realm of possibility.

SUMMARY AND CONCLUSIONS

In summary, this investigation has examined the contact of Norse and Eskimo peoples on the island of Greenland during the time period of 1000 to 1500 A.D. Documentation through archaeology, history, ethnography, literature, and legend has shown that expressive culture exchange through game, dance, and song took place. Similar play activities known and shown to be practiced by both Norsemen and the Thule Inuit in Greenland during this time included: ball games of keep-away and football, circle dancing, gymnastics, hopping-stones, roulette, "rowing to seal," skipping over rope, songs of European origin, and wrestling (strength contests of arm pull, hand pull, neck pull). Thule dolls with European dress and miniature (model) toys of European objects show observation and imitation of Norse items. Wooden draught (checker) gaming pieces found in Thule sites may indicate only trade items and not actual knowledge of the game. The notion of indirect contact offers a plausible explanation of these items. However, Egede's (1741, 1745/1818) eye-witness reports of the Thule participation in pastimes also common to the medieval Norsemen support the theory of direct contact in expressive cultural exchange. The relatively greater number of Norse expressive culture items found in northern Thule sites and the relative dearth of such items found in both Norse and Thule southern sites indicate primarily a Norse to Thule diffusion process and suggest friendly relations between these people in the early northern contact and hostility or at least neutral quality of contact in the later medieval period.

In conclusion, the evidence suggests:

- The Norsemen and the Thule peoples both colonized the island of Greenland during the medieval period.
- These two groups had contact and exchanged expressive culture items as evidenced by similar pastimes of games, dance, and songs.
- The diffusion of these pastimes appears unidirectional from the Norse to the Thule peoples.
- Evidence of pastime exchange in northern Greenland sites indicates early friendly contact between these peoples, and the lack of exchanged artifacts in the southern sites implies later hostile relations.

Notes

1. The Thule Eskimo culture, which appears to have had its origin in North Alaska, is named after Thule in northwestern Greenland where the culture was first identified (McGhee, 1978). In Greek antiquity the same "Thule," apparently a Celtic term, was given to Scandinavia. In poetry, the "ultimate Thule" referred to the farthest frontiers of man's explorations. As the Vikings moved westerly from the Faroe Islands to Iceland and then to Greenland, the term "Thule" iden-

tified each successive outpost; therefore, Greenland became known as the legendary "Thule." (Gilberg, 1976). It is also intriguing that as very young men, Danish Knud Rasmussen and Peter Freuchen called their northwest coastal trading post Thule and it was from there they launched their extensive explorations of the Arctic peoples (Freuchen, 1961; Rasmussen, 1912-1952).

2. The Arctic region is the northernmost culture area in North America and one of the relatively few exceptions to the general patterns of independently distributed race, language, and culture. The Eskimos and Aleuts of the Arctic differ physically from American Indians, and they have a distinctive linguistic family known as Eskimo-Aleutian or Eskaleutian. The Arctic culture area extends from the Aleutian Islands of southern Alaska on the west, north around the coasts and tundra of Alaska, across the barren grounds of Canada, to the ice-free coastal lands of Greenland. There are many distinctive smaller patterns of Eskimo and Aleut culture, but the area as a whole differs culturally, linguistically, and physically from comparable areas to the south (Manitoba Museum of Man and Nature, Human History Information Sheet 34, n.d., p. 1 — Introduction to North American Indians and Eskimos).

3. Fortunately, the Icelanders had a compelling interest in history. Their narratives recounted heroic achievements and, when written down after 1200 A.D. became known as "sagas." These Norse adventures and family histories helped flesh out the Greenland tale. The sagas, although not agreeing in details, outlined the major persons, places, dates, and events, thus providing starting points for verification.

4. The Eskimo peoples of arctic regions speak dialects of a single Eskimo language, Inuktitut, in which they refer to themselves as "Inuit" or "the people," by which they prefer to be known. Inuit in this paper is used to refer to the present occupants of the area between the Bering Strait and Greenland and to their archaeological ancestors of the past thousand years (McGhee, 1978).

5. My thanks to Ase Everstevedt of Bergen, Norway, for identifying the Norwegian term *Ganga Heljarbrui*, ora Hel-bridges, which is called in this paper Hopping Stones (Personal communication, May 26, 1982).

6. The possibility of Inuit-Norse indirect contact was cogently argued by Henry Stewart, Waseda University, Tokyo, Japan. I appreciate his help in my thinking about this alternative to my direct cultural exchange notion (Personal communication, August 21, 1983).

7. "Boothsitters" was the name given to Icelandic colonists. Booth means tent or dwelling place.

REFERENCES

Birket-Smith, K. (1924). Ethnography of the Egedesminde District. *Meddelelser om Gronland, 66.*

Birket-Smith, K. (1929). The Caribou Eskimo. *Report on the 5th Thule expedition 1921-24, 4,* Part 2. Copenhagen: Gyldendalske Boghandel, Nordisk Lorag.

Birket-Smith, K. (1936). *The Eskimos.* (W.E. Calvert, Trans, revised by C.D. Forde). London: Methuen & Co.

Bruun, D. (1918). The Icelandic colonization of Greenland. *Meddelelser om Gronland, 57.*

Collins, H.B. Jr. (1943). Eskimo archaeology and its bearing on the problem of man's antiquity in America. *Proceedings of the American Philosophical Society, 86*(2), 220-235.

Culin, S. (1907). *Games of North American Indians.* Twenty-fourth Annual Report of the Bureau of American Ethnology. Washington, D.C.: Government Printing Office.

Duason, J. (1941). *Lankonnun og landnum Islending i Vesturheimi.* Reykjavik: Pretad, isafoldarprentsmidju H.F.

Egede, H. (1741). *Det gamle Gronlands nye perlustration eller naturel-historie* & c. Copenhagen. (As quoted by Birket-Smith, k. 1924).

Egede, H. (1818). *A description of Greenland.* London: T. and J. Allman. (Originally published 1745)

Freuchen, P. (1961). *Book of the Eskimos.* Cleveland: World Publishing Co.

Gad, F. (1971). *The history of Greenland I: Early times to 1700.* (E. Dupont, Trans.) Montreal: McGill-Queeens University Press.

Giddings, J.L. (1961). Cultural continuities of Eskimos. *American Antiquity, 27*(2), 155-173.

Giberg, R. (1976). Thule. *Arctic, 29*(2), 83-86.

Glassford, G. (1976). *Application of a theory of games to the transitional Eskimo culture.* New York: Arno Press.

Gotlind, J. (Ed.). (1933). Idrott och lek, *Nordisk Kulture, 24.* Stockholm: Albert Vonniers Forlag.

Instad, H. (1969). *Westward to Vinland.* New York: St. Martin's Press.

Jenness, D. (1940). Prehistoric culture waves from Asia to America. *Journal of the Washington Academy of Sciences, 30*(1), 1-15.

Jenness, D. (1955, winter). Enter the European ... Among the Eskimos. *The Beaver,* pp. 24-30.

Kendrick, T.D. (1968). *A history of the Vikings.* New York: Barnes & Noble.

Knudsen, F. (1906). Den Islandske Boldleg. *Danske studier,* Copenhagen: Udgivne af Marius Kirstensen og Axel Olrik.

Lloyd, L. (1870). *Peasant life in Sweden.* London: Tinsley Brothers.

Manitoba Museum of Man and Nature. (n.d.). Human history information sheet 34, Winnipeg, Canada: author.

Mathiassen, T. (1930). Ingusuk, A medieval Eskimo settlement in Upernivik District, West Greenland. *Meddelelser om Gronland, 77,* 145-340.

McGhee, R. (1970). Speculations on climatic changes and Thule culture development. *Folk, 11*(12), 173-184.

McGhee, R. (1978). *Canadian Arctic prehistory.* Toronto: Van Nostrand Reinhold Ltd.

Mehl, E. (1948). Baseball in the Stone Age. *Western Folklore, 7*(2), 145-161.

Nielsen, H.G. (Ed.). (1933). Dans. *Nordisk Kulture, 24.* Stockholm, Sweden: Albert Vonniers Forlag.

Norlund, P. (1924). Buried Norsemen at Herjolfsnes. *Meddelelser om Gronland, 76,* 1-10.

Oleson, T.J. (1963). *Early voyages and northern approaches (1000-1632).* Toronto: McClelland and Stewart Ltd.

Oswalt, W. H. (1977, autumn). The Eskimo people: The earliest accounts. *The Beaver,* pp. 21-27.

Persson, I. (1969). The fate of the Icelandic Vikings in Greenland. Man. 4(4), 620-628.

Rasmussen, K. (1912-1952). *Report of the Fifth Thule Expedition 1921-24. The Danish expedition to Arctic North America in charge of Knud Rasmussen.* Vol. I-X. Copenhagen: Glydendalske Boghandel, Nordisk, Forlag.

Rink, H. (1875). *Tales and traditions of the Eskimo.* London: William Blackwood and Sons.

Rink, H. (1974). *Danish Greenland.* Montreal: McGill-Queens's University Press. (Original work published 1877, London: Henry S. King Co.)

Rowley, G. (1940). The Dorset culture of the Eastern Arctic. *American Anthopologist, 42,* 490-499.

Schledermann, P. (1975). *Thule Eskimo prehistory of Cumberland Sound, Baffin Island, Canada.* Archaeological Survey of Canada, Paper No. 38. Ottawa: National Museums of Canada.

Schledermann, P. (1981). Eskimo and Viking finds in the high Arctic. *National Geographic, 159*(5), 575-601.
Stanford, D.J. (1973). *The origins of Thule Culture.* Unpublished doctoral dissertation, University of New Mexico, Albuquerque.

Stewart, H. (1983, August). *Carbon-14 dating and the origins of earliest eastern Eskimo cultures.* Paper presented at the meeting of the XIth International Congress of Anthropological and Ethnological Sciences, Vancouver, British Columbia, Canada.

Taylor, J.G. (1974). *Netsilik Eskimo material culture (The Roald Amundsen collection from King William Island).* (The Norwegian Research Council for science and the humanities). Oslo: Universitesforlaget.

Taylor, W. E. (1963) Hypothesis on the origin of the Canadian Thule culture, *American Antiquity, 28*(4), 456-464.

Thalbitzer, W. (1914). Ethnographic collections from East Greenland. *Meodelelser om Gronland, 39,* 319-755.

Thalbitzer, W. (1924). Cultic games and festivals in Greenland. *XXI Congres International des Americanistes.* Goteborg. *21,* 238-255.

Thalbitzer, W. (1941). The Ammassalik Eskimo: Contributions to the ethnology of the East Greenland natives. *Meddelelser om Gronland, 40,* second part, second half vol., pp. 565-740.

Thalbitzer, W. & Thuren, H. (1911). Dans i Gronland. *Feilberg fra nordiske sprog-og folkemindeforskere.* Copenhagen: Stockholm & Christiana.

Turner, L. (1894). *Ethnology of the Ungava District.* 11th Annual Report of the Bureau of American Antiquity, Smithsonian Institution, 1889-1890. Washington, D.C. Government Printing Office.

Wahlquist, B. (1980). *Ville Vikinger I lek of idrett.* Oslo: Tiden Norsk Forlag. (Original work published 1978 in Swedish, *Vikingarnas Vilda Lekar)*

VIDEO GAME PLAY AND THE FLOW MODEL

David R. Chase
The Pennsylvania State University

Games were among the earliest forms of human interaction and, according to some authors, foreshadow social change (Harris, 1981). One category of game, the video game, was developed in the early 1970s and by the beginning of 1980 had become an established part of a worldwide popular culture. As with much of popular culture, video games have been called a fad, an outrage, a nuisance, and a waste of time by proponents of traditional culture. Video game enthusiasts and proponents of technological change find video games challenging, fun, a positive addiction, and potentially stimulating for personal growth. To date, there has been little thoughtful debate on the merit of these positions and even less empirical research conducted on the issues. This paper offers a studied perspective of the video game phenomenon. The central question investigated in this study is: "Why do many people find video game play enjoyable?" Selected findings from a study of 175 video game players are presented to provide tentative answers to this question. The final section of the paper deals with the general phenomenon of video gaming. The possibility of a transformation in current styles of video play and future approaches to the study of video games is discussed.

EMPIRICAL RESEARCH RELATED TO VIDEO GAMES

A search of academic journals and phone conversations with researchers interested in video gaming indicated that there is little published research. However, the phone conversations indicated that several studies are in progress. Fridgen (1982) of Michigan State University has presented initial results of the observation of video game play. At MIT, Terkle (personal communication, November 1982) is in the process of interpreting her observations of video play in the Boston area. Ng (personal communication, December 1982) of Waterloo University is completing a video game study, while Kuby (personal communication, November 1982) at the University of Chicago is proposing a video game play study using the flow model of experience proposed by Csikszentmihalyi (1975). As can be seen, it is too soon to determine if and how the research in progress will address the positive and negative aspects of video play discussed in the previous section.

The published research that deals specifically with video games has focused on the design of video games to assist in the learning process. Malone (1981a) has studied the use of computer games in the educational environment. His work first examined the question, "What makes computer games fun?" Three intrinsically motivating characteristics—challenge, curiosity, and fantasy—are found to be the factors stimulating the subjects' playing of computer games. These motivational factors are quite different from the extrinsic motivators of money, power, and status. Malone (1981b), using these three intrinsic motivators and their subcomponents, outlines the characteristics of an intrinsically motivating computer learning environment. Additional research on the use of microcomputers in educational settings can be found in a conference report edited by Malone and Levin (1981).

A point not explicated in Malone's (1981a) paper is the relationship between intrinsic motivation and fun. That is, why do people report an activity to be enjoyable. Are all intrinsically motivated activities fun? Malone's work, which focuses more on the motivating properties of the environment (i.e., the structure of computer games) than on the subjective experience of the player, does not provide ready answers to these questions. A more phenomenological approach, as in Csikszentmihalyi's (1975) work on the flow experience, provides the basis for addressing these questions. This work contains subjective recall of experience during intrinsically motivated activities such as rock climbing, chess, and rock dancing. Under the intrinsically motivating condition of a balance between perceived challenge and appropriate skill to meet the challenge, Csikszentmihalyi (1975) states a person "is in control of his actions, and there is little distinction between self and environment, between stimulus and response, or between past, present, and future" (p. 36). He calls this state of consciousness "flow" because, "In the flow state, action follows upon action according to an internal logic that seems to need no conscious intervention by the actor" (p. 36). The individual experiences the flow state as enjoyable. The question that arises is whether an environment can offer motivators that are both necessary and sufficient for enjoyment. According to Csikszentmihalyi (1975), more than extrinsic motivators are required: "It is to be stressed again that whether a person will experience flow at all and, if he does, whether it will be at a complex or at a simple level depends only in part on the objective conditions in the environment or the concrete structure of the activity. What counts even more is the person's ability to restructure the environment so that it will allow flow to occur. Artists, poets, religious visionaries, and scientists are among those who have learned to use cognitive techniques to order symbols so that they can "play" with them any time and anywhere, to a certain extent regardless of environmental conditions. Ideally, anyone could learn to carry, inside himself the tools of enjoyment" (p. 53).

The ideas presented above may convey the impression that a person searches the environment, is appropriately challenged, acts, experiences a degree of flow, feels a certain amount of enjoyment, then stops the activity. Based on the observed persistence of intrinsically motivated behavior, the impression of a linear, causally linked sequence of events leading to enjoyment is misleading. This becomes clearer when the concept of emergent goal mentioned by Csikszentmihalyi (1978) is considered. An emergent goal is a goal not visualized at the outset of the activity that arises during that activity. This suggests that some behavioral processes (activities) are self-perpetuating not as the result of habit but as the result of the actor's continually constructing and responding to new challenges.[1] An appropriate conceptualization of an intrinsically motivated behavioral process is as an open system that is driven by emergent goals. Such a system is difficult to study from reductionist and causal perspectives because these perspectives do not readily encompass the paradoxical report of a rock dancer who described the dancing experience as: "You feel relaxed, comfortable, and energetic" (Csikszentmihalyi, 1975, p. 39).

One study has drawn upon the flow model to help explain the fascination of playing Pac-Man (Bowman, 1982). Although Bowman sees some aspects of video game play as extrinsic, such as score, which may become a peer group status symbol, he finds that the challenge involved is a strong intrinsic motivator. Expanding on the challenge factor, Bowman (1982) following Csikszentmihalyi (1975), states: "The Pac-Man's addictiveness would be explained as follows: it is an action system where skills and challenges are progressively balanced, goals are clear, feedback is immediate and unambiguous, and relevant stimuli can be differentiated from irrelevant stimuli. Together, this combination contributes to the formation of a flow experience" (p. 15). Drawing on these ideas, Malone's (1981b) findings on the motivational effect of fantasy and curiosity, the idea of emergent goals, and the fact that enjoyment comes from experiencing flow, it is easy to understand why some persons play video games with extreme persistence. For some, video gaming appears to be a self-perpetuating experience, a type of creative behavior.[2] The following section reports on a video game study conducted by the author in which certain aspects of the flow model are investigated.

A VIDEO GAME STUDY

In the spring of 1982, a study of 175 video game players at three arcades in central Pennsylvania was conducted. The study was designed to explore and test some of the concepts and relationships mentioned in the previous section. Besides questions on demographic data, playing patterns, and motivational items, there were six questions designed to measure the degree of flow experienced by a video game player during a typical session of play. The intent here is to examine a portion of this data in order to discover if the video game experience can be described by the model of flow experience. Specifically, it is hypothesized that experiencing flow in video play is positively related to satisfaction with play, and that experiencing flow is related to frequency of play, time of play, and money spent per visit.

The data were collected by trained student interviewers who approached persons in the video arcades and asked them to participate in a study of video game playing by answering a few questions and then filling out a questionnaire. Realizing that the time of day and the day of the week might affect the representativeness of the sample, respondents were contacted in the morning, afternoon, and evening, Wednesday through Saturday. Once inside the arcade, the interviewer took a central position, closed his or her eyes, turned around, and then opened his or her eyes. The nearest person in direct line of sight was the person selected to be interviewed. The usable sample of 167 derived from this process was 75 percent male and 25 percent female, 77 percent college students and 10 percent high school students, with a mean age of 20.

The degree to which an individual either experiences flow or experiences ordinary awareness when playing video games is measured by a six-item scale reflecting three elements of the flow experience (Csikszentmihalyi, 1975).[3] A person's score on this scale is calculated from these six items by reversing the scoring on items 4 and 5 and then summing the six individual item scores. Using this scoring system, a score of 30 indicates the maximum amount of flow, and a score of 6 indicates a maximum amount of ordinary awareness. The scale mean is 20.7 with a standard deviation of 4.0. The alpha coefficient of reliability for this scale is .68. Table 1 presents the six items arranged according to the three elements of the flow experience along with the standards, deviations, and item to total correlations.

To examine the first hypothesis concerning the relationship between flow and satisfaction, a Pearson product moment correlation coefficient between flow and five point Likert scale measuring satisfaction in video play was calculated. There was a moderate positive correlation between flow and satisfaction in video play ($r=.42$). The prediction that flow relates to frequency of play, time of play, and

money spent per visit was tested with chi-square analysis. For this
analysis, individuals indicating a more pronounced experience of
flow were contrasted with those who experience video game playing
at an ordinary level of awareness. Thus, individuals falling from one
point below the mean (ordinary awareness side) to one point above
the mean (flow side) of the scale were dropped from the analysis.[4]
This resulted in a sample (n) of approximately 125 for the relationships examined. The relationship of flow with frequency of play and
time of play per visit are presented in Tables 2 and 3 respectively.

Table 1. Type of Experience Scale Items with Means, Standard Deviations, and Item-Total Correlations

Item	Mean	Standard Deviations	Item-Total Correlation
Delimit Reality			
- Daily routines and concerns are part of another world while I play pinball/video games	3.66	1.11	.47
- I would say the world seems smaller when I play pinball/video games.	2.90	1.02	.31
Control Aspect of Reality			
- I feel in control of the game as I play.	3.35	1.08	.41
- When I play pinball/video games, there is a lot of luck involved when I get a good score.	3.10[a]	1.24	.35
Respond to Feedback as if All Else Were Irrelevant			
- When I play, I often think of other things.	3.76[a]	.98	.45
- When I play pinball/video games, I concentrate totally on what is happening in the game.	3.76	1.01	.45

[a]Scoring reversed on these items

Table 2. Relationship Between Type of Experience and Reported Number of Video Game Sessions a Week

| | Type of Experience | |
| | Ordinary | |
Number of Sessions a Week	Awareness	Flow
Less than 1	35%	10%
1	10	24
2	26	19
3	10	21
4	19	26
Total %	100	100
Number	(62)	(62)

Note. χ^2 = 16.7; $p < .002$; eta = .21 (with Number of Sessions dependent).

Table 3. Relationship Between Type and Experience and Length of Session

| | Type of Experience | |
| | Ordinary | |
Length of Session	Awareness	Flow
Less than ½ hour	48%	12%
½-1 hour	38	56
1-2 hours	11	28
More than 2 hours	3	3
Total %	100	100
Number	(61)	(64)

Note. χ^2 = 19.6; $p < .000$; eta = .33 (with Number of Sessions dependent).

Tables 2 and 3 show a statistically significant relationship between flow and frequency of play per week and time spent per visit. Respective *etas* of .21 and .33 indicate the relationship is moderate and positive. In Table 3, the small percentage of respondents in row 4 may indicate an upper limit for the amount of time spent on a single visit.

Table 4. Relationship Between Type of Experience and Money Spent on Session

| | Type of Experience | |
| | Ordinary | |
Money Spent	Awareness	Flow
Less than $1	45%	25%
$1.00-$2.99	42	50
$3.00-$4.99	11	19
$5.00-$6.99	2	6
Total %	100	100
Number	(62)	(64)

Note. χ^2 = 7.0; $p < .07$ eta = .23 (with Money Spent dependent).

The relationship between flow and money spent per visit, as presented in Table 4, is not as definite as the relationships flow has with frequency and time of play. Still, there is a tendency for those who experience flow to spend more money per visit. The strength of this relationship is surprising because the probable high skill level of those who spend the most time playing (i.e., people who experience flow) means that they could play longer for less money. Since the data contain no direct measure of skill level, it is not possible to clarify the interrelationships among flow, time spent playing, money spent, and skill level.[5]

DISCUSSION

The results from this study of video game players fit the predictions of the flow model quite well. Those who were classified as experiencing flow found both the most satisfaction with video play and showed the most persistence in their play, as evidenced by time and money spent on play. Within the framework of the flow model, these findings suggest that playing video games, for some, is largely an intrinsically motivated behavior that has emergent goals and tendencies toward self-perpetuation.[6] Other preliminary findings from this data derived from questions on mood states before and after play and from additional questions on playing patterns support this contention.

Csikszentmihalyi (1978) has suggested characteristics of the activity or environment that facilitate the occurrence of flow. Bowman (1982) has argued that video games, at least Pac-Man, have these characteristics. Yet, as the data from this study indicate, there are many people who play video games and do not find them to be a flow activity. Can this be explained by denying that video games possess the necessary features to induce flow? Or should an individual's cognitive approach to video games be used as an explanation? The former explanation suggests possibilities for research on the structure of video games and the ways in which they may or may not meet the environmental characteristics that facilitate the flow experience. The latter explanation leads to research on how individuals cognitively process their interaction with a video game. It also suggests the possibility that such variables as locus of control and the self-efficacy concept postulated by Bandura (1977) affect that interaction.

Other areas for future research within the framework of flow include refinement of the measurement of flow. For example, can the occurrence of flow be reliably and validly measured through use of respondent recall, as in paper and pencil tests and face-to-face interviews? Would the measurement of brainwave patterns during play provide clues to understanding the state of flow? In order to achieve immediate reports on flow states, subjects could be interrupted at random times during play and asked to report their experience of flow. A final area that has not been examined is the physiological state of persons experiencing flow and ordinary awareness while playing video games. How would the physiological state of playing a video game while experiencing flow compare to the physiological state of a meditator? Does experiencing flow in video play reduce overall levels of stress?

CONCLUSION

For the past 3 to 4 years video games have been an ever-growing form of recreational activity that has been called a fad, the electronic age's answer to gaming, and a plague affecting American youth. A review of the literature on video games indicates there is a paucity of work that addresses these claims. The majority of the work encountered, including the findings reported in this paper, explains video game playing in terms of the flow model (Bowman, 1982; Fridgen, 1982). An exception is Malone's (1981b) research, which presents the most complete analysis of how to design a computer game that is fun to play.

In spite of the enormous increase in players and an initial understanding of what makes video games enjoyable, there is partial truth in the contention "that computer games are boring" (Wanner, 1982, p. 8). Wanner argues that the fantasy worlds created by computer graphics and manipulated with a joystick are an updated version of prior arcade games and that the same skills apply. If this is the case, as recent downturns in gross income from arcade games and a slackening market for home video game cartridges suggest, it portends not necessarily the demise of video games but most likely a transformation that will take advantage of the gaming potential of microcomputers.

Such a transformation might be a stimulus to examine the structure of video gaming and gaming in general. For example, who is the opponent: the machine, Kong of Donkey Kong, the designer of the game, or the player him or herself? Whom the player considers to be the opponent could have an effect on the mode of play and the feelings after play. If the machine is the opponent, the player might approach play with a competitive, aggressive attitude designed to pummel an external, generalized opponent into submission. In contrast, one advanced player the author knows has discovered that playing video games is an experience in learning about himself and that the true opponent is oneself. This player's style of play is characterized by words such as "understanding," "discovery," and "spontaneity."

Another possible structural change in video game play would be to allow the player to alter the rules of play. Allowing the player access to the rules of the game through limited programming statements would prompt what Farrer (1981) identifies as contesting: "the playing with play during the playing" (p. 195). A video game might be played under existing rules until such time as a rule change emerges that introduces a desired challenge or novelty. Changes could be left for future players to discover and then alter. One would be interacting with others both known and unknown through playing with play; that is, in an emergent, creative manner. The study of video game playing in this style, or a playful variant, offers possibly valuable insights regarding the interaction between games and culture.

Notes

1. It is readily acknowledged that a self-perpetuating activity is not a closed system and thus is subject to termination as the result of factors external to the activity. The word "habit" is used in the sense of stimulus-response behavior in which a repetition of the stimulus produces a repetition in response.

2. An example of creation in video play is the discovery of unique and challenging routes up the elevator board in Donkey Kong. When experienced players discuss "their game" they commonly mention new and interesting challenges that were discovered while playing.

3. Flow is conceptualized as one end of the dimension of individual awareness, the other end being ordinary awareness. Ordinary awareness is characterized by the self mediating between stimulus and response. It is an ego-involved state of awareness in which the individual may experience the extremes of anxiety and boredom (Csikszentmihalyi, 1975). The design of the scale does not allow for the determination of the degree of anxiety or boredom for persons experiencing an activity at the level of ordinary awareness.

4. The purpose of contrasting the extremes is to highlight the differences between the ideal types, flow experience, and ordinary awareness. Other analyses were run using more extreme ideal typing (contrasting the top and bottom 10 percent of the distribution) and no ideal typing (Pearson Correlations with no cases excluded). The various analyses showed that persons falling between the extremes of flow and ordinary awareness tended to have scores near the mean on the variables, frequency of play, time of play per visit, and money spent per visit.

5. Discussions with Joe Fridgen have led to the speculation that some of these relationships are related to the learning curve. For example, after an initial adjustment phase in which a person will not spend much time but a moderate amount of money, a player will begin to develop skill rather rapidly and will increase both his or her time of play and money spent. A final stage, stabilization, may be achieved when the growth in skill level flattens out, money spent has declined to a stable level, and the time spent playing has declined from previous peaks.

6. The term self-perpetuation is used here rather than the value-laden term addiction because addiction can have both a positive and negative meaning, for example, Glasser's (1976) use of the term positive addiction. Also, describing a behavioral sequence as addictive suggests that habit is the mechanism for behavioral continuance. Self-perpetuation more precisely describes experience construction that is intrinsically based and has emergent goals.

REFERENCES

Bandura, A. (1977). Self-efficacy toward a unifying theory of behavioral change. *Psychological Review, 84,* 191-215.

Bowman, R.F. Jr. (1982, September). A "Pac-Man" theory of motivation: Tactical implications for classroom instruction. *Educational Technology,* pp. 14-16.

Csikszentmihalyi, M. (1975) *Beyond boredom and anxiety.* San Francisco: Jossey-Bass.

Csikszentmihalyi, M. (1978) Intrinsic rewards and emergent motivation. In M.R. Lepper and D. Greene (Eds.), *The hidden costs of reward: New perspectives on the psychology of human motivation.* (pp. 205-216). Hillsdale, NJ: Lawrence Erlbaum Associates.

Farrer, C.R. (1981). Contesting. In A.T. Cheska (Ed.), *Play as context* (pp. 195-208). West Point, NY: Leisure Press.

Fridgen, J.D., & Taber, M. (1982), October). *Video arcades: Implications for leisure study and research.* Paper presented at the Leisure Research Symposium, Louisville, KY.

Glasser, W. (1976). *Positive addiction.* New York: Harper and Row.

Harri, J.C. (1981). Beyond Huizinga: Relationships between play and culture. In A.T. Cheska (Ed.), *Play as context* (pp. 26-36). West Point, NY: Leisure Press.

Malone, T.W. (1981a). Toward a theory of intrinsically motivating instruction. *Cognitive Science, 4,* 333-360.

Malone, T.W. (1981b, December). What makes computer games fun? *Byte,* pp. 258-274.

Malone, T.W., & Levin, J. (Eds.). (1981, March). *Microcomputers in education: Cognitive and social design principles* (summaries). Conference Report, University of California, San Diego.

Wanner, E. (1982, October). The electronic boogeyman. *Psychology Today,* pp. 8-11.

MALE BORDER WARS AS METAPHOR IN CAPTURE THE FLAG

Jay Mechling
University of California, Davis

The game of Capture the Flag remains a puzzling embarrassment for a male youth organization that for nearly 75 years has been denying it is a paramilitary movement. Capture the Flag, Color Wars, Capture the Staff, and their variants are war games as old as the Boy Scout movement itself. The organized game's roots are in the folk game of Scots and English, a self-conscious reenactment of the 18th-century border wars in the North. Across two centuries the game retained its vocabulary of "enemy," "enemy territory," "prisoner," "flag raiding," and its central object of seizing and carrying off the property of others. Baden-Powell's Boy Scout movement in England quite purposefully began as a corrective to the poor performance by young British soldiers in the Boer Wars. Ernest Thompson Seton, whose Woodcraft Indians was one of the youth movements combined to form the Boy Scouts of America in 1910 and who resigned from the latter organization in 1915 when it became too militaristic, enjoyed the game enough to propose in a 1906 letter to Baden-Powell a "capture-the-flag" competition between Eton and Harrow and to include a version of the game in his "Games and Athletic Standards" chapter of the first Boy Scouts of America *Handbook for Boys* (1911).

The puzzle of the attraction of this mock war game extends into the 1980s. It is difficult to imagine a Boy Scout troop less militaristic than the California Central Valley troop with whom I have done my fieldwork. And yet this troop plays Capture the Flag regularly. The male adults who have defined the movement since the beginning of this century and the boys who give life to the movement apparently see in this game something beyond the war game its formal characteristics define. Discovering the "something beyond the war game" is the goal of this essay. After sketching briefly the history of the game of Capture the Flag, I present a description of the game as it is played by a troop of Boy Scouts at their annual summer encampment in the

Sierra Nevada. The communications approach to play provides a means for unfolding the dialectic between the game text and the contexts that ground its meanings. Finally, I comment on the metaphorical borders suggested in my title, especially the male gender display made possible through the medium of this game.

HISTORY OF THE GAME

The roots of the modern game of Capture the Flag lie in 18th-century England, but even the earliest accounts of this game—sometimes known as "French and English" and sometimes as "Scots and English"—meet the strict anthropological definition of a true game. That is, the early accounts describe "a recreational activity characterized by (1) organized play, (2) competition, (3) two or more sides, (4) criteria for determining the winner, and (5) agreed-upon rules" (Roberts, Arth, & Bush, 1959, p. 597). Gomme (1964) describes the earliest version of this romantic model of border warfare between the Scots and English:

> Boys first choose sides . . . . The parties being at length formed, are separated by a real or imaginary line, and place at some distance behind them, in a heap, their hats, coats, . . . They stand opposite to each other, the object being to make a successful incursion over the line into the enemy's country, and bring off part of the heap of clothes. It requires both address and swiftness of foot to do so without being taken by the foe. The winning of the game is decided by which party first loses all of its men or its property. (p. 183)

The formal structure of this game as described by Gomme has remained remarkably stable over 200 years. It is a game of chase and capture, with the goal of penetrating the "enemy's" territory, seizing the enemy's property, and returning to safe territory without being captured and taken prisoner. Prisoners must remain in a "jail" until freed by a teammate, and in some versions a prisoner must be rescued before any more booty may be taken (Opie & Opie, 1969). The booty varies from clothing to handkerchiefs (as in Gomme's [1964] description of "French and English"), to sticks (Newell, 1963).

The historians of this game see as part of its attraction the romantic model of maurauding raids of the Borderers" (Opie & Opie, 1969, p. 147), and the English versions feature traditional taunts at the crucial border between friendly and enemy territory. Gomme (1964) offers two examples of taunts:

> King Covenanter, come out if ye daur venture!
> Set your foot on Scots' ground, English, if ye daur! (Chambers' Popular Rhymes, p. 127)

and "Here's a leap into thy kingdom, dry-bellied Scot" (pp. 183-184). The Opies (1969) add another taunt: "Here's a leg in thy land, thieving Sassenach" (p. 147).

The name "Capture the Flag" apparently appears only when the game passed from being a spontaneous self-structured game to being an "organized game," which means organized by adults for children with some adult end in mind. The organized version appeared almost simultaneously in the British and American Boy Scout Handbooks. In fact, there was considerable acrimony between Lord Baden-Powell and Ernest Thomson Seton over who brought into the movement a number of games, including "Flag Raiding," the Scout precursor to Capture the Flag. Thus, both Seton's chapter on "Games and Athletic Standards" for the first Boy Scouts of America *Handbook for Boys* (1911) and editions of Baden-Powell's *Scouting for Boys* (1915) from the same period have near-identical descriptions of "Flag Raiding." But in this case the game of French and English has been transformed into a game that better suits the goals of both Seton and Baden-Powell to train young men in the skills of scouting, stalking, and observing. In "Flag Raiding" there are two or more patrols of boys to a side, protecting in their own territory three flags (or, at night, three lanterns). An "outpost" protects the flags, while each side "sends out scouts to discover the enemy's position" (Boy Scouts of America, 1911, p. 306). As in war games, a scout seen by a stronger party is "out of action." At the end of play, sides tally points for flags captured, for sketches of enemy outposts, and for reports of movement of enemy scouts. With the stalking skill at its core, this is much more a game of strategy than of seizing property.

By 1917 the Boy Scouts of America *Handbook* described the modern game of Capture the Flag. The play is between two troops or two teams chosen in a troop and distinguished between those with a handkerchief or neckerchief tied to the arm and those without. A single flag mounted on a staff is placed within 100 paces of the center boundary. Boys guarding the flag may stand no closer than 50 feet from the flag unless an "enemy" enters that circle. Scouts caught in "enemy territory" are captured if the captor can grasp and hold the intruder while shouting "Caught, Caught, Caught." The captor accompanies the prisoner to the guard house, where he must keep a foot or hand on the prison base. A "friend" can free a prisoner by touching him, whereupon the two hold hands and have a "safe" return to their home territory. If an enemy seizes the flag but is caught before crossing into safe territory, the flag remains where the enemy is captured. A team wins by seizing the enemy flag and carrying it safely back to home territory or, if the flag is never captured, by having more prisoners than the other side at the end of the time limit.

It is clear from both the *Handbook for Boys* and from the *Handbook for Scoutmasters* from 1917 well into the 1930s that the intent of this game is to reinforce Scout skills and cooperation while providing healthy, strenuous physical activity. This overt adult agenda for the game is important to keep in mind when we examine the game as it is actually played by a troop of Boy Scouts, for the boys are able to do to this game what they do to so many games planned according to the official Scout agenda—namely, they transform the game into a highly personalized text that serves the boys' social and psychological needs rather than the adult goals. They turn a highly structured game into a multivocal performance celebrating the overthrow of structure.

THE GAME PERFORMED

Sutton-Smith (1971) complains that a chronic lacunae in the study of games is detailed accounts of games as they are actually played, as opposed to the formal accounts of their rules. Nowhere is this admonition better taken than in the study of Capture the Flag, for the "emergent" qualities of this game tend to be far more important than its official structural features. The following description is of games played by a troop of California Boy Scouts at their summer encampment high in the Sierra Nevada in 1979 and in 1981.

The game is a favorite of the boys, played by them at least once a week after dinner and before the evening campfire. The main players are the Scouts, ages 11 to 14, and occasionally a few of the Seniors, the older Scouts (ages 14 to 17) who are the camp staff and supervise most activities. Rarely do the adult Staff appear at the game site, so generally the game is played away from adult scrutiny, but supervised by one of the senior scouts.

The play space is rather rugged, liberally sprinkled with trees, logs, and granite boulders. It is a dangerous place to be running, by any sane judgment, and the danger increases as the light fades. But the boys view this as an ideal playing field for Capture the Flag, providing sufficient cover to make stalking as important a strategy as outright running. In fact, this feature of the play space is an equalizer of sorts. Whereas in flat, open field the fastest runners have a decided advantage, in this terrain the slower runner can rely upon slow stalking, camouflage, and cheating to compensate for speed.

The Senior in charge indicates the game boundaries as an official public announcement. The main center line, a dirt road, divides the space into two equal areas, the total playing area being a rectangle approximately 200 yards by 100 yards. The Senior in charge selects two younger Scouts as team captains who alternately select players until everyone is chosen. To distinguish the teams, one side takes off its shirts or wear neckerchiefs while the other does not. Each team then huddles to make some crucial decisions and assignments. The flag (in 1979 a neckerchief, in 1981 a frisbee) must be placed within a team's own territory where it is both visible and within the reach of the smallest Scout. Each team must select a spot for its jail, and each team must assign positions.

The forwards are the players who cross into enemy territory, usually for one or more of the following purposes: to capture the flag of the enemy and carry it back across the center line into safe territory without being caught; to divert the enemy defenders in such a way that another forward has a better chance to capture the flag; or to free the prisoners held in the enemy jail. The guards are the players who stay within their own territory to defend the flag. They are allowed to cross the center line (as are all players), but their game role is to chase and capture enemy forwards who encroach upon the defenders' territory. Some guards may be assigned specifically to guard the flag. The troop rule is that these guards must stand "at least a Cadillac's length away" from the flag unless they are chasing an enemy forward. This rule, among others, is the subject of many disputes during the game.

The third position is that of a jailer, a position sometimes occupied by a Scout with a physical impairment that keeps him from running. The jailer stands by the team's jail and watches over the captured enemy. The prisoners may not escape unless they are freed by a free forward, who must reach the jail, tag a prisoner for the count of three, and walk him hand-in-hand safely back across the center line.

Capturing is an important activity within this game. The capture of the enemy's flag is, of course, the goal of the game, the act that determines the winning side. Far more frequent is the capture of other players in enemy territory. The defender must chase, grab, and hold the enemy forward long enough to say "Troop Blahity-Blah," essentially the count of three that the official *Handbook* versions specify. The captured player must then cease resisting and go peacefully to jail, where he must wait until he is freed or the game ends.

This normative description of the capture glosses too quickly the features of a capture as actually performed. The space over which the game is played is so large that it is really very difficult for the Senior in charge to supervise the game. Away from scrutiny, the capture can become an invitation to violence. An explicit rule, "no fighting," confirms this invitation. At the very least, the capture is an event ripe for dispute, the word of one boy against another whether or not the one was held for the count of three. The act of freeing prisoners creates similar disputes, as does the capture of the flag. Scouts dispute over whether or not a defender was "at least a Cadillac's length" away from the flag. Since forwards capturing the flag are allowed to pass the flag while attempting to get it back into safe territory, there are disputes about whether a boy in possession of the flag was caught for the count of three before he passed it. And so it goes. The Senior referee sometimes steps in to resolve a dispute, especially if it appears that the parties involved are really angry about some infraction, but the usual course is to view the disputes as unimportant and enjoyable events in the game. I saw several boys throw considerable energy into arguing each capture and freeing, just to see how far they could push the rules.

This description so far has been about the roles, rules, and dispute of the game. At least as interesting is the matter of style that the boys bring to their play. First, the game is surprisingly verbal. Forwards taunt each other across the center line, though never in the couplets recorded in histories of the game. Forwards shout changes of strategy to one another, and guards shout warnings or call loudly for help when they see an incursion. Prisoners shout to their own forwards to free them and shout taunts like "base sticker" to the jailer or guards who hover near the jail. And, of course, the endless disputes are also highly verbal.

A second observation of the style of play is that each boy seems to want to seek out a role that suits his talents and personality. Forwards take joy in fast, elusive running or in slow, sneaky stalking. Both strategies entail a great deal of risk of capture, and therein lies the excitement of the forward's role. Also, Capture the Flag sometimes provides a boy the chance to openly sacrifice himself as a diversion so that others may have a better chance to capture the flag. Guards tend to be no less athletic than forwards. But being a guard entails no direct risk of being captured and, consequently, of being out of action for some time. The guard is always "in play" so to speak. His pleasure comes not from risk but from defense and the act of capturing another. The jailer is, as I have said, the most passive player in the game, and is almost always a hurt or minimally capable player. Yet the job is an important one and provides the player with some sense of identity in the game. The Opies (1969) are correct in their observation that in Capture the Flag every player is important.

The game ends either when one team captures the other's flag and returns it safely back to home territory or at the end of a time limit, in which case the winning team is the one with the most prisoners. The troop I observed often played two or three games within an hour's time, sometimes switching stronger players from one side to another if the initial choosing somehow created an imbalance of talent.

The game finished, the boys return to camp to prepare for the evening's program, either a patrol campfire or a troop campfire (Mechling, 1980), and then to bed in patrol campsites. The game of Capture the Flag was a brief suspension of their normal grouping as patrols, a source of identification to which they return later in the evening as confirmation that this is their "home" loyalty within the troop.

CONTEST AND ANTI-STRUCTURE

To see something more than the war game in Capture the Flag requires that we ask the sort of questions posed by the communications approach to play and games. Play is a framed subuniverse of experience that produces paradoxical statements about itself, about other subuniverses of experience, and about the taken-for-granted everyday world. If the highly structured, everyday world of the Boy Scout camp is communicated in the simple, declarative mood, and often in the imperative, then the games of these boys are in the subjunctive. The "as if" mood of play gives it the power to comment upon everyday life in ways that would be too frightening or too disruptive if done "for real." "We face then two peculiarities of play," writes Bateson (1972) in a characteristic understatement, "(a) that the messages or signals exchange in play are in a certain sense untrue or not meant; and (b) that that which is denoted by these signals is nonexistent" (p. 183). The play frame is metacommunicative, creating a class of messages that comment upon other classes of messages. Further, although he does not quite say so, Bateson (1972) seems to suggest in his analogy between a game of canasta and psychotherapy that what distinguishes games from less formal play frames is the fact that the explicit rules of a game more or less reduce the realm of rules-in-use subject to the metacommunication necessary to sustain the play frame.

It is the power to generate paradoxical statements about persons, objects, and events (Schwartzman, 1979) that makes games and related secular rituals particularly self-reflexive (Handelman, 1982). For Handleman (1977), the special quality of the play frame is that it doubts the social order upon which it comments, while ritual frames more often confirm and integrate that order. Mary Douglas' (1975) analysis of jokes similarly stresses the self-reflexive power of the play frame.

Like jokes, play selects not just any aspect of routine existence for its self-reflexive comment, but chooses especially conditions of confict. Abrahams' (1972) rhetorical approach to play and games, resting as much upon Kenneth Burke as upon Bateson, reminds us that the dramatization of conflict is play's most powerful mode of self-reflexivity. Games and other expressive folk genres give "a 'name' to the threatening forces both within and without the group," presenting "these names in a contrived, artificial form and context, giving the impression that the forces are being controlled" (p. 18). The *agon,* or conflict, gives dramatic structure to play, but the formal characteristics of games make them particularly efficacious frames for the dramatization of conflict.

The characteristic of games that make them good models of conflict would seem to be as threatening as the everyday world they are meant to dramatize if it were not that games often use disorder to affirm order of a different kind. Handelman (1976) observes in the natural setting games that he studies "the encapsulation of opposition within boundaries of solidarity in a manner which encourages the exhibition of conflict in order to demonstrate the strength and viability of cohesion and integration" (p. 439). Games remind the players of the most amazing paradox of culture—"that social cohesion is most fully sensed in terms of the antagonisms felt within the group" (Abrahams, 1968, pp. 147-148). This cohesion is doubtless the sort found in Turner's (1969) *communitas.* Douglas (1975) makes this same claim for jokes. How a game, one of the most structured forms of play, can lead the players through the conflict of competition, through disorder and doubt, to a new integration of *communitas* is surely among the most miraculous transformations of play.

A final point to be made about games as framed message systems is that the dramatization of conflict in the game is stylized, which is to say that the messages within the frame take full advantage of the expressiveness of metaphors and other tropes (Fernandez, 1974) and even of the "affecting presence" of the game experience as it presents itself as itself rather than standing for something else (Armstrong, 1981). Thus, not only does the symbolism of the game encode something about the structures and relationships of other realities, but as importantly about moods (Geertz, 1973). The taunts across the center line in Capture the Flag, for example are pure expressions of mood, but mood stylized. Abrahams' (1972) point is that this stylization contributes to the players' perception that conflict and chaos are under control, thereby creating "an atmosphere in which pleasure may occur because the feeling of control is transferred magically from the formal expression to the situation itself" (p. 18).

The communications approach to games suggest that Capture the Flag is a frame of stylized dramatic performances within which the Boy Scout players objectify contradictory and threatening elements of the institution, comment upon those elements through the structure and moods of the game, and finally confirm their *communitas* through the impression that they have controlled or tamed the anxiety-producing contradictions and conflicts in the social order of the Boy Scout camp. This much said, what might be the contradictions and conflicts this particular group of boys best work out through the medium of Capture the Flag?

The conflicts turn out to cluster around two of the "emotional bonds of modern society" (Sennett, 1980): authority and fraternity. Richard Sennett (1980) calls authority "the emotional expression of power" (p. 4), and it should surprise nobody that a good deal of what goes on at a Boy Scout camp has to do with male power and authority (Mechling, 1981). Among other things, games are dramatic models of power (Sutton-Smith, 1971), so let us look at what the game of Capture the Flag does to and for the ordinary patterns of authority and power at a Boy Scout camp.

At its outset, the game suspends the normal identities and rules of the camp. Normal identity in the troop is ascribed through the patrol, one of the four subgroups (Bear, Eagle, Snake, or Tiger) to which a boy belongs in this troop. Capture the Flag is one of the few games in camp where the contest is not between patrols. The game could be played two patrols to the side, but it is not. Instead, choosing sides destroys the normal lines of affiliation and loyalty within the troop and creates new, temporary loyalties. The game also plays with identity in another sense, to the degree that the game provides three sorts of roles—forward, guard, jailer—to which the boys might gravitate. Each game role requires a different sort of skill level and temperament, as described earlier, and it is likely that these game roles (chaser, chasee, jailer) allow the boy to experiment with relative proportions of aggression and passivity in her personality.

Similarly, the game casts doubt upon the normal rules of camp. The certain, inflexible rules of camp life are set against the dispute-ridden rules-in-use of the game. The pervasive testing of rules and outright cheating in the game are a disorderly comment upon the rigid rules of camp. Moreover, there are specific camp rules the game challenges. Most obvious are the camp rules against running and fighting. The nature of the game space and its central element of capture make the game an easy outlet for violence. Still another camp rule challenged by the game is the right of territory. The patrols generally respect each other's territory and belongings in camp, but a central feature of the game is penetrating the other's territory and carrying off his property. The symbolism of the flag is relevant in this regard, as each patrol campsite features its patrol flag. Seizing a symbolic flag, be it neckerchief, signal flag, or frisbee, is a violation of the other's symbol of patrol identity in the troop.

There are two sources of authority among the boys in the troop, authority through rank and authority through office. Each of these is subject to comment in the game of Capture the Flag. Authority by rank arises out of the boy's acquiring badges of rank (Tenderfoot, Second Class, First Class, on up to Eagle Scout) that represent levels of knowledge, skill, and achievement. Authority by rank represents some mixture of intelligence and physical skill, but a good deal more of the former. The boys comment quite frequently how much like school are the advancement classes at camp, and the boy's attitude toward advancement as well as his actual advancement depend largely upon his attitude toward school. The game of Capture the Flag nicely cuts through matters of strategy and "school smarts." Although the *Handbook* and its adult goals appreciate the chance for the boys to exercise stalking skills and strategy, the fact is that the game favors physical ability. The two main activities, running and physically capturing another boy for the count of three, are the key to success or failure in the game. So, just as this troop's Treasure Hunt game undercuts the myth of strategy and skill with the game-determining reality of chance (Mechling, 1984), so Capture the Flag undercuts the ideology of strategy with the game-determining reality of physical skill. Put differently, the athletic boy who does poorly in school and struggles with his Scout advancement through the ranks has the opportunity for unqualified success in this game of physical skill.

The game of Capture the Flag also comments upon the authority of office. Each patrol has its patrol leader and assistant patrol leader, and the camp itself has a distribution of offices among the Seniors, such as Senior Patrol Leader, Scribe, Quartermaster, Head of Commissary, Campfire Director, Advancement Director, and the like. The game undermines the authority of office in several ways. Choosing sides along lines that erase patrol identifications means that in the game's space and time the normal authority of patrol leaders and assistant patrol leaders no longer applies. This makes possible not only verbal aggression through taunts but physical violence toward a bossy patrol leader or Senior. Disputes over rules in this game also tend to make irrelevant the power of the central interpreter of rules, the Senior in Charge.

This discussion of the ways in which the game of Capture the Flag provides a frame for doubting the normal lines of authority and power in the Boy Scout troop might lead us to conclude that this is only a game of disorder and inversion, but such is not the case. The game dramatizes fraternity. It contributes powerfully to the *communitas* the boys create in the face of the adult agenda for the organization. The game provides two dramatic displays of self-sacrifice for the group, one an explicit feature of the game and the other a peculiar feature that, at first glance, appears to be not a part of the game at all.

The first symbolic display of self-sacrifice is provided by the game strategy that requires that a forward draw defenders away from the flag so that a comrade has a better chance of capturing the flag. This is a central strategy even in the official versions of the game, for example in the 1917 *Handbook for Boys*. The second dramatic display of self-sacrifice is a good deal more subtle. Every time I have witnessed the troop play Capture the Flag, there is at least one case of moderate injury. Boys trip and fall and hurt one another in capture. Once a boy fell victim to a severe insect sting. The "natural attitude" of the game participants on the occasion of a relatively severe injury is to "break frame" and suspend play until the injured boy is cared for or leaves the playing field. Like the boys, I took these injuries to be outside the play frame, events that are natural outcomes of the conditions of play but that follow rules different from the game's.

I now believe that these "injury events" are most likely "injury displays" that are as much a part of the game as asides are crucial aids in framing and interpreting a verbal narrative (Georges, 1981). I call them "injury displays" not because the boys "fake" the injuries, but because the injured boy becomes the center of a symbolic ritual easily as complex and important as the game itself. Consider what happens when a boy stumbles over a log and goes sprawling across a stretch of granite and brush. Play stops; rules are suspended. Those closest to the boy, including his pursuer (or pursued) stop to see if he is hurt. If he is, the Senior referee and others administer first aid (an important Scout skill), sending for the camp first-aid kit if necessary. Others stand nearby, awaiting the outcome of the diagnosis. Boys express concern and encouragement. Sometimes the boy will "walk it off" and resume play; at other times, a severe or convenient injury will mean the boy retires from the game. Often he stays in the game area to watch with the Senior referee. What has happened?

The injury and response, the "injury display" text, is a necessary element of the game of Capture the Flag. It is necessary as a cybernetic correction to keep contest under control. The game is highly competitive and violent, features that serve useful functions in the play frame as the occasion for metacommunication about matters of power, rules, and identity in everyday life at Scout camp. But these same qualities that make the game a useful metaphor for dealing with these other issues also threaten to run out of control if not checked by some process intrinsic to the game itself. The injury display is that check. Totally unpremeditated but equally inevitable, the injury event stops the contest and the violence long enough to permit the boys to show the nurturance and the caring that the institution values so much. There is a lesson in androgyny in this cybernetic process, the developmental task of males being to some extent learning how to "mitigate agency with communion" (Spence & Helmreich, 1978, p. 18).

There is one other important function served by the "injury performance" in Capture the Flag. To be injured in team sports, as in battle, is to have earned the badge of courage and sacrifice. The injured boy most likely feels justified in terms of the game: he was hurt in service of his fellows. "Walking it off," that is, enduring the hurt and resuming play, is a sure sign of masculine courage.

MALE BORDERS

Borders are the "hot" culture zones where the business at hand is the symbolic display of difference, and the literal "border crossings" in this game are as aggressive and violent as one is likely to find in other verbal and physical displays of dominance in adolescent male groups. The game creates its anti-structure through mockery and inversion of the everyday structures of Boy Scout camp life. The game destroys normal patterns of authority and makes accessible to some boys the power and prestige not normally theirs. The game is a perfect model of the male contest (Gouldner, 1965, p. 13), in which one wins by "putting down" the other through physical violence (Dundes, 1978). As a male model of power, the game favors physical skill over strategy and chance (Sutton-Smith, 1971, Robinson, 1978). Some players even use the game to "mask" the violence and revenge that are their real motives for playing the game (Sutton-Smith, 1983).

The problem is that the game's mockery and inversion, its disorderliness, tend to spill over into the realm of fraternity, of friendship, thereby becoming dysfunctional. Not even Abrahams' generous view of the cohesive possibilities in the dramatization of conflict is much help in seeing the anti-structure of Capture the Flag as anything other than disorderly, violent, and destructive of fraternity. Contest seems a poor medium for the expression of male friendship. Is there no way to see anti-structure as something more than the inversion of normative social order, as something more like the authentic bonding Turner apparently means when he writes of the fraternity of *communitas*?

The answer lies, I believe, in the game text itself, in the self-sacrifice and injury events that affirm fraternity. Sutton-Smith (1977) wants us to call "proto-structural" that part of the anti-structure that "is the precursor of innovative normative forms . . . . the source of new culture" (p. 25). What I would call proto-structural in the game of Capture the Flag are those moments and performances of sacrifice and nurturance we ordinarily associate with the feminine. The fraternity of *communitas* requires some androgeny in its male communicants, and I am one of those people who considers innovative the American male's recapturing of portions of his experience he heretofore relegated to females (Miller, 1976). In a real sense, one of the male borders crossed in this game is that between the masculine self and the feminine. This is the wonder of the game of Capture the Flag, that in the midst of an aggressively male mockery and inversion of authority there is glimpsed the possibility of fraternity based upon qualities considered feminine in American culture. For the boys to value these qualities is a male border crossing far more significant than any other.

REFERENCES

Abrahams, R.D. (1968). Introductory remarks to a rhetorical theory of folklore. *Journal of American Folklore, 81,* 143-158.

Abrahams, R.D. (1972). Personal power and social restraint in the definition of folklore. In A. Paredes & R. Bauman (Eds.), *Toward new perspectives in folklore* (pp. 16-30). Austin: University of Texas Press.

Abrahams, R.D. (1981). Shouting match at the border: The folklore of display events. In R. Bauman and R.D. Abrahams (Eds.), *"And other neighborly names": Social process and cultural image in Texas folklore* (pp. 303-325). Austin: University of Texas Press.

Armstrong, R.P. (1981). *The powers of presence: Consciousness, myth, and affecting presence.* Philadelphia: University of Pennsylvania Press.

Baden-Powell, R. (1915). *Scouting for boys.* London: C. Arthur Pearson, Ltd.

Bateson, G. (1972). A theory of play and fantasy. In *Steps to an ecology of mind* (pp. 177-193). New York: Ballantine. (Reprinted from American Psychiatric Association, *Psychiatric research reports, 11,* December 1953)

Boy Scouts of America. (1911). *The official handbook for boys.* Garden City, NY: Doubleday, Page & Company.

Boy Scouts of America. (1917). *The official handbook for boys* (16th ed.). Garden City, NY: Doubleday, Page & Company.

Boy Scouts of America. (1928). *Revised handbook for boys.* New York: Boy Scouts of America.

Boy Scouts of America. (1934). *Handbook for scoutmasters* (Second handbook). New York: Boy Scouts of America.

Boy Scouts of America. (1938). *Handbook for scoutmasters* (Third handbook). New York: Boy Scouts of America.

Douglas, M. (1975). Jokes. In M. Douglas, *Implicit meanings* (pp. 90-114). London: Routledge and Kegan Paul.

Dundes, A. (1978). Into the endzone for a touchdown: A psychoanalitic consideration of American football. *Western Folklore, 37,* 75-88.

Fernandez, J. (1974). The mission of metaphor in expressive culture. *Current Anthropology, 15,* 119-145.

Forbush, W.B., & Allen, H.R. (1927). *The book of games for home, school, and playground.* Philadelphia: John C. Winston Company.

Geertz, C. (1973) *The interpretation of cultures.* New York: Basic Books, Inc.

Georges, R.A. (1981). Do narrators really digress? A reconsideration of "audience asides" in narrating. *Western Folklore, 40,* 245-252.

Gomme, A.B. (1964). *The traditional games of England, Scotland, and Ireland.* New York: Dover Publications, Inc. (Originally published, vol. 1, 1894, vol. 2, 1898)

Gouldner, A.W. (1965). *Enter Plato: Classical Greece and the origins of social theory.* New York: Basic Books, Inc.

Handelman, D. (1976). Rethinking "banana time": Symbolic integration in a work setting. *Urban Life, 4,* 433-48.

Handelman, D. (1977). Play and ritual: Complimentary frames of metacommunication. In A.J. Chapman & H.C. Foots (Eds.), *It's a funny thing, humour* (pp. 185-192). Oxford: Pergamon.

Handelman, D. (1982). Reflexivity in festival and other cultural events. In M. Douglas (Ed.), *Essays in the sociology of perception* (pp. 162-190). London: Routledge and Kegan Paul.

Mechling, J. (1980). The magic of the boy scout campfire. *Journal of American Folklore, 93,* 35-56.

Mechling, J. (1981). Male gender display at a boy scout camp. In R.T. Sieber & A.J. Gordon (Eds.), *Children and their organizations: Investigations in American culture* (pp. 138-160). Boston: G.K. Hall & Co.

Mechling, J. (1984). Patois and paradox in a boy scout treasure hunt. *Journal of American Folklore, 97,* 22-42.

Milberg, A. (1976). *Street games.* New York: McGraw-Hill.

Miller, J.B. (1976). *Toward a new psychology of women.* Boston: Beacon Press.

Newell, W.W. (1963). *Games and songs of American children* (New York: Dover Publications, Inc. (Originally published, 1883)

Opie, I., & Opie, P. (1969). *Children's games in street and playground.* Oxford: Clarendon Press

Roberts, J.M., Arth, M.J., & Bush, R.R. (1959). Games in culture. *American Anthropologist, 61,* 597-605.

Robinson, C. (1978, spring). Sex-typed behavior in children's play. The Association for the Anthropological Study of Play *Newsletter, 4,* 14-17.

Schwartzman, H.B. (1976). The anthropological study of children's play. In B.J. Siegel, A.R. Beals, and S.A. Tyler (Eds.), *Annual Review of Anthropology* (pp. 289-328). Palo Alto, CA: Annual Reviews, Inc., Vol. 5.

Scwartzman, H.B. (1979). The sociocultural context of play. In B. Sutton-Smith (Ed.), *Play and learning* (pp. 239-255). New York: Gardner Press, Inc.

Sennett, R. (1980). *Authority.* New York: Vintage Books.

Smith, C.F. (1934). *Games and game leadership.* New York: Dodd Mead and Company.

Spence, J.T., & Helmreich, R.L. (1978). *Masculinity and femininity: Their psychological dimensions, correlates, and antecedents.* Austin: University of Texas Press.

Sutton-Smith, B. (1971). Play, games, and controls. In J.P. Scott & S.B. Scott (Eds.), *Social control and social change* (pp. 73-102). Chicago: University of Chicago Press.

Sutton-Smith, B. (1977, fall). Games of order and disorder. The Association for the Anthropological Study of Play *Newsletter, 4,* 19-26.

Sutton-Smith, B. (1983). The masks of play. In B. Sutton-Smith & D. Kelly-Byrne (Eds.), *The masks of play.* West Point, NY: Leisure Press.

Turner, V. (1969). *The ritual process: Structure and anti-structure.* Ithaca, NY: Cornell University Press.

SYMBOL, CELEBRATION, AND THE REDUCTION OF CONFLICT: WOMEN'S FIELD HOCKEY, A GAME IN TRANSITION

Roberta J. Park
University of California, Berkeley

A growing number of scholars who have contributed to our understanding of games and sports in sociocultural contexts have demonstrated that such phenomena are likely to be far more complex than was once assumed (e.g., Geertz, 1972; Blanchard, 1981; Morris, 1981; Azoy, 1982; Lever, 1983). A number of these studies have attained a more powerful level of analysis and interpretation by developing due attention to the historical developments. There have been several recent attempts by some historians and anthropologists to achieve new ways of viewing and presenting evidence in which intellectual insights from both disciplines are utilized. Historian Natalie Davis (1982), for example, has declared that anthropological studies, especially those concerned with symbolism, have been especially useful in causing historians to pay attention to and rethink events that they had formerly tended to dismiss as arbitrary or inconsequential, and anthropologist Clifford Geertz (1980) has informed his study of state organization in 19th-century Bali by interpreting historical documents, inscriptions, and texts "in terms of ecological, ethnographic and sociological processes" (p. 6).

John MacAloon's *This Great Symbol: Pierre de Coubertin and the Origins of the Modern Olympic Games* (1981) makes creative use of intellectual insights from the fields of "history, anthropology, sociology, psychology, literary criticism, and classical studies" (p. xii). Expanding upon and extending Bateson's (1972) work concerning play frames, contexts, and meta-communication, and Goffman's (1974) analyses of keyings, transformation, and the laminating of organizing and interpretive frames, this elegant study offers a penetrating analysis of the layers of symbolic frameworks in which the athletic contests of the 1896 Olympic games were embedded. Noting that athletes, spectators, and organizers were often confounded by numerous ambiguities, MacAloon (1981) points out that it would take many years before the Games would become established as a "consensual and predictable" cross-cultural category of performance of the type that "Gregory Bateson and Erving Goffman have taught us to recognize in culturally framed performances" (p. 270).

In a related paper dealing with the nature of spectacle in modern societies, MacAloon (1984) proposes a multidimensional analytical model for studying the mulitiplicity of performative layers that constitute the more recent Olympic Games. In this paper the author points out how various developments that have occurred since the 1920s and 1930s have threatened to "break the frame" of the Games, and in doing so have transformed the frames from "the indicative to the interrogative mood."

The present investigation deals with women's field hockey, a sport that has undergone considerable transition since the mid-1970s. It uses methods and insights derived from both history and anthropology. It focuses upon both change and persistence within the "total universe" of the sport of women's field hockey in the United States, especially in the late 1970s and early 1980s, a period during which the traditional "frames" in which the game was embedded were abruptly broken. Specifically, it looks at ways in which both the United States Field Hockey Association (USFHA), the main governing body, and individual players have sought to maintain something of the former sense of "ideal community" (cf. Turner, 1974, 1977) of the world of women's field hockey, while acknowledging and supporting the importance of preparing a small elite group for international competitions and implementing major structural changes to make the preparation of such a team possible.

The study focuses on the Northern California Field Hockey Association (NCFHA) and its involvement in Association, Sectional, and National competitions during the 1982 season. Participant observations were carried out during eight Sundays of regular season Association level play, the 2-day Pacific Southwest Region (PSW) Tournament, and the 3½-day National Region (PSW) Tournament, and the 3½-day National Hockey Festival. A pilot study, conducted during the 1981 playing season, had suggested that because the sport of women's field hockey was in transition, it would be useful to devote particular attention to the framing contexts (cf. Bateson, 1972; Goffman, 1974; MacAloon, 1981, 1984) in which the competitions were held. The author's acquaintance with earlier (i.e., prior to mid-1970s) methods employed for selecting the "national team," the well-specified transitions through Association, Sectional, and National competition, and the nature of the awards ceremonies and banquets suggest that Turner's (1969, 1974, 1977) work on *com-*

munitas was relevant. These are the theoretical backdrops against which the data of this study have been examined.

The investigator has been a member of the NCFHA for nearly 3 decades. While this has been useful in helping inform the historical aspects of the study, the personal connection raises problems of possible distortion and bias. In an effort to correct for this, the views of other players who had been connected with the NCFHA in the 1950s, 1960s, and 1970s have been obtained. Individual players may be competent to express their personal views of past events; however, these need to be checked against documentary sources. Moreover, individual players do not necessarily represent the "official" position of governing bodies. In an effort to obtain such information, a variety of written documents was consulted. These included such ephemeral material as: the "Hockey Briefs," a mimeographed mailing by which the NCFHA has usually informed its membership of tournament games, team standings, forthcoming tournaments, the names of "selected" players, a variety of tournament and banquet programs, and miscellaneous reports. *The Eagle,* the official journal of the USFHA, provided the most substantial source of evidence for the official position of the organization. Generally, *The Eagle* must be seen as a publication that reflects the opinions of individuals whose views are in concert with those of the elected—or the acknowledged—power structure of the USFHA. However, occasional commentaries, even articles, can be found that were critical of the official position.

BACKGROUND TO THE LATE 1970s

In the United States, until quite recently field hockey has been an almost exclusive domain for girls and women. It is broadly agreed that Constance M.K. Applebee introduced the game from England at the 1901 Harvard Summer School. Club hockey was soon established in the Philadelphia area, and colleges and universities in the early 1900s included field hockey among those sports that were appropriate for young women. A United States team, organized by Ms. Applebee, visited Britain in 1920. An English team returned the visit in 1921. In 1922 the USFHA was established, and from the very beginning it adopted many structures and ideologies from the All-England Women's Hockey Association (e.g., "U.S. Team Tour," 1930; "International Federation," 1937; USFHA "National Tournament Program," 1940; "International News," 1951; "West of England," 1952; "All England," 1961; MacKay, 1963; Park, 1976; "Passing of an Era," 1981). Over the decades summer hockey camps, the best known being Ms. Applebee's at Mt. Pocono, frequently featured English coaches.

Touring teams from Great Britain and Commonwealth countries were invited to visit and play exhibition games in various parts of the United States, and *The Eagle* often included information about hockey in Great Britain and Commonwealth countries.

Starting in the 1960s, some attention was also given to those teams from the Continent that were beginning to capture a larger share of the victories in international competitions. Two styles of team play were noted: "The Classic," which was described as "flowing and graceful," exemplified by British and Commonwealth teams; and "The Continental," which was characterized as strong and aggressive play, the type of hockey mostly played by Western European teams (Stewart, 1971). A growing rift between these two styles of play, and between what was perceived by some to be a different value structure regarding the importance of winning vis-a-vis adherence to conventional values of sportsmanship, became clearly evident at the 1971 IFWHA Conference in Auckland, New Zealand.[1] In general, however, a connection between field hockey in the United States and in the United Kingdom, especially regarding the official "attitudes" toward the game, continued to be reinforced through participation in the quadriennial International Federation of Women's Hockey Association's (IFWHA) tournaments. These were heavily dominated by ideologies derived largely from 20th-century distillations of 19th-century English "public" (private) school sport.[2]

The organizational structure of the USFHA traditionally was intensely pyramidal, and constant efforts were made to reinforce something akin to "normative" and ideal *communitas"* (Turner, 1974, 1977). This structure included: Club Teams, Associations, Sectional Tournaments, and a culminating National Tournament at which the US and Reserve Teams were chosen. The transitions of individual players at each of these stages were often marked by a series of events that drew attention to their more elevated status. Men, and women who had never been players, were largely excluded from the "inner lore" of the game.

In 1975, in response to dramatically changing attitudes regarding women in sports, as well as pressures from Title IX legislation and anticipated litigations, this longstanding structure of the USFHA underwent rapid and in some ways dislocating changes. In particular, the selection of a US team was dissociated from the traditional sequence of connected steps from Club team to National Tournament. The route to the US team was now achieved by nomination to participation at an ascending series of developmental camps. It was no longer necessary for individual players to pass through the various tournaments as part of an actual and ideal communal whole (i.e., on Association and Sectional teams).

In spite of its commitment to the support of an elite team for international, especially Olympic, competitions, the USFHA (now part of a more broadly conceived "USA Field Hockey," the US Olympic

Committee-appointed national governing body for women's field hockey) has sought to implement various programs aimed at maintaining something of the traditional ideal community within the world of women's field hockey (e.g., Junior Hockey and Masters, both of which literally and symbolically extend the ideal). Pragmatically, Junior Hockey also may serve to improve the pool from which an elite national squad may be drawn. In addition to efforts on the part of the USFHA, the players themselves also engage in a variety of practices that attempt to reinforce the concept of community. It is primarily the activities of the players at each level of competition during the 1982 season that are discussed in the following sections.

THE NCFHA

When the NCFHA was officially founded in 1929, local Club competitions had already taken place for several years. For the past 5 decades NCFHA has conducted an autumn season (Park, 1976). The season traditionally terminated in time for the PSW tournament and the USFHA National Tournament at Thanksgiving. Players attend from a radius of up to 100 miles, and a few come from longer distances. The standard of play among the strongest NCFHA teams has become quite good. During the 1982 season, 130 players were affiliated with the nine teams that made up the Association. A few of these have played with the NCFHA for at least 25 years; the majority have been with the Association between 3 and 10 years. About 15 percent are still in college. The vast majority are physical educators. Five are attorneys, and one is a medical doctor. A weekly "Hockey Briefs" is mailed to all members, informing them of game scores, team standings, playing schedules, and news of forthcoming local, sectional, and national events. In general, players tend to remain with the team with which they first affiliated. Efforts over several years to divide the Association in order to reduce travel distances have been repeatedly resisted on the grounds that players do not want to break away from their teams. In recent years, new players have been assigned to teams by means of a "draft." While this does help somewhat equalize the playing strength of the teams, many object that they would prefer to be on teams with their friends. The total number of teams has remained constant for several years. The reasons for this are not entirely clear, but the general impressions of the current membership are that: newer players are not made to feel welcome unless they have a friend who can help them develop strong bonds with a particular team, one major reason for objection to the "draft"; a 10- to 12-week commitment is too constraining; and those who have experienced a highly structured and intense intercollegiate program find the relative informality of the NCFHA incompatible with their ideas of competitive sports. It should be noted, however, that the actual competitions are often very intense, and the standard of play can be quite good. What these individuals seem to object to are the absence of regular training sessions, the lack of intensity in pregame preparations, a sense that it is unnecessary to make a deep commitment, and poor fields.

The fields where the majority of the NCFHA games are scheduled are in rather poor condition. They are adjacent to the local university's football stadium. After important games, they are littered with garbage, broken bottles, and other more offensive refuse. A different team is assigned each week to line the fields and set up the goal cages. The NCFHA is not permitted to use the excellent women's intercollegiate field nearby. In addition to problems created by wear and tear, the implication in part is that Club hockey, which literally is open to any woman, is nowhere near as meritorious as are elite intercollegiate teams that now select, if not recruit, their members. However, the Association has for years steadfastly rejected committing itself to generating the funds to obtain its own fields, and only pays a small annual sum for rental.

Each Sunday during the season players arrive by car (singly or, more often, with one or two friends) about a half hour before their games. Acknowledgments of recognition and brief conversations occur at the parking area. Players then head with their equipment to the wall of the small structure that abuts on the field. Many meet each other at the rest rooms, the early morning trip having taken an hour or more. Several stop at a display of sportswear that features hockey equipment and an array of logos set up by the owners of a local sporting goods store who are NCFHA players. Players form loose little groups as they change their shoes, stretch, and warm up by hitting the ball. Talk centers on sports topics, not necessarily hockey, and conversations about friends and associates.

Usually, games start and end more or less on time, and teams are not required to have a full complement of 11 players. In general, the teams that have been in existence the longest are thought to be the best teams. They tend to dominate in the season's standing, but some newer teams are becoming very strong. Traditionally, NCFHA teams have taken the names of dogs: Foxies (Fox Terriers) Pups (once, but no longer, composed of some of the youngest players), Irish (Terriers). Unless it is pointed out to them, newer players are not aware that "Irish," for example, stands for Irish Terriers. Former players, now retired but still affiliated with the NCFHA, are called "Setters." Evidently, during the formative years of the NCFHA many of the members owned dogs and this stimulated the naming trend *(Pacific Coast Sectional Hockey Tournament Program,* November 29-30, 1935).

Each team has its distinctive uniform consisting of a shirt of one color and a kilt of another. Most of the players appear for their Sunday Club games in uniform, but it is not unusual to see some in shorts or sweat suits. As long as this does not cause confusion for the other team or for the umpires, no one seems to mind very much. In general, the games are contested in a spirited manner. Some teams are known for complaining about the officiating and arguing with each other during play. Other teams are known for being "fun" to play because the players are both "good sports" and, in general, well skilled. After a game, team members usually come together briefly to cheer the other team, the game itself, and unless there has been some highly disputed call, the officials. Most teams shake hands with several of their opponents; some teams rarely do so. After the games many players hang around to talk about their just-finished games and watch other games. Some drive off to local quick-service food stands and return with food and drinks to watch other games or wait for the Selection "trials" that will occur later in the day.

Few men watch the games, but one, whose wife is a former national player and now a member of the NCFHA, is actively involved in officiating. During the past few years both the uniform and the "symbols of office" of field hockey have changed. Whereas the former official uniform was a plain white blouse, dark skirt, and jacket bearing the emblem of the USFHA and the individual's achieved officiating level (e.g., Sectional "A", National), the new uniform features a shirt of broad black and white stripes. Previously, umpires used only a whistle, hand signals, and voice instructions. Now they also carry green, yellow, and red "warning cards." These changes reflect practices in international field hockey that in turn reflect men's international soccer practices. The assumed need for warning cards in place of the former and rare verbal admonishment is seen by some of the older players as yet a further indication of an undesirable trend toward a relaxation of the sportsmanship standards that were traditionally supposed to be integral to the game.

At the end of the 1982 season the NCFHA perpetual trophy was awarded, at an informal ceremony, to the team with the best "win-loss" record. This trophy is rarely seen until about a week before the end of the season, when it is casually displayed. Sometimes there has been no actual presentation, only the announcement of the winning team in the "Hockey Briefs." The customary practice is for the captain to take it home for the year. No one seems to be very impressed by the trophy itself, an inexpensive silver-plated dish upon which the names and dates of the season's winners are engraved. There is, however, a fairly intense rivalry among many of the teams to be declared the NCFHA "winner." Tempers sometimes flare, especially between members of teams that have been high in previous season's standings or that are in close competition for the present season's trophy.

Until the late 1970s, the only way a player might become a member of the USFHA National team was by being "selected" on the basis of observed playing performance at the Association, then the Sectional, then the National tournaments. This system was often criticized on the grounds that selector's decisions regarding who was the best player at each position were too subjective and idiosyncratic, if not explicitly biased. Others felt it was ridiculous to have a "national" team that had only played together on a few occasions (e.g., "Letter to the Editor," 1976). As the United States moved toward greater involvement in women's international sports competition, new ways were needed to prepare elite teams.

With the establishment in 1976 of a program of increasingly selective Developmental Camps for the selection of a US squad, the traditional route to an elite national team was eliminated ("First Developmental Camp," 1976). It might seem, therefore, that there would be no reason to continue the Sectional Tournament or to have some type of "national" event. This has not yet been the case. The Pacific Southwest Sectional Tournament continues, and the USFHA has retained its sponsorship of a national event. The form that the latter takes, however, has changed markedly. NCFHA players who wish to "stand for selections" remain after the club games and participate in additional games constructed for this purpose. Several years ago players were selected during the regular club games. This was abandoned for three reasons: watching so many players was cumbersome; selectors were often engaged in their own team's games or were needed to officiate; and a few individuals felt this tended to interfere with "club team" spirit, as a player might be more interested in "looking good" for selectors than in contributing to the team's efforts.

THE PWS TOURNAMENT

The Pacific Southwest Sectional Tournament, which now brings together teams from the Los Angeles Field Hockey Association, the San Diego Field Hockey Association, and the NCFHA has traditionally taken place 2 or 3 weeks before the USFHA National Tournament — now the National Hockey Festival. It alternates between the north and the south of the state, a pattern that has existed for several decades. Three "Sectional" teams were chosen in 1982. These, and the Sectional Masters team, represented the PSW at the National Festival.

It is perhaps understandable that the Sectional Tournament involves more conspicuous symbolism than that which is evident during the regular season. First, it is a kind of culmination of the season's efforts. Second, the teams are composed of players who have undergone the trials of the local Association "selections" process and have emerged "transformed" into 1st, 2nd, and 3rd Association team players. This new team affiliation remains important from the beginning of the tournament until the PSW teams are named at the conclusion. Third, the competitions are against comparable groups from outside the Association clan. On the "Sectional" teams (1st, 2nd, and 3rd) that will emerge at the conclusion of the PSW tournament, individual players will again be incorporated into new teams on which they will now identify with the larger Section, rather than the smaller Associations.

A variety of things occur that establish and reinforce a sense of community that "frames" team within Association, Association within Section, and Section within the total field-hockey world. For the Sectional Tournament, players devote much more attention to proper uniform. The number-one teams receive the best (usually newest) NCFHA uniforms. (Each of the three Association teams will have its distinct uniform.) If the venue is sufficiently far away, team members usually stay at the same motel and "hang around together," talking hockey and giving each other emotional support (e.g., "You can fake X out and beat her to the ball"). The PSW banner, symbolic of the "Sectional" nature of the tournament, is displayed. So is the national Masters Trophy, won by the PSW Masters Team the three years the award has existed.[3] Badges, pins, and clothing with a variety of hockey logos are worn, and the ubiquitous hockey bags, which announce the owner's achievements—or aspirations—adorn the sidelines.

Pregame activities are similar to those that accompany the Association games, but the atmosphere is much more intense. Immediately prior to their match, team members come together, ostensibly to discuss strategy but more often to provide each other with moral support and reinforce "team unity." (There is much positive chatter and some backslapping, and comments like "We can *do* it" are frequent.) For the duration of the game, and for some time before and after it, team members are literally transformed into a small, intense community. "Applebee Bear," a brown and gold teddy-bear (brown and gold are the PSW colors)—named for the "mother" of American women's field hockey, Ms. Constance M.K. Applebee—is brought out. Although some individuals register disdain for "that dumb bear," others seem reluctant to offend too greatly the clan totem.

During closely contested games, especially those between 1st teams, the very limited number of spectators often exhibit a considerable amount of involvement. Even so, sideline chatter is rarely as frequent or intense as is that which so often occurs in connection with other team games. However, it is rarely abusive. Older spectator/players in particular occasionally criticize what they interpret to be an unnecessarily rough or unsporting tactic. No NCFHA team has a male coach. In fact, relatively few women's field hockey teams do yet. At the 1982 Sectional Tournament the venerable "elder" of the NCFHA—who left England many decades ago but has retained a strong sense of English "fair play" concerning game conduct—pointed out to a young male coach that "coaching from the sidelines" was not within the "spirit" of the game. Although the young coach declared that the rule book made no such prohibition, he subsequently limited his sidelines comments to players.

At the conclusion of a game team members are likely to come together to cheer. This is often followed by a general shaking of hands between opponents, a pattern similar to that which concludes the Association Club games. Players depart the field, hanging around the sidelines, talking about the just completed game in general and their own play in particular as they slowly reincorporate themselves into the normative world. Some players who have had a particularly satisfying game talk repeatedly about the various plays in which they were involved, seemingly in an attempt to relive the more satisfying moments. Their positive comments often suggest experiences somewhat similar to those that Csikszentmihalyi (1975) has called "flow."

NATIONALS

Traditionally, the USFHA National Tournament was conducted in an atmosphere of austere dignity that bore many resemblances to English "public" schoolgirl sport. Afternoon "teas" were often scheduled at which players, umpires, organizers, and the small numbers of spectators could socialize. There was no official effort to identify a winner, although most players informally acknowledged a "winner" depending upon the successes of the most prestigious teams. Scores that were "tied" at the conclusion of playing time stood. While team success was certainly not unimportant, the selection of the US and Reserve teams was the highlight of the Tournament. A formal banquet, which followed a more or less prescribed format, culminated the 3 days of play. The announcement of the US Reserve teams was the final and much-awaited event.

In 1976 the structure of the National Tournament began to change as winners in various playing pools were named. A considerable debate ensued regarding how "tie" games should be decided (cf. "The New Pitch," 1977). It was also in 1976 that the new, and separate, structure of a series of Developmental Camps was instituted. Henceforth, players aspiring to selection for the elite National Squad ascended through "invitations" issued on the basis of their performance at these Camps rather than by "selection" at Association, Sectional, and National tournaments (*Hockey Festival '81*, 1981; *Hockey Festival '82*, 1982; USFHA, to: Administrative Council, 1982). These changes were intensified by efforts to have women's field hockey sanctioned as an Olympic sport. In 1977 the USFHA was named to an "A" classification within the USOC ("Women's Hockey to

Enter Olympics," 1976; "International Scene," 1977). The establishment in 1981 of the National Sports Festival and the American Cup Tournament were important steps in America's bid for a 1984 Olympic Championship in women's field hockey. With "Olympic" recognition ensured, USFHA efforts and funds were largely directed to the development of an elite US squad.

The quantitative changes in field hockey since the late 1970s have been substantial. An evaluation prepared by the executive director in 1982 noted that the membership identified as belonging to the USFHA, Inc. had risen from 2,300 in 1978 to 16,000 in 1982. In 1978 the US team had played four international matches; in 1982 the number had risen to 39. The National Tournament in 1978 had included 350 participants. The Hockey Festival in 1982, it was estimated, would attract 1,500 (USFHA, To: Administrative Council, 1982).[4]

Not everyone approved of this changed emphasis, however. In an article in the July/August 1979 *Eagle*, a USFHA Honorary Member pointed out that since it was no longer "imperative or even considered important for players to attend the National Tournament," it was "no wonder that young players think of loyalty to the squad as their sole responsibility and allegiance to the coach as their primary concern. Without intent, the USFHA has allowed itself to become less important than the squad it created!" ("Views on Hockey," 1979).

Since the US team was no longer chosen by the traditional process, the National Tournament lost a major reason, perhaps the major reason, for its existence. However, there was reluctance on the part of both the USFHA and many individual players to abandon a concept that had been instrumental in holding together for over half a century an idealized concept of "hockey-playing community." In 1981 the Hockey Festival (not to be confused with the National Festival) was created.

"Festival" was indeed the appropriate term for the new format, for it was in effect a series of attenuated sports tournaments embedded within a larger carnivalesque framework. The 1981 Festival included a Junior and High School Jamboree, the Sectional Tournament, a College All-American Tournament, the Masters Competition, and a Club Championship. Although codified rules eliminate ambiguities regarding how the games should be played, the larger "festival" frame tends to create uncertainties regarding just how seriously one should take the athletic contests. Mixed (coed) competition was added in 1982, further "breaking the frame" of traditional ideal hockey *(Hockey Festival '82*, 1982; "Hockey World," 1983).

At the 1982 Hockey Festival, the USFHA banner with the shield of all 10 Sections and the names of recent Sectional winners of national competitions was inconspicuously displayed inside the registration area. Other team trophies (e.g., Club and Masters) were displayed below the banner. At the fields, however, a host of symbols prominently announced the "new" face of women's field hockey.

Twelve-foot-long banners proclaimed "U.S.A. Hockey," the new umbrella field hockey organization that is headquartered at the Colorado Springs Olympic Development site, and Mitchell and Ness, a sporting goods manufacturer that sponsors a "College All-American" squad. Strategically placed near the entrance to the fields were gaily striped and decorated stands of a circus-like appearance that offered for sale an assortment of hockey books, equipment, clothing, and memorabilia. Rock music blared from loudspeakers during much of the play and a 20-foot-high vinyl inflated balloon announced the dispensing of fruit drinks. All this was a far cry from the pristine atmosphere and "frames" of the traditional USFHA National Tournament.

The venue of the first two Hockey Festivals was Orlando, Florida, which offered the possibility of warm weather and adequate housing for the 900 or so participants. Fields were little better than pastures, however, causing some players to complain that this message proclaimed that the Festival was not really a very important athletic competition. Most players appeared to have a quite good time, however, and took such inconveniences in stride.

Most of the members of the four PSW Teams traveled together to the 1982 Hockey Festival, stayed at the same motel, and spent a good deal of time together, both on and off the fields. Since there is no longer a culminating banquet, the PSW teams arranged their own at a local restaurant. During the meal, a good deal of horseplay and general chatter reinforced the sense of belonging to the PSW "community." Uniforms of the four teams (PSW I, II, III, and Masters), though different from each other, all bore the sectional colors gold and brown. The Sectional totems "Applebee Bear" and the PSW banner were again displayed, now inconspicuous in the welter of other graphics, banners, tents, and the like. The general tone was one of support for members of the Section regardless of which team a player was on, and sectional members, upon seeing each other, usually asked each other: "How was your game? What was the score?" It is rare that teams from the same Section compete against each other at the National level. On those few occasions when this does occur, players usually are quite disappointed, and respond with comments like: "It's a bummer!" or "Who in the h--- wants to play your own teams!"

CONCLUSION

This paper is about a sport that seems to be in a state of flux and some of the ways that both the governing body (the USFHA) and individual players, specifically those connected with the Northern California Field Hockey Association, have sought to adapt to a variety of events precipitated by changing attitudes regarding women and sports during the late 1970s and early 1980s. It is also about the persistence of values that Turner (1974, 1977) has associated with *communitas*. As Cohen (1974) has pointed out, in modern industrial societies sports seem to be one of the more salient ways by which individuals may create and recreate "oneness through partaking in the symbolism that articulates the corporate organization of the group of which he is a member." Symbols may help achieve a "measure of continuity-in-change by their ambiguity and multiplicity of meanings" (pp. 134-135). Traditionally, women's field hockey in America had been "framed" (cf. Bateson, 1972; Goffman, 1974) in value-laden structures that borrowed heavily from British organizational patterns and ideals concerning how—and why—games were to by played. The ideological concept of a "community of women hockey players" was reinforced by means of an organizational pattern in which a player belonged to an Association, which was part of a larger Section, which was itself part of the larger USFHA. Tournament competitions were organized in accordance with this pattern, Ideologically as well as actually, membership on the national team was achieved by means of outstanding competitive play, in proper sequence, at each of these levels. Theoretically, any local Association club player ultimately could be named to the national team. Every 4 years this was extended to a worldwide concept through the participation of the United States in the quadrennial conference of the International Federation of Women's Hockey Associations competitions.

Even though this pattern for nomination to the national team was abandoned in the late 1970s, the Association and Sectional tournament competitions have persisted. The National Tournament, however, has been replaced by a national Hockey Festival. The new "festival" frame, with its strong elements of merrymaking and celebration, seeks to provide an encompassing event for the "whole world of women's field hockey." However, as MacAloon (1984) has shown, frames can be transformed from the declarative to the interrogative when "frame breaking" (Goffman, 1974) occurs. This seems to be what is occurring in women's field hockey, a sport in transition.

Notes

1. The author was a nonplaying member of the United States delegation to the 1971 IFWHA Conference and Tournament, and witnessed the opening game between New Zealand and Germany (host country for the preceding 1967 IFWHA). During this match a number of plays occurred that many of the several thousand spectators described as "most unsportmanlike," "shocking," and not in the true spirit of hockey. A major topic of conversation for the duration of the Conference was the differences in playing style between the Continental Associations,

which were members of the FIH (Federation Internationale de Hockey), and those associations that had been strongly influenced by the style of play that predominated in the United Kingdom. It was also frequently implied, if not actually stated, that a quite different "ethic" underscored the two styles, with fair play being fundamental to the British concept of games playing—so fundamental, in fact, that a moral victory was more worthy than a literal (winning game score) victory. Much concern was also voiced that because the FIH was the governing body for both men's and women's teams (the IFWHA governed only women's teams), the women's game was being tainted by masculine values. Some individuals were also aware that there was growing pressure among some countries to have women's field hockey placed on the Olympic program. Should that happen, it was believed that the IFWHA might be eliminated because national Olympic governing bodies recognized only one official governing body for each sport in a country.

2. The importance of a "games-playing" ethic in English "public school" education has by now been discussed by numerous authors. Much of the most recent and best work has been done by James A. Mangan (1981, 1982a, 1982b, in particular). Mangan has also correctly pointed out that games-playing is an important aspect of elite "public school" education for girls. It is worth noting that the game of field hockey for women in the United States has had what some might describe as an elitist flavor. This has been especially prevalent in small northeastern women's colleges, in colleges and universities at which there were women physical educators who had had some type of contact with these colleges or individuals who had been trained at such institutions, and in secondary schools that have had similar contacts. A careful study of the diffusion of the game and what might fairly be described as "a hockey-playing ideology" in America awaits some interested investigator.

3. In keeping with the concept of "Masters," the stick which adorns this trophy is the older "English" version.

4. The NCFHA membership has also been urged to help the USFHA defray a debt of several hundred thousand dollars, incurred largely through the rapid expansion of elite women's field hockey during the past few years.

REFERENCES

All England women's hockey association touring team to U.S.A., 1961. (1961, August). *The Eagle,* pp. 5-8.

Azoy, G.W. (1982). *Buzkashi: Game and power in Afghanistan.* Philadelphia: University of Pennsylvania Press.

Bateson, G. (1972). A theory of play and fantasy. *Steps to the ecology of mind* (pp. 177-200). New York: Ballantine.

Blanchard, K. (1981). *The Mississippi Choctaws at play: The serious side of leisure.* Urbana: University of Illinois Press.

Cohen, A. (1974). *Two-dimensional man: An essay on the anthropology of power and symbolism in complex society.* Berkeley: University of California Press.

Csikszentmihalyi, M. (1975). *Beyond boredom and anxiety: The experience of play in work and games.* San Francisco: Jossey-Bass.

Davis, N.Z. (1982). The possibilities of the past. In T.K. Rabb & R.I. Rotberg (Eds.), *The new history: The 1980s and beyond—Studies in interdisciplinary history* (pp. 267-275). Princeton, NJ: Princeton University Press.

First developmental camp program held; Canadians attend A level. (1976, July). *The Eagle,* p. 13.

Geertz, C. (1972). Deep play: Notes on the Balinese cockfight. *Daedalus,* *101*(1), 1-37.

Geertz, C. (1980). *Nagara: The theatre state in nineteenth century Bali.* Princeton, NJ: Princeton University Press.

Goffman, E. (1974). *Frame analysis: An essay on the organization of experience.* New York: Harper & Row.

Hockey festival '81 (official program), November 25-29, 1981.

Hockey festival '82 (official program), November 24-28, 1982.

Hockey world. (1983, January). *The Eagle,* pp. 8-9.

International federation plans for 1939 triennial conference. (1937, December). *The Eagle,* p. 3.

International news. (1951, October). *The Eagle,* p. 6.

International scene. (1977, September). *The Eagle,* p. 11.

Letter to the editor. (1976, June). *The Eagle,* p. 6.

Lever, J. (1983). *Soccer madness.* Chicago: University of Chicago Press.

MacAloon, J.J. (1981). *This great symbol: Pierre de Coubertin and the origins of the modern Olympic games.* Chicago: University Press.

MacAloon, J.J. (1984). Olympic Games and the theory of spectacle in modern societies. In J.J. MacAloon (ed.), *Rite, drama, festival, spectacle: Rehearsals toward a theory of cultural performance.* Philadlephia: Institute for Study of Human Issues Press, 241-280.

MacKay, H.T. (1963). *Field hockey: An international team sport.* Englewood Cliffs, NJ: Prentice-Hall.

Mangan, J.A. (1981). *Athleticism in the Victorian and Edwardian public school.* Cambridge: Cambridge University Press.

Mangan, J.A. (1982a). The education of an elite administration: The Sudan political service and the British public school system. *International Journal of African Historical Studies, 15*(4), 671-699.

Mangan, J.A. (1982b). Philathlete extraordinary: A portrait of the Victorian moralist, Edward Bowen. *Journal of Sport History, 9*(3), 23-40.

Morris, D., (1981) *The soccer tribe.* London: Jonathan Cape.

Pacific Coast sectional hockey tournament program. November 29-30, 1935.

Park, R.J. (1976). Ladies, gentlemen and 'ruffians': The origins and development of hockey, cricket and rugby in the San Francisco area. *Proceedings of the Seventh International Congress of the International Association for the History of Sport and Physical Education,* (pp. 458-472).

Passing of an era: "The Apple" dies January 27, 1981. (1981, January-February). *The Eagle,* pp. 3, 14.

Stewart, H. (Ed.). (1971). *Selected field hockey and lacrosse articles.* Washington: AAHPER (pp. 56-73).

The new pitch. (1977, October). *The Eagle.* pp. 2-3.

Turner, V. (1969). *The ritual process: Structure and anti-structure.* Ithaca, NY: Cornell University Press.

Turner, V. (1974). Liminal to liminoid, in play, flow and ritual: An essay in comparative symbology. In E. Norbeck (Ed.), *Rice University Studies: The Anthropological Study of Human Play, 60* (3), 53-92.

Turner, V. (1977). Variations on a theme of liminality. In S.F. Moore & B.G. Myerhoff (Eds.), *Secular ritual.* Amsterdam: Van Gorcum.

U.S. team tour to the far west. (1930, March). *The Sportswoman,* pp. 26; 28.

U.S.A. Field Hockey, To: Administrative Council, November 17, 1982.

USFHA national tournament program, November 21-23, 1940.

USFHA national tournament program(s), 1960-1972.

USFHA, To: Administrative Council, November 17, 1982.

Views on hockey today. (1979, July-August). *The Eagle,* pp. 6-9.

West of England. (1952, October). *The Eagle,* p. 3.

Women's hockey to enter Olympics. (1976, June). *The Eagle,* pp. 12.

DOES THE REFEREE MAKE ANY DIFFERENCE? AN OBSERVATION STUDY OF A RECREATION BASKETBALL LEAGUE

C. Roger Rees
Adelphi University

Robert D. Hammond
Fort Worth, Texas

Gerald W. Woodruff
Texas Christian University

In a recent article, Csikszentmihalyi (1981) decries the artificial dichotomy between instrumental activity (work) and expressive activity (leisure). He suggests that the integration of instrumental and expressive roles are essential for the survival of our society. While noting that expressive rewards are available in leisure activities such as hobbies and sports, he warns us that such activities are in danger of losing their expressive enjoyment because this enjoyment becomes replaced by instrumental goals. Thus in societies where instrumental activity is highly valued even leisure takes on an instrumental meaning.

This point of view is acceptable to many sociologists and anthropologists who have studied the role of play and games in socialization. If games do act as socialization models, then the social values important in the society will be reflected in the games and sports of that society. This has been shown consistently with different types of games (Roberts & Sutton-Smith, 1962), with aggressive and nonaggressive societies (Sipes, 1973), and in the way particular games become representative of a particular society. Compare for example the game of "taketak" played by the Tangu of New Guinea (Leonard,

1973) with the game of basketball or football in America. In the first case the game cannot finish until each side has an equal number of points and in the second everyone knows that "a tie is like kissing your sister." Contrast this with cricket, the national sport of England, which invariably ends in a tie, if it ends at all. Usually it rains, and the match has to be abandoned.

The enculturation value of games and sports is shown by the way they are changed when they are transported from one culture to another. Thus, when an egalitarian chasing game was introduced to a Mexican village, it was changed to reflect the authoritarian structure of that society (Maccoby et al., 1964), and in urban Zulu soccer the coaching role is filled by a "witch doctor" (Scotch, 1961). Closer to home, one of the first changes made by the Intercollegiate Football Association in 1876 when they adopted the game of rugby for American colleges was "the introduction of two judges and a referee to decide disputed points" (Davis, 1911, p. 467). In the English version of the game at that time such "external" law enforcement was considered superfluous because any difference of opinion would be settled by the two captains in a "gentlemanly" manner (McIntosh, 1968, p. 73).

In the games and sports of our society the concern with instrumental rather than expressive values has been well documented. According to Webb (1969), the transition from play to games to sport is part of this move toward instrumentality. Webb showed that through the course of this development children expressed increasingly "professionalized" attitudes toward participation and emphasized the importance of victory over the importance of fairness. More recent evidence supports the contention that the higher the degree of involvement the greater the concern with instrumental criteria (Theberge et al., 1982).

The possibility that instrumental reasons replace expressive reasons for participation in games and sports at all levels of involvement has been raised by sociologists and psychologists. This includes lifelong involvement in physical activity (Snyder & Spreitzer, 1979a), international sport (McIntosh, 1963), intercollegiate and high school athletics (Rees, 1980), and recreational sports programs for young children (Halliwell, 1980; Martens, 1976). These researchers would probably share Csikszentmihalyi's concern for the survival of expressive experiences in instrumentally oriented societies.

In an attempt to counter this instrumental emphasis it has been suggested that responsibility for the organization and control of sports and games be returned to the participants. Leagues have been organized in which team members do their own coaching and officiating. Furthermore, attempts have been made to reduce the negative and zero sum characteristics by de-emphasizing league standings and knocking out competitions and play-offs. The argument is that this will allow participants to be more involved from an intrinsic perspective and play the game more for its own enjoyment than for extrinsic reward (see, for example, Duthie & Moriarty, 1976). While these experiments have been attempted primarily with children's games and sports (Orlick et al., 1978), there has not been much research on the effects of this approach upon adult involvement. The lack of knowledge of how adults react to such change motivated the present study.

METHODS

The setting for this study was a church recreation intramural basketball league composed of members of the church and the local community. The league was formed to provide an opportunity for these individuals (many of them poor) to play basketball without paying the high fees of the city leagues, and to promote interracial friendships among the members of the church and the community that surrounds it. Four teams were chosen by the participants with some effort to equalize abilities. Numbers on the team varied from five to nine players. All members of the league were male.

Concerned by the level of competition and aggression that had typified the league during previous seasons, the recreation director (also a member of the research team) decided to try to reduce the emphasis on instrumental values (victory) by de-emphasizing league standings (no records were kept during the season) and by not having referees and coaches. Thus players were responsible for calling their own fouls and settling all game-related disputes. They did have the benefit of an official time-keeper and scorer.

With the cooperation of the league director the researchers were able to conduct a quasi experiment with the recreation basketball league. Specifically, each team played every other team under the "nonreferee" condition. At the midpoint of the season the referees were introduced and the games were repeated in the same order. The same officials refereed all the games. Thus, a total of eight games were observed, four without the referee and four with the referee. Theoretically, the only difference between the two "halves" of the season was the introduction of the referee.

Three forms of data collection were employed by the researchers. They observed the games and collected information on the number of fouls, the number of arguments, the time elapsed, and the number of points scored. While this observation occurred the researchers recorded on tape their comments and impressions of incidents in the games as these incidents happened. This methodology is similar to that used by Polgar (1976) in her study of children's games in two social contexts. At the end of the last game the players

responded to a questionnaire in which they were asked their perceptions of what difference, if any, the referee made to the game.
Responses were received from 27 players, about 95% of the total
group.

RESULTS

A summary of the observational data collected in the study is given in
Table 1. The values were calculated for each quarter of play and the
means and standard deviations were reported. The only significant
difference between the nonreferee and referee condition occurred in
the number of arguments. While there were many more arguments in
the nonreferee condition, these arguments did not appear to affect
the flow of the game, particularly as represented by the number of
fouls called, the number of points scored, and the time elapsed. This
finding is reinforced by examination of the tape recordings, which
revealed several remarks about arguments taking place while the
game was in progress. Thus players seemed to be able to assume
the refereeing role without adversely affecting the game.

The actual behavior of the players during the games was
reflected in their answers to the questionnaire. Table 2 shows their
perceptions of the difference made by the referee. The only such difference was that the players felt that the number of arguments
decreased when the referee was introduced. There was, however,
some change in the perceptions of the reasons for playing basketball
under the two conditions. These data are shown in Table 3.

Table 1. Comparison of Nonreferee and Referee Conditions

| Conditions | Nonreferee | | Referee | | |
	M	SD	M	SD	N
Time elapsed per quarter in minutes	12.00	1.9	12.39	1.55	16
Fouls per quarter	6.37	3.07	5.75	3.15	16
Arguments per quarter	2.31	1.78	.56	.63	16
Points per quarter	17.7	5.29	17.9	8.9	32

**Table 2. Players' Perception of Changes Occurring
When Referee Is Introduced**

Changes	Increase	Stay the Same	Decrease
Number of Fouls	22%	41%	37%
Number of Arguments	15%	18%	67%
Interruptions in Play	26%	37%	37%
Physical Contact	15%	41%	44%
Total Points Scored	41%	41%	18%

**Table 3. Ranking of Reasons for Playing Basketball
with and without Referee**

	Quarter			
	1st	2nd	3rd	4th
Nonreferee	Win(2.15)	Fun(2.19)	Fair(2.54)	Well(2.85)
Referee	Fair(1.88)	Win(2.23)	Fun(2.54)	Well(3.08)

Note. The mean of the ranking is given in parentheses, the lower the ranking the more important the reason.

One item on the questionnaire asked respondents to rank reasons for playing basketball in the referee and the nonreferee condition. Following Webb (1969) and others who have extended his research (see particularly Snyder & Spreitzer, 1979b), respondents were asked to rank the following reasons: "play for fun," "play to win," "play fair," and "play well." The results showed that while "fun" did increase in importance under the nonreferee condition, the greatest change involved the ranking of "fair." This moved from third in the nonreferee condition to first in referee condition. However, it is not suggested that this is evidence of a decrease in professionalization of attitudes during the referee condition. Instead, victory seems to be the dominant motive for participation in both conditions. In the referee condition one needs to be more concerned with fairness than in the nonreferee condition because if one does not play fair one will be penalized and consequently one's chances of victory are jeopardized.

DISCUSSION

The motive for removing the referee was to reduce the instrumental nature of the competition. The evidence from the researchers' observations and the players' perceptions was that this did not occur. An extrinsic orientation was maintained by the participants in both conditions. However, the players were able to integrate their playing roles with their officiating roles. This was done at the cost of an increase in arguments between players, but these arguments had little effect on other aspects of the game. Throughout the study a record was kept of the intensity of the arguments on a quasi-ordinal scale that had the following categories: "verbal," "push," "swing," "fight (1 on 1)," and "brawl." There was one "near fight" during the nonreferee condition and one during the referee condition. Interestingly enough, on both occasions the players dealt with the problem themselves. Even in the referee condition it was the players who decided that one team member, clearly the aggressor, should cool down on the sidelines.

One other difference between the two conditions is worth noting. While a similar number of fouls per quarter was committed in the referee and nonreferee conditions, there was a great difference in the type of fouls called. In the referee condition the mean ratio of shooting to nonshooting fouls was 9.5 to 13.5. The equivalent ratio in the nonreferee condition was 5.7 to 19.75. Clearly, players did not call shooting fouls in the nonreferee condition. Several reasons may be advanced for this finding. Perhaps free throws were considered an "easy" way of scoring, although they were frequently missed by the players. Perhaps players did not want to interrupt the flow of the play by taking free throws when they could simply take the ball out of bounds and start another offensive maneuver. It seems that there was some informal norm that controlled the mode of behavior in the nonreferee condition.

Thus, while removing the referee did not change the instrumental nature of the game, there was evidence of an "expressive" commitment by the players to maintain the flow of the game. The frequent and sometimes very loud arguments were usually kept within tacitly agreed upon limits so that the action could be maintained. In this sense the study failed to find tension between the instrumental and expressive values that Csikszentmihalyi (1981) suggested is characteristic of our involvement in leisure experiences. While instrumental reasons seemed important, the players did seem to be able to control the action and seemed to get enjoyment from this control.

REFERENCES

Csikszentmihalyi, M. (1981). Leisure and socialization. *Social forces, 60,* 332-340.

Davis, P.H. (1911). *Football the American intercollegiate game.* New York: Charles Scribner.

Duthie, J.H., & Moriarty, R. (1976). Retreading sports organizations. In T.T. Craig (Ed.), *The humanistic and mental health aspects of sports, exercise and recreation* (pp. 66-68). Chicago: American Medical Association.

Halliwell, W. (1980). Intrinsic motivation in sport. In W.F. Straub (Ed.), *Sport psychology: An analysis of athletic behavior* (2nd ed.) Ithaca, New York: Mouvement Publications.

Leonard, G.B. (1973). Winning isn't everything. It's nothing. *Intellectual Digest,* 45-47.

Maccoby, M., Modiano, N. & Lander, P. (1964). Games and social character in a Mexican village. *Psychiatry, 27,* 50-61.

Martens, R. (1976). Kid sports. A den of iniquity or a land of promise *79th Proceedings of the NCPEAM,* 102-12.

McIntosh, P. (1963). *Sport in society.* London: C.A. Watts Co. Ltd.

McIntosh, P. (1968). *Physical education in England since 1800.* London: G. Bell and Sons.

Orlick, T.D., McNally, J., & O'Hara, T. (1978). Cooperative games. Systematic analysis and cooperative impact. In F.L. Smoll & R.E. Smith (Eds.), *Psychological perspectives in youth sports.* (pp. 203-324) Washington: Hemisphere.

Polgar, S.K. (1976). The social context of games: Or when is play not play? *Sociology of Education, 49,* 265-71.

Rees, C.R. (1980). Motivation-hygiene theory and sport participation. Finding Room for the "I" in "team." *Motor Skills Theory into Practice, 4,* 24-31.

Roberts, J.M., & Sutton-Smith, B. (1962). Child training and game involvement. *Ethnology, 2,* 166-85.

Scotch, N.A. (1961). Magic scorcery and football among urban Zulu. *Journal of Conflict Resolution, 5,* 70-74.

Sipes, R.G. (1973). War sports and aggression: An empirical test of two rival theories. *American Anthropologist, 75,* 64-86.

Snyder, E.E., & Spreitzer, E. (1979a). Lifelong involvement in sport as a leisure pursuit. Aspects of role construction. *Quest, 31,* 57-70.

Snyder, E.E., & Spreitzer, E. (1979b). Orientation toward sport: Intrinsic, normative and extrinsic. *Journal of Sport Psychology, 1,* 170-175.

Theberge, N., Curtis, J. & Brown, B. (1982). Sex differences in orientations towards games; Tests of the sports involvement hypothesis. In A.O. Dunleavy, A.W. Miracle, & C.R. Rees (Eds.), *Studies in the sociology of sport* (pp. 285-308). Fort Worth, Texas: TCU Press.

Webb, H. (1969). Professionalization of attitudes toward play among adolescents. In G.S. Kenyon (Ed.), *Aspects of contemporary sport sociology* (pp. 161-178). Chicago: The Athletic Institute.

STRATEGY AND COMPETENCE: PERCEIVED CHANGE IN THE DETERMINANTS OF GAME OUTCOMES

Garry E. Chick
University of Illinois

John M. Roberts
University of Pittsburgh

Games have generally been viewed as nondynamic entities, bound by rules and not subject to change under most circumstances. This paper reviews literature that indicates that this is not the case at the cultural level and introduces data suggesting that the perceptions of game structures change at the individual level as well. These changes in perception occur as strategic competence and input rise concurrent with increasing player expertise.

It is well known, based on cross-cultural studies, that games covary with other cultural traits. Primarily, this covariance is between the number and types of games in a culture and various measures of cultural complexity. Roberts and Sutton-Smith (1962) suggested that this covariance comes about, in part, through a social learning process wherein conflicts induced through child training or other forms of socialization are expressed in cultural models of those conflicts. Involvement in these expressive models, which include games, riddles, folktales, art, music, dance and other forms, provides a "buffered" learning context in which enculturation takes place and assuagement of the conflicts is provided. This "conflict-enculturation" hypothesis of model involvement (Roberts & Sutton-Smith, 1962) suggests that types of games (e.g., games of physical skill, of strategy, or of chance) will not be adopted by or developed in cultures where the antecedent conflicts that are instrumental in their involvement do not exist. Where the antecedent conflicts do exist, appropriate game-types should persist.

One model of the relationship between culture and games is that of a "cafeteria line," where members of cultures select traits, such as games, to fit their needs. Games are adopted or rejected as culture change brings about new needs (Heider, 1977). In this case, culture is regarded as dynamic, but games are treated as static traits to be either accepted or rejected, as required. A second model consists of situations where culture remains constant and games change in order to achieve mutual consistency. This situation is best exemplified in studies by Maccoby, Modiano, and Lander (1964) wherein a game was purposely introduced into a Mexican village in an attempt to alter a submissive social character, and by Heider (1977), who looked at the changes that took place in a game introduced from Java to the Dani, a highland New Guinea group. In both of these cases, the games were quickly altered to accord with general cultural values. In the Mexican case, the game apparently was dropped completely after the researchers left the village, while the Dani altered the structure of the game to the extent that it no longer possessed the attributes of competition, scorekeeping, and strict adherence to rules. In general, however, the plasticity of games in relation to culture has not been well explored.

At the individual level, maturation leads children or adolescents to drop many games, such as tag, hide-and-go-seek, and tick-tack-toe, because they have exhausted the limited potentials of these activities (Sutton-Smith & Roberts, 1967). Adults often drop games as well, even though they apparently have not so thoroughly mastered them that the games no longer present a challenge. Roberts and Chick (1984) found that conflicts may arise in the play of a game itself, that is, within the expressive model. In a study of dropouts from a pool league, they found that individuals who were uncertain about continuing their participation in the league exhibited high levels of both approach and avoidance attitudes toward play. Those who indicated that they definitely would continue to play showed high approach and low avoidance attitudes while those who were certain that they would not continue to play displayed low approach and high avoidance attitudes. The authors suggested that the above sequence may demonstrate a developmental process of becoming involved in, playing, and disengaging from a game.

COMPETENCE AND GAME OUTCOME DETERMINATION

Roberts and Barry (1976) suggested that the existence of different game types in combination may have mutually interactive effects (i.e., games of physical skill may be qualitatively different depending on whether or not they coexist with games of chance and/or strategy). They indicated as well that games of one type, such as football, a game of physical skill, may also strongly emphasize another attribute, such as strategy. Inept players may treat games of strategy, such as poker, as games of pure chance. Indeed, strategy and player competence in games of mixed types (i.e., physical skill and strategy or strategy and chance) are strongly related, and dissatisfaction with such games may take place when the amount of strategy that a player inputs assumes precedence over the component of physical skill or chance for which the game was originally selected. Hence, the perceived nature of the game can change with the increased competence of the player even though there is no overt alteration in its actual structure. The game of blackjack provides an illustration.

Blackjack is the only casino game in which the gambler can significantly influence the likelihood of winning through choice behavior. Keren (1982) enumerated five possible strategies that the gambler can follow: "the blind gambler" (the player who hits or stays at random) advantage: -28%; "never bust" (the player who always holds when his total has reached 12 or above) advantage: -8%; "follow the dealer" (hit until one has reached a total of 17 or more) advantage: -6%; "basic" (play a strategy based on a probability table that indicates whether to hit or stay depending on the dealer's total showing and the player's total) advantage: -.4%; and "basic plus card counting" (same as basic except the player keeps track of the number of 10s and non-10s that have been played) advantage: +1.5%. This last strategy permits the player to estimate the likelihood of getting a 10 or non-10 and to manage the bet, wagering a larger sum when the ratio of 10s to non-10s is high. More sophisticated card-counting methods, such as also keeping track of aces, which can be either ones or 11s, can result in an even greater advantage for the player.

Obviously, few if any players use the first strategy, while the second and third strategies may be used to some degree. Most players, however, use some form of basic or a "system" such as doubling bets after a loss. Less experienced players may use their intuition about the probabilities while more experienced players may well use the actual probability table. Only extremely sophisticated players will use some combination of basic and card counting. Nevertheless, it is clear that the game of blackjack can range from one of complete chance to one of extremely sophisticated strategy where chance plays a part only in normalizing, over many hands, the total count on the first two cards received by players.

STRATEGY, FUN, AND COMPETENCE IN THE MONDAY NITE POOL LEAGUE

This report is the result of ongoing research in the Monday Nite Pool League of Western Pennsylvania and furnishes results not presented in earlier publications (Robert & Chick, 1979; 1984). Pool is a game of physical skill, involving fine motor movement, and strategy, the careful planning of an optimal sequence of shots much as a chess player plans his own and anticipates his opponent's moves. The ability to successfully execute the various shots is the primary skill necessary in any of the permutations of pool (e.g., seven-ball, eight-ball, nine-ball, or straight pool). Beginning players typically take the easiest and most obvious shot available to them. This manner of play is virtually devoid of strategy and is inadequate for skilled performance in pool, much as failing to plan several moves ahead would be in chess. Competent pool players utilize strategies that permit them to take shots that are as simple as possible to execute while providing them with good cue ball position for the next shot in the sequence they have planned. Again as in chess, increased competence depends on developing the ability to plan as many shots ahead as possible and to revise the plan quickly should something go awry. This is not to say that skill in shotmaking becomes less important, but that strategy becomes more important at high levels of play.

In a study of the cognitive and expressive aspects of pool play, Roberts and Chick (1979) used cluster analysis and multidimensional scaling to determine how players structured a sample of 60 behaviors that occur during play of the game. Thirty-five behaviors (Table 1) fell into a "seemly" group (i.e., they were appropriate within both league and game contexts and were not errors that could lead to losing the game). A second group of 15 behaviors (Table 2) was termed "unseemly" inasmuch as it was composed of errors, risky shots, or lucky shots. The final 10 behaviors comprised a "set-up" group.

Behaviors that occur during the course of the game of pool may consist primarily of decision making (i.e., strategy) or primarily of skillful execution, although most behaviors are likely to combine the two. Of the 35 seemly behaviors, three competent league players judged, by consensus, that 11 were principally strategic and 11 others demanded only skillful execution, while the remaining 13 involved both strategy and skill for successful performance.

The 35 seemly behaviors had been scaled from 0 (low) to 100 (high) in terms of how much fun they were to execute and how much concentration was experienced in performing them by a small sam-

Table 1. Thirty-Five "Seemly" Pool Behaviors Categorized in Terms of Implied Strategy, Physical Skill, or Strategy and Physical Skill.

Primarily Strategic	Strategy and Skill	Primarily Skill
1. Playing defense	1. Shooting combination off opponent's ball	1. Making the eight ball
2. Leaving ball sitting in (blocking) a pocket	2. Shooting with right or left "English"	2. Making a shot
3. Determining best sequence in which to shoot remaining balls	3. Drawing the cue ball	3. Using high "English"
4. Choosing which of the object balls (high or low) to shoot	4. Breaking the opponent's ball out of a pocket	4. Running a ball down the rail
5. Calculating the angle on cut shots	5. Shooting a combination shot	5. Shooting a cut shot
6. Calling the pocket	6. Using low "English"	6. Shooting the object ball
7. Shooting a dead combination	7. Running the table	7. Shooting with the rake
8. Shooting for position	8. Winning the game	8. Shooting off the rail
9. Shooting for a breakout	9. Making the eight ball on the break	9. Shooting the bank shot
10. Shooting softly	10. Banking off the diamonds	10. Shooting a massé shot
11. Shooting safe	11. Shooting a kiss shot	11. Shooting a reverse bank
	12. Stopping the cue ball	
	13. Following with the cue ball	

Table 2. Fifteen "Unseemly" Pool Behaviors with Mean Scale Values for Fun Experienced and Concentration Broken for Expert and Average Players

| | | Mean Scale Values | | |
| | | Experts | | Average Players |
Behaviors	Fun	Concentration Broken	Fun	Concentration Broken
1. Making a slop shot	80.0	11.7	88.4	8.5
2. Shooting hard	57.4	29.3	79.0	20.7
3. Blasting	55.2	30.9	84.5	17.9
4. Getting a double kiss	36.7	35.7	45.3	38.8
5. Making a table scratch	24.8	57.7	24.3	65.5
6. Missing a shot	24.1	46.4	21.8	49.5
7. Scratching on the break	22.8	33.4	21.4	41.3
8. Making a table foul	21.4	39.6	20.1	56.4
9. Scratching	20.6	62.2	19.2	76.0
10. Making a bad hit	18.3	69.1	10.8	66.8
11. Calling a table foul	10.3	7.7	24.5	34.6
12. Making a miscue	9.3	72.7	13.1	71.5
13. Calling a bad hit	8.3	21.3	17.0	51.9
14. Losing the game	4.0	36.3	4.9	74.3
15. Scratching on the eight ball	2.9	80.9	1.3	94.8

ple of players who were judged to be either expert (n=9) or average (n=11) by league standards. Roberts and Chick (1979) found that fun varied significantly for both experts and average players depending on whether the behaviors were characterized by strategy, physical skill, or a combination of strategy and physical skill. Behaviors that primarily involved decision making (i.e., strategy) were judged to be lowest in fun by both expert and ordinary players, whereas those that required both strategic input and physical skill for successful execution were judged to be highest in fun by both groups.

With the concentration-experienced variable there was a significant difference between experts and average players in addition to significant differences among the groups of behaviors. Here, the behaviors that required little or no strategy but necessitated substantial physical skill were experienced with the most concentration and those that were primarily strategic provided the least. Expert players reported experiencing greater concentration than did the average players for each of the three groups of behaviors, with the greatest difference occuring in the primarily strategic behavior group.

The relationship between fun, concentration, and player expertise can be further evaluated by looking at the group of 15 unseemly behaviors (Table 2). These behaviors were also scaled by the expert and ordinary players from 0 to 100 in terms of how much fun they are to perform, as well as in terms of how much they break one's concentration when they occur. As might be expected, fun was negatively correlated with concentration broken, although, interestingly, some unseemly behaviors (i.e., lucky shots and risky shots) were thought to be high in fun. The strength of the correlation between concentration broken and fun was significantly lower for experts ($r = -.45$) than for ordinary players ($r = -.88$; $z = 1.65$, $p > .05$). Although fun correlated positively with concentration experienced for both groups of players for the 35 seemly behaviors, again the relationship was weaker for experts ($r = .34$) than for average players ($r = .40$), although this difference is not statistically significant.

These results suggest that both fun and concentration are related to the levels of skill and strategy inherent in pool behaviors, with those having the largest degree of strategy being the least fun and entailing the lowest concentration. Concentration is related to competence as well, with experts consistently reporting higher levels than average players, regardless of the nature of the behaviors. Indeed, fun and concentration appear to be less strongly related for experts than for average players. Good players, it seems, can sustain concentration even in the absence of fun. Perhaps that is part of why they are good players.

EXPERTISE AND STRATEGIC COMPETENCE

Research on the game of chess has indicated that experts (masters and grand masters), after observing a chess board with 25 or so pieces from an actual game for 5 to 10 seconds can reproduce the positions from memory with about 90 percent accuracy. Beginning players do well to replace five or six pieces correctly. However, if a board with pieces ordered at random is shown to experts and novices, their performances are not significantly different. This suggests that the difference between experts and novices is not in the ability for visual imagery, but in the recognition of familiar situations or patterns that occur in chess (Chase & Simon, 1973). A similar situation exists in the game of pool. Expert players have the capacity to scan a pool table covered with randomly scattered balls and to quickly select the optimal sequence in which to shoot the balls into the pockets such that each successive shot is as simple to execute as possible while maximum control over the positioning of the cue ball for the next shot is maintained. As in chess, the more skilled the player, the more "moves" (shots) ahead the player can anticipate.

As part of a study concerned with why some skilled, experienced players drop out of the pool league and, in many cases, quit playing the game almost entirely, data were gathered on player competence, perceived competence, and strategic ability (Roberts & Chick, 1984). Player competence, in terms of league standards, was judged by team captains on a three-point scale (below average, average, above average). Individual players (n = 47) were asked, via questionnaire, "How good a money player do you consider yourself to be?" This question, measured on a 5-point scale, was taken as an assessment of perceived competence. Strategic competence was gauged by players' responses (on a 6-point scale) to the question, "In general, how many of the shots that you took during your game at the pool league match can you remember the next day?" Memory of shots is taken here to represent players' abilities to sequence shots after observing the spread of balls on the table, that is, strategic competence.

Competence, as judged by team captains, and perceived competence were highly correlated (Kendall's tau c = .402, p = .001, gamma = .629). Perceived competence was also significantly associated with the reported ability to recall shots the day after one's game (Kendall's tau c = .353, p = .002, gamma = .489). However, team captains' judgments of player ability were not significantly associated with players' recall of shots, although the result was directional (gamma = .17).

The association between the measures of perceived competence and strategic competence suggests that players who believe themselves to be good players also view themselves as superior strategists. It is probable that perceptions of general competence and strategic competence develop simultaneously, leading players increasingly to recognize the importance of strategy for successful outcomes. This increased recognition of the importance of strategy at higher levels of competence is not without cost, however. The findings of Roberts and Chick (1979) that, in general, the strategic aspects of pool are less fun and entail less concentration than the physical skill characteristics of the game may mean, for some players, that the game becomes less enjoyable as they become more expert. As shown above, expert players in the Monday Nite Pool League appear to be more able than average players to divorce fun from concentration on the game, a capacity that may not be compatible with continued participation by some individuals.

CONCLUSION: STRATEGY AND THE CONFLICT-ENCULTURATION THEORY

The conflict-enculturation theory of game involvement holds that antecedent conflict produced through childhood training in achievement, obedience, or responsibility leads individuals to participate in games of physical skill, strategy, or chance respectively later in life. However, the relationships that have been pointed out in this paper indicate that, as players' levels of competence increase, the outcomes of combined-type games become more a function of strategy while physical skill or chance becomes less significant in comparison.

The conflict-enculturation theory generally accounts for a significant amount of the variance in game involvement, but it may be that more of the variance could be explained by considering player expertise as an intervening variable in the relationship between game involvement and conflict. As players become more expert, certain games may no longer function to assuage conflicts because they are no longer of the appropriate type. That is, an individual may initially participate in a game because of its requirement for physical skill but later lose interest because the outcome of the game becomes increasingly dependent upon strategy.

Roberts and Chick (1984) found that players who quit the Pool League often do so because of a buildup of approach-avoidance conflict that is engendered during the course of participation in the league. While some of this conflict is clearly due to the league context of play, it is also possible that some measure of dissatisfaction is a result of the increasing strategic requirement involved in high level tournament play, especially since each individual plays only one game per evening and thus cannot effectively concede a game with the intent to recoup it later. Indeed, many of the players who dropped out of the pool league went on to join a local machine bowling league that operates in some of the same taverns as the pool league. This latter game is virtually devoid of strategy at any level of expertise and may better suit the antecedent conflicts of players than pool, which for many of them had become a game of strategy first and physical skill second.

Thus, it is argued here that games cannot be viewed as static and immutable, either from a cultural or an individual perspective. It appears to be true that the game inventories of various cultures match members' needs and that introduced games are altered in accordance with those needs. Similarly, individuals play certain games, depending on personal needs, and when the games no longer satisfy those needs the games are dropped. Aside from the obvious structural changes that can occur in games (e.g., changes in rules, equipment, etc.) the most significant other change that can take place is the increasing importance of strategy in determining the outcome as players become more competent.

The research reported here also indicates the need for more study of the relationships among player expertise, fun, and concentration, an area of concern that could provide information on problems of how ordinary players become experts. As Roberts and Chick (1979) have pointed out, the fact that experts and average players appear to have different cognitive maps of the same game also has implications for the study of cultural patterns other than games.

REFERENCES

Chase, W.G., & Simon, H.A. (1973). Perception in chess. *Cognitive Psychology, 4,* 55-81.

Heider, K.G. (1977). From Javanese to Dani: The translation of a game. In P. Stevens, Jr. (Ed.), *Studies in the anthropology of play.* West Point, NY: Leisure Press.

Keren, G. (1982, November). *Blackjack — Chance or skill?* Paper presented at the Psychology-Business Administration Colloquium series, University of Illinois at Jrbana-Champaign, IL.

Maccoby, M., Modiano, N., & Lander, P. (1964). Games and social character in a Mexican village. *Psychiatry, 27,* 150-162.

Roberts, J.M., & Barry III, H. (1976). Inculcated traits and game-type combinations: A cross-cultural view. In T.T. Craig (Ed.), *The humanistic and mental health aspect of sports, exercise, and recreation* (pp. 5-11). Chicago: American Medical Association.

Roberts, J.M., & Chick, G.E. (1979). Butler County eight ball: A behavioral space analysis. In J. Goldstein (Ed.), *Sports, games and play: Social and psychological viewpoints* (pp. 65-99). Hillsdale, NJ: Erlbaum.

Roberts, J.M., & Chick, G.E. (1984). Quiting the game: Covert disengagement from Butler County eight ball. *American Anthropologist, 86,* 549-567.

Roberts, J.M. & Sutton-Smith, B. (1962). Child training and game involvement. *Ethnology, 1,* 166-185.

Sutton-Smith, B., & Roberts, J.M. (1967). Studies of an elementary game of strategy: Tick-tack-toe. *Genetic Psychology Monographs, 75,* 3-42.

7

CONCLUSION

INTRODUCTION

Kendall Blanchard

One of the disadvantages of interdisciplinary research is the tendency for central issues to be muddled by a plethora of theoretical conceptualizations and models. In the case of play research, anthropologists, historians, psychologists, sociologists, and others all come to the problem of definition armed with an arsenal of preconceptions and methodological constraints characteristic of their particular disciplines. Some amount of confusion is to be expected. Conceptual meanings are usually most problematic and agreement regarding terms most elusive when a particular discipline is attempting to define its key concepts. For example, anthropologists are probably less certain of the meaning of "culture" than sociologists. This is within single discipinary units. Imagine the babble generated by the convergence of several disciplines. The concept of play continues to be bandied about both within and between the many disciplinary camps that make up the large, diverse world of play research.

On the other hand, there are advantages in the interdisciplinary approach to concepts. Discussion takes on more of a universal quality, disciplinary biases are more quickly seen for what they are, and conceptual issues are more likely to develop a history of their own, independent of the politics and fads of particular disciplines. Perhaps most importantly, interdisciplinary research has a vitality to it that keeps conceptual issues constantly fresh.

Meier's paper addresses this dilemma, the disadvantages and the advantages. It notes the various ways in which TAASP theoreticians have "talked about each other" in a pattern characteristic of conceptual development in science generally. In many ways, "play" remains a mystery to many who devote much of their scholarly energies to its study. Nevertheless, one of Meier's major points, though it may be only an implicit one, is that play as a subject of scholarly investigation has a continuing, irrepressible vitality. Also, he admits that the "talking around" has given way in some instances to "talking to." It is this rare but critical communication that suggests those who study play are beginning to ask more appropriate questions than they were asking 10 years ago.

The Meier paper is candid, at points controversial, and in some cases deliberately overdramatic. However, the author has done an excellent job of summarizing the key conceptual issues underlying contemporary play research and forces those who struggle with these issues to step back for a moment and rethink. For this reason the paper provides a fitting conclusion to this collection.

PLAY AND PARADIGMATIC INTEGRATION

Klaus V. Meier
University of Western Ontario

This paper was occasioned by two discrete incidents, one of a sweeping metatheoretical nature, the other of a more limited scope and applied purpose. First, in her 1982 presidential address to The Association for the Anthropological Study of Play (hereafter, TAASP), Cheska discussed the published proceedings of the Association's annual meetings from 1975 to 1982. She asserted that herein "we have developed a fine treasure chest of . . . literature representing the current [state of the art of] research in play" (Cheska, 1982, p. 9). Second, the provocative, metasystematic analysis of the nature and structure of revolutionary changes in science, originally conducted by Kuhn (1962) slightly more than 20 years ago, has been the basis of much reflective activity and serious discussion in the intervening period of time. Although Kuhn's investigation focused upon the natural sciences, numerous attempts have also been made to utilize his framework to analyze the current state of the art in the social sciences. Friedrichs' *A Sociology of Sociology* (1970) is but one example of such theoretical reconnoiterings. Efforts of this type provide considerable impetus to additional scientific inquiry, including anthropological research primarily concerned with human play.

As a result of the previous two occurrences, it appears that this is an appropriate time to employ an adaptation of Kuhn's basic model to investigate a substantial portion of the accumulated body of research dedicated to the aforementioned topic. Consequently, in an attempt to ascertain the true "state of the art" of the anthropology of play literature, I decided to undertake a detailed content analysis of all of the 169 articles contained within the seven proceedings published to date by TAASP.[1]

The four specific major problems and areas of concern for the present investigation are as follows: to analyze the concept of play as delineated by the various perspectives representative of differing research paradigms to be found in the writings; to note its evolution and historical development within the specialized environment of TAASP; to evaluate both the nature and merit of its current theoretical structure; and to suggest directions of amelioration for any perceived inadequacies in order to enhance the possibility of paradigmatic integration.

To accomplish these objectives, this paper addresses, sequentially, the three particular items: the nature of scientific paradigms and their constituent components; the infrastructure of play, in particular the different images and definitions of the basic subject matter promulgated within the literature; and three specific issues intimately connected with the debate on infrastructure. Following these deliberations, the concluding section utilizes the derived conceptual framework and findings to present final reflections on the current state of the art and to offer both recommendations and prognosis designed to facilitate and contribute positively to future anthropological research in the area.

ON PARADIGMS AND PLAY

Despite the fact that "revolution" is the titular theme of Kuhn's (1970) volume, it is clear that "paradigm" is the key term of his entire analysis. For the moment, the term may be defined, following Friedrichs (1970), as "a fundamental image a discipline has of its subject matter"[2] (p. 55). The importance of the concept may be clearly seen in the following representation (Ritzer, 1980, p. 3) of Kuhn's model of scientific changes:

Paradigm 1 → Normal Science → Anomalies →
Crises → Revolution → Paradigm II

A brief explanation of this scheme is in order. According to Kuhn (1970), the period labelled "normal science" is entered into when one specific paradigm has established a hegemonic position. In addition, normal science is a restricted, "puzzle-solving" enterprise. It is:

a period of accumulation of knowledge in which scientists work and expand the reigning paradigm. Such work inevitably spawns *anomalies*, or things that cannot be explained by the existing paradigm. A *crisis stage* occurs if these anomalies mount, which ultimately may end in *revolution*. The reigning paradigm is overthrown and a new one takes its place at the center of the science. A new reigning *paradigm* is born. The stage is set for the cycle to repeat itself. (Ritzer, 1980, p.4)

The foundations of the coherence and unity of normal scientific research are thus to be found in shared paradigms. Unfortunately, despite the obvious importance of this pivotal concept, it is most elusive. In fact, even Kuhn was remarkably lax in his use of the term. Indeed, as Masterman (1970) has pointed out, Kuhn used it in at least 21 different ways. As a result, both clarity and parsimony are significant problems in his work. Further, negative consequences are often produced by such a state of affairs. For example, Ritzer (1980) has asserted that Friedrichs' earlier-mentioned work is severly "marred by the fact that he is forced to work with Kuhn's definition, or rather Kuhn's 21 different definitions of a paradigm. Working with such a muddled definition, it is little wonder that Friedrichs comes to such a muddled conception of the paradigmatic status of sociology" (p. 190).[3]

The self-admitted, "gratuitious difficulties and misunderstandings" (Kuhn, 1970, p. 174) caused by this regrettable imprecision notwithstanding, it is possible to forward an adequate characterization of a paradigm that is faithful to the major thrust and insights contained in the remainder of Kuhn's original work. Therefore, the following definition is employed both to act as a framework for and to inform the substance of the present study.

A paradigm is a fundamental image of the subject matter within a science. It serves to define what should be studied, what questions should be asked, and what rules should be followed in interpreting the answers obtained. The paradigm is the broadest unit of consensus within a science and serves to differentiate one scientific community (*or subcommunity*) from another. It subsumes, defines, and interrelates the exemplars, theories, and methods and instruments that exist within it. (Ritzer, 1980, p.7)[4]

Thus a paradigm is composed of not one, but four basic components: an examplar; an image of the subject matter; one or more theories; and appropriate investigative methods and instruments (Ritzer, 1975).

At this stage, it must be pointed out that I am not prepared to defend further herein the full definition just presented.[5] Instead, I wish to use it as an appropriate organizing or heuristic device within which to address the primary issues of this paper—namely, to locate the role played by, to understand the nature of, and to emphasize the importance of the second component delineated above.[6] That is, since a paradigm clearly dictates what is eligible for and what is excluded from the proper area of study for a particular field, the main thrust of this study is to determine the character of the basic subject matter of the anthropology of play as depicted in the TAASP literature. In other words, the focus of the analysis is limited to the topic of anthropological definitions of and postulations about the nature and essence of the concept of play.

The accumulated research under perusal demonstrates that social scientists concerned with play—similar to those working in other areas and disciplines—rather than always listening seriously to, frequently "talk through each other" (Kuhn, 1970, p. 109) when discussing the relative merits of their research or respective paradigms. Consequently, the writings are replete with recurring contradictions, definitional circles, repeated questionable and even fallacious dichotomies, inappropriate paradigmatic shifts, and additional incongruities. However, on the other hand, instances of significant conceptual growth and obvious theoretical maturity and sophistication are also in evidence. Of course, substantial documentation is necessary both to support the first, rather negative assessment and to assist in the further development of the second, more positive aspect of play theory research. I now wish to direct my attention to this dual task.

THE INFRASTRUCTURE OF PLAY

Not surprisingly, in the writings of a scholarly society dedicated to the study of play, praise of this phenomenon is ubiquitous. Norbeck's (1976) comments in the opening article of the first proceedings are indicative of this general state of affairs: "play should not be regarded as interlude in human behavior, a dispensable if refreshing indulgence, but as a vitally important activity of human life that in fact exists among the members of all human societies" (p. 15). Similarly, Csikszentmihalyi (1981) asserted that playfulness "is not an expendable luxury. It is the stuff of life, it is what gives us the experience of freedom, of transcendence, of growth" (p. 24). However, before the positive consequences of this general position may be fully explored, it is necessary to delineate the pertinent conceptual infrastructure.

The demanding preliminary task of "defining primary conceptual frameworks," as Fox (1980) pointed out, "becomes particularly problematic when the definitions must be both broadly applicable and contextually meaningful" (p. 52). As might reasonably be expected in an association that entitles the keynote presentation at its annual meetings "The Johan Huizinga Address," many social scientists acknowledge and support, either in their entirety or with only slight modifications, the definitions tendered originally in *Homo Ludens* (1955). In fact, in the inaugural Huizinga lecture, Norbeck (1976) listed at least 15 traits or descriptive characteristics of play identified in that seminal volume. Further, although he rejected some cardinal attributes, such as agonism or competition, he contended that Huizinga provided a "richer working base" (p. 19) for formulations about play than that to be found elsewhere.

Obviously, this assessment is shared by numerous other anthropologists and social scientists in both their theoretical and field studies. For example, Conn and Marquez (1983) utilized Huizinga's altered social context component to label pinball play as a public game. In addition, Salamone's (1976) study of "friendly" witch doctors postulated that since Huizinga's major play characteristics of order, tension, movement, change, rhythm, solemnity, and rapture are also traits embodied in religious beliefs and experiences, it is possible to conclude that religion is a game and thus play.[7] Further, Fox (1980) utilized Norbeck's modification of Huizinga's play definition— namely, that play "transcends ordinary behavior" because it is a "voluntary pleasurable behavior that is separated in time from other activities and that has a quality of make-believe" to assert that play and ritual are very similar in terms of function in many cultural contexts" (p. 52). Similarly, Goldberg (1982), citing Handleman's work on metacommunicative frames, noted that although play and ritual are multiple, complementary frames within different transmissions, the two share numerous important characteristics.

Not unexpectedly, Caillois receives almost as much acknowledgment and support in the anthropological literature. This is based predominantly upon the brief discussion of play and the more comprehensive classification system of games presented in his influential book *Man, Play and Games* (1961) and closely echoed in several articles published separately. In the first proceedings volume, for example, Olofson (1976) utilized Caillois' formulations, although mistaking his game categories for elements of play,[8] to discuss selected activities of the Hausa society of Nigeria. In the same set of writings, Mouledoux (1976), also mistaking game categories for types of play, championed and utilized Caillois' definitions, albeit supplemented by Huizinga among others, as the basis for the development of a descriptive play observation instrument. In the second volume, Mouldedoux (1976) again appropriated Caillois' scheme, this time to supplement Piaget's model, for developmental research. Finally, in the latest volume, Jorgensen (1983) utilized Caillois' explication of the "make believe" or "second reality" element of play to investigate speech play and antischool parodies.

Admittedly, most social scientists are no longer ensconced at the stage of appealing to Huizinga and Caillois as almost canonical authorities. However, others have been substituted. Although numerous famous explorations of play are often referred to in the literature — including the pertinent works of Freud and Erikson (e.g., Cheska, 1978)—I will limit the discussion to only a brief mention of Piaget's studies and a more extensive perusal of Bateson's writings.

Numerous research papers acknowledge the contributions of Piaget's typologies, from his tripartite classification of play types (sensory motor, symbolic, and games) to the previously mentioned model of child development. In one of his papers, for example, Duthie (1976) supported Piaget's basic model, but added the dynamic feature of sensoristasis (that is, the desire to activate the recticulate arousal system) to compensate for its static nature.

However, Piaget has also come under attack. For one, it has been argued that since "the structure of play is an inevitable outcome of the structure of the child's mind," it is clear that in Piaget's view play represents immature cognitive functioning; consequently, adult play is relegated to the status of being perceived as merely an "infantile remnant" (Guilmette & Duthie, 1982, p. 87). In addition, Sutton-Smith (1971) provided extended criticism and attempted to repudiate major components of Piaget's models. Finally, Post's (1978) review of the critical literature on Piaget delineated additional points of incompleteness and contention.

On the other hand, the theoretical formulations forwarded by Bateson in a variety of scientific and popular sources are just beginning to attract dissenting critical opinion. Indeed, within the last 15 years in general and certainly within the specific studies under discussion, it has been the vogue for anthropologists to praise Bateson's contributions to play theory. His conception of play as a signal or "meta-message"—best understood as a frame demarking a class of behaviors not to be taken seriously or often about something that does not exist, rather than as the sum of messages or contents to be found therein—has achieved wide recognition and remarkable support. In fact, Bateson's signal "this is play" has become a "buzz-phrase" not only for TAASP, but in other contexts as well.

Bateson's efforts have inspired and oriented many of the papers contained within the proceedings, including the following representative but by no means exhaustive selection: Grayzel's (1978) study of play behavior in state penitentiaries; Gorfain's (1983) discussion of Shakespeare's Hamlet as a ludic event; Handelman's (1980) interpretation of the Naven ritual as a metacommunicative activity, which he presented and structured as an unabashed, "appreciative commentary" on Bateson; and finally, J. Schwartzman's (1981) appreciation of Handelman's appreciation of Bateson's theory to explore the paradoxical nature of post-modern or anti-realist literary works of fiction, which are "created by the interplay of several logical levels of communication, which negate one another and are contingent on the context of that communication, and not reducible to the sum of the messages that compose them" (J. Schwartzman, 1980, p. 39, paraphrasing Bateson). In fact, J. Schwartzman (1980, 1981, 1982) was so enamoured by Batesons' framework that he utilized it to analyze the same topic in three consecutive articles published in the fourth, fifth, and sixth TAASP proceedings.

Perhaps the most interesting aspect of Bateson's message about play is the overwhelming support and partisanship that it has produced. Indeed, remarkably few of the pertinent writings criticize it at all. Denzin's 1982 keynote paper is one such rare challenge. Although he concurred that play is the name of a "frame for action," Denzin contended that the paradox of play does not lie at the Batesonian level of the message "this is play." He insisted that "there is more to play than the recognition of a paradox of logical types"; that is "play transcends communicative and metacommunicative contradictions." Denzin (1982) found unsupportable and thus rejected Bateson's notions of, and Goffman's subsequent elaborations on, the frames and messages of play, which he argued assume "a recurring eidos, or essence to the play frame experience" (pp. 13-23).

In the process of forwarding his own symbolic interactionist conception, Denzin (1982) adopted Simmel's approach and designated play to be an emergent, emotionally laden, social process; specifically, it was postulated to be a "recurring interactional form whose content and substance must be established on every occasion of its occurrence" (p. 13). Further, he asserted that play is a necessarily competitive process, thus apparently leaving little if any room for individual play. This led Denzin (1982) to make the intriguing claim that "boasting and threatening are basic to play" (p. 20).

But there are more significant conceptual problems at hand in Denzin's paper. Within the short space of three paragraphs, he made the following two contadictory assertions: first, "the world of play is *not* — as Caillois, Huizinga and others would have it — distinct from and apart from everyday taken-for-granted reality. It occurs in the immediately experienced here-and-now"; and second, only 19 lines later, "In playing, persons suspend tones of seriousness and ... detach themselves from literal, taken-for-granted reality; they fool around, tell funny stories, laugh and tease one another, although they may do so with a studied seriousness" (Denzin, 1982, p. 13-14). The presence of such contradictions is a handicap to be surmounted before it is possible to consider seriously Denzin's treatment of the paradoxes of play" suggested in the article's title.

Csikszentmihalyi (1981) offered a more substantive criticism. Although he agreed that play involves the acceptance of an alternative set of rules and goals—that is, we play only when we "learn' to shift from one set of rules to another, and are able to communicate that shift to others"—he refused to accept Bateson's implied hierarchy attributing "higher epistomological status to one set of goals and rules over the other." In direct contrast to Bateson, he asserted that "an activity is not play because it suspends or evades the rules of reality, but because the player freely accepts the goals and rules that constrain his or her actions, knowing full well that he or she need not do so" (pp. 19-20). In other words, play does not consist of the "moratorium on reality" implied in Bateson's message "this is not real." Csikszentmihalyi (1981) argued that it is questionable indeed to hold the "assumption that the arbitrariness of play can be contrasted to a solid, permanent, objective reality" (p. 15). Such activities as rock climbing, spelunking, and sky diving, whose "consequences affect life directly, and thus are not at all removed from so-called 'reality'," clearly demonstrate that it is untenable to assert that these play activities are not to be taken seriously or are about something that does not exist. "Is climbing a vertical face of rock at the risk of one's life" in any manner "not real"? By changing goals, play restructures reality to, at times, "risk the things that matter most in ordinary life, such as life and money, for a set of different goals" (Csikszentmihalyi, 1981, pp. 16, 17).[9] In summary, play is not necessarily based upon an avoidance of directly dealing with reality. Rather, it involves a change of perspective on the part of the participant to effect a temporary transformation or suspension of normal social dictates.

Needless to say, the entire issue of clearly identifying the differences between the "real"and "unreal" world is in need of further detailed investigation. Although it is possible to concur with Csikszentmihalyi that Bateson's assertion "this is play" necessarily implies that this is, somehow, "not real" is incorrect, considerable additional analysis is required to establish the nature and boundaries of any such epistemological uncertitude.

The previously described conceptual efforts are needed important steps in the right direction. However, it is also apparent that some of the postulations are in need of further detailed study. In other words, much more of this type of analysis and discourse—aimed at clarifying the basic parameters and issues of the debate by, for example, closely investigating the merits of competing premises—is required for this field of inquiry to continue to advance.

Unfortunately open critical scrutiny is frequently supplanted by unquestioned, even dogmatic, theoretical and paradigmatic allegiances. This state of affairs often serves as a strong factor inhibiting the reconciliation of differences or the productive advancement of new models. Nonetheless, as Kuhn (1970) noted in the original version of his treatise, "the battle between paradigms is not the sort of battle that can be resolved by proofs" and, further, "the transfer of allegiance from paradigm to paradigm is a conversion experience that cannot be forced" (pp. 148, 151). In fact, Ritzer (1980) contended that sociologists, for example, "are often more interested in winning a victory for their paradigm than expanding sociological knowledge" (pp. 31-32).

Despite this somewhat pessimistic evaluation of the problems raised by intractable political allegiances, particularly within multiple paradigm sciences such as sociology and anthropology, perhaps it is still feasible to call for the resolution of the difficulties resulting from competing theoretical positions,. Kuhn (1970), in his revised work[10] advocated the utilization of criteria usually listed by philosophers of science to arbitrate differences—namely, "accuracy, simplicity, fruitfulness, and the like"—to achieve this desirable end (p. 199).

With this directive in mind, I wish to focus upon three specific, exemplary, and recurring problems in the literature, to which additional critical reflection would be profitably addressed, and that require satisfactory resolution before additional growth is manifested in the field: first, the question of the interchangeability of the concepts of "play" and "game"; second, the feasibility of a "play-work" dichotomy; and third, the persistent utilization of circular reasoning.

THE INTERCHANGEABILITY OF "PLAY" AND "GAME"

The literature is replete with both overt and covert support for assertions similar to the one that was forwarded by Adams (1980) in his study of the Basotho domain of games, namely, that "playing and games are not categorically differentiated activities" (p. 151). Beran (1977), for example, defined play and games as "systematic cultural patterns" that are one and the same (p. 81). Similarly, Duthie (1980) claimed that sport is "an extension of play" and, further, that both sport and games "are simply enduring play forms" demonstrating wide appeal (pp. 93, 91). Finally, Blanchard (1980) contended that sport may be classified as a game form and that it may be defined as "a form of play that involves physical exertion, formal competition, and an explicit set of rules" (p. 83).

This frequent interchanging of categories — of course, abetted by the fact that Huizinga, Caillois, and other "classic" scholars often treated play and games as virtually synonymous terms naturally falling into the same category—has resulted in the tendency for investigators of play to report and study predominantly formalized games (H. Schwartzman & Barbera, 1976). For instance, Salter (1977), in his study of the activities of Eastern Woodland Indians, freely interchanged playforms and games without providing a substantive definition of either.

The problem that arises here is that the occurrence of such equations or collapsing procedures is at least questionable. For one, they presume exactly what should be questioned, explored, and resolved. Similar to the incompatible characteristics often attributed to play itself—for example, Piaget suggested that play is often spontaneous and unorganized, whereas Huizinga stressed the necessary presence of rules and social organization in play—it is possible to contend that play and games possess significantly different components. In the way of illustration, whereas games invariably possess a rule structure, play does not. Stevens (1977b), for one, questioned the inclusion of rules in both Huizinga's and Caillois' definitions of play. Bamberg (1983), in his paper on the use of metaphor and play in young children, distinguished play from games by asserting that the former is necessarily spontaneous while the latter "follow highly routine and/or stereotyped rules" (p. 139).[11] Finally, Sack (1977) stated that such activities as a child joyfully rolling down a grassy embankment have little or no constitutive or normative regulation. Any attempt to claim that an implied social structure is unconsciously present in occurrences of the type immediately preceding is simply a matter of begging the question, without assisting in its resolution.

The claim that I wish to forward here is not that spontaneity is an essential component of play—at the very least, such a notion is contestable—but rather that, although games may at times possess important manifestations of play, it is better to differentiate these activities completely. Contrary to any postulations specifying a necessary identification or equation of play and games, it is possible for a game, or for that matter a sport (which is a different category again), to fulfill all of the requirements of "gamehood" without demonstrating any play characteristics whatsoever.[12] In other words, a game is not invariably, as it is sometimes claimed to be, "the ultimate play form" (Robinson, 1978, p. 144). On the other hand, models that attempt to argue for major differentiation or even absolute discreteness among the three concepts—such as Edward's (1973) "play-game-sport" continuum (p. 57)—present their own significant conceptual difficulties.

In concluding this section of the analysis, it is necessary to emphasize two points: first, the lack of resolution of this issue is by no means a unique characteristic of the literature under investigation;[13] second, the issue is certainly worthy of and would benefit greatly from additional theoretical efforts directed toward rectification.

THE PLAY-WORK DICHOTOMY

It has been strongly contended that, in anthropological investigations at least, "studies of play cannot be separated from studies of work" (H. Schwartzman, 1980, p. 315). Indeed, it appears as if the nature of the relationship between these two forms of human endeavor has been particularly problematic in this field. Two distinct and contradictory positions are readily identifiable in the literature: the first supports the establishment of a dichotomy between play and work; the second petitions for the elimination of just such a notion.

Mergen (1977) cited Bowen's (1909) work as one of the earliest instances of a championing of a psychological (i.e., attitudinal) continuum with work and play occupying opposite poles. Guilmette (1976) differentiated the "play dimension" (characterized by fun, relaxation, and intrinsic rewards) from the "nonplay dimension" (involving emphasis on winning, the pursuit of trophies, etc.). Mouledoux (1976) also distinguished play from nonplay forms such as art or work. Finally, Sack (1977) argued for the maintenance of a major distinction between sport as play and sport as work. He asserted that an activity may be perceived as play as long as the primary motivation is independent of extrinsic rewards and the demands on which these rewards are contingent. On the other hand, the more the activity is oriented toward utilitarian or obligatory concerns, the more it approximates a work orientation.

The contrary position was supported by Lancy (1976), who contended that play and work are "integrated." Daher (1981) utilized the writings of Thoreau to support a notion of the possibility of the fusion of work and play in a single activity. Humphrey (1981) suggested that there is a very hazy (in fact, nonexistent) line that separates work, play, life, and cosmology.[14] Finally, Mergen (1978), in a study of American shipyard workers, claimed that the postulated dichotomy is false because the "flow experience" frequently manifested during play is also often present in the rhythm of work activities.

Stevens (1980) chose to make the previously mentioned dichotomy the focus of his 1978 presidential address. He began his attempt "to bring some clarity to [definitional] waters that are now pretty muddy" by emphasizing what he termed the "apparently forgotten attribute" of Huizinga's classic definition of play, namely, that of "absorbing the player intensely and utterly" (p. 317). Stevens then proceeded by equating this characteristic with Csikszentmihalyi's description of the "flow experience," that is, the process of intense involvement and optimal harmonious interaction with the environment.[15] Subsequently, reference to selected studies indicating that a significant number of people have flow experiences during their work endeavors, or even during moments of front-line warfare, led him to quote a line from a piece of personal correspondence with Csikszentmihalyi in which the latter bluntly asserted "so much for the dichotomy of play and work" (Stevens, 1980, p. 319).[16] Stevens (1980) concurred completely with this assessment and terminated his address with the contention that "much of our investigations into what constitutes 'play' has been bounded by a false conceptual dichotomy" between play and work that has stood "in the way of meaningful advances in several aspects of our field of study" (pp. 322, 318).

However, despite Stevens', and for that matter Csikszentmihalyi's dismissals of the bifurcation, the previously delineated arguments may be questioned. At best, all that has been demonstrated is that one particular experiential characteristic chosen for discussion—namely, the participant's intense absorption in an activity—may not be an attribute in and of itself sufficient to differentiate play from work. However, this may not invalidate the dichotomy, since it is clearly possible to contend that the two classes of activities may be radically discriminated on other, and perhaps more important, necessary components. It is readily apparent that Stevens unjustifiably assumed as a given exactly what he had to prove, namely, that the specific characteristic chosen for his discussion is the one and only essential attribute that defines play. Indeed, not even Huizinga forwarded such a restrictive claim.

As H. Schwartzman (1980) pointed out in her introduction to Stevens' address, his paper elicited some interesting responses, including a brief note from Bateson[17] in which he argued, in part, that "the dichotomy of play and work is not necessarily a false one" since the actions of individuals in many cultures are both "premised" and guided by a radical work-play distinction (p. 315-316).[18] However, and contrary to the previous statement, it is readily apparent that a dichotomy, or for that matter a principle of conduct, may indeed be false even if belief in it guides action.[19]

At this point, it is necessary to present a brief note of clarification and purpose. I do not necessarily wish to either support or refute the contention that there is a viable and legitimate dichotomy between play and work.[20] On the contrary, my intention is far more modest in scope; namely, to point out that the issue of bifurcation has not yet been successfully resolved, despite the numerous postulations to be found in the literature that tend to convey such an impression. Additional efforts to attain this desideratum would be of significant benefit.

ON CIRCULAR REASONING

Similar to most areas of scientific endeavor, the utilization of circular reasoning in arguments presented in support of specific theories or paradigms can have a substantial constraining effect on the satisfactory development of play theory. In its simplest form, the procedure consists of asserting that previously forwarded conceptions of play are inadequate because they do not successfully incorporate certain characteristics demonstrated within or by a specific form of human activity, say 'X', that represents a type of behavior that the author claims to be an instance of play. Consequently, 'X' is delineated, its selected traits specified, and a call for a new conception of play that accommodates the activity at hand is stridently championed. However, as the following discussion attempts to illustrate, the reliance upon such technique may cause problems.

In their paper on play and the emotions, based predominantly on the affect theory forwarded by Jungian analysis and psychotherapy, Stewart and Stewart (1981) asserted that "if there is any characteristic of play that has achieved general recognition . . . it is that play is voluntary activity engaged in just for the fun of it, for the joyful pleasure that is play" (p. 42). Further, they emphatically contend that "play must be motivated by the affect of joy." (p. 45). It is precisely this ubiquitous notion of the necessary intertwining of joy and play that Sutton-Smith (1983) attacked in his study of the playground activities of 19th-century New Zealand children. In this brief paper, he presented several instances of "furtive, brutal and cruel" (p. 103) activities that he claimed were not entered into voluntarily and did not necessarily produce positive effects. As a consequence of these observations, Sutton-Smith concluded that previous notions of play must be repudiated. In other words, because of these manifestations of children's behavior, he argued that the "romanticized" idealization of play as a voluntary, intrinsically motivated activity must be significantly altered if not totally discarded.

Unfortunately, Sutton-Smith's assertions are less than suasive for simple reasons similar to those advanced in the immediately preceding section on the premature dismissal of the work-play dichotomy. That is, he granted at the start of his discussion specifically what he needed most to demonstrate; namely, that the activities described are indeed play activities and, as such, serve as substantial evidence clearly arguing against the previously forwarded notions of play. But how was it determined that the activities described were instances of play in the first place? That is, how were they recognized as play, if not in conformity with an appropriately encompassing criterion accepted prior to the observation? In other words, it appears as if Sutton-Smith simply presumed exactly what he most had to prove.[21]

It is not an altogether difficult task to construct a defense of "traditional" play characteristics and definitions against Sutton-Smith's charges. It may be contended that if children participate in a certain activity due to coercion, peer pressure, status seeking, or the desire to attain social acceptance, or if such engagements continue to produce negative rather than positive effects, the activity under consideration, in whatever form it takes, is simply not an instance of play behavior. That is, if compulsion and the desire to attain social respectability are the major causes of participation or if intrinsic rewards are negated—no matter if induced, controlled, and sustained by the children engaged—the activity lies outside of the play realm.[22] Such activities, however, may most assuredly be games or sports since these enterprises do not necessarily have play, in the manner previously outlined, at their core.[23] To presume that all children's activities conducted on the playground, even under their volition, must necessarily be instances of play is somewhat akin to suggesting that whatever actions a cook undertakes in the kitchen is related to, if not an integral part of, the activity of food preparation. Thus, if the cook writes checks on the sideboard, participates in conversation with another person, or even engages in sexual relations, voluntarily or through coercion, on the butcher block island, these ventures must all be accommodated in a revised definition of cooking.

On a somewhat related issue, it is readily apparent that there are additional assumptions to be unearthed in the literature that may profitably be challenged. There is at times, for example, a failure to recognize the importance of content and reference distinctions between noun and adjectival word forms; for instance, Nardo (1982) simply assumes that because John Donne's poetry is playful, it is *ipso facto* play. However, this is a point to be won, not simply granted.

Hopefully, this discussion has demonstrated that it is necessary to direct further research efforts toward the clarification and resolution of important issues concerned with the nature and application of the concept of play. The successful completion of such ventures undoubtedly will be of substantial benefit to the entire area of anthropology of play.

CONCLUDING NOTES

At this point, it is helpful to use the conceptual framework developed by Kuhn and Ritzer to place the intent and result of the present study in proper perspective, as well as to offer concluding reflections on future endeavors in the area.

Many, if not most, of the truly important differences and paradigmatic splits to be found in the anthropology of play, as in numerous other scientific disciplines, relate to and are based upon varying conceptions of the basic subject matter of the field. It is evident from the preceding analysis that there is indeed "considerable diversity of opinion regarding the salient characteristics of play which distinguish it from other behaviors or activities" (Harris, 1981, p. 27). However, to condone the perpetuation of such a state of affairs is counterproductive. After all, if the fundamental definitions, images, and interpretations of an area of research are confused or contradictory, meaningful discourse and the advancement of a common core of knowledge are handicapping. Thus, it appears as if research efforts directed toward the open questioning of the basic tenets and assumptions, both explicit and implicit, of competing definitions, the reduction of conceptual fragmentation and the achievement of a reasonable level of consensus concerning both past accomplishments in and the present status of the field are important to the study of play.

Although the task of adequately delineating the essential nature and structure of the phenomenon of play is surely not a conundrum, the studies previously surveyed at times tend to support such a conclusion. Therefore, I would issue a call for the undertaking of a careful, unbiased critical analysis of the duplicity of terms and formulations evidenced in the play literature.[24] There is a need for precise definitions and tightly drawn parameters, as well as the clear identification of models and positions no longer tenable. A request for tightly drawn and clearly defined analyses, aimed toward clarifying the variables inherent in play, is not "theoretically destructive to the development of a minimally distorted understanding of play," as H. Schwartzman (cited by Harris, 1981, p. 27) has suggested. [25] On the contrary, to urge the elimination of unnecessary and unproductive conceptual contradictions and paradoxes, continued support of incompatible attributes, and the utilization of circular reasoning is to call for clarity and enhancement.

In conclusion, it may be asserted that the anthropology of play is a vibrant field of inquiry with significant future potential. However, to progress beyond the current state of the art, it will be necessary to achieve a greater level of paradigmatic integration through the resolution of several substantive difficulties, including the three specific concerns previously delineated. In other words, there is a necessity to reduce some of the chaos in the anthropology-of-play brickyard by moving toward amelioration through the provision of clearer conceptual maps than some currently in evidence. Hopefully, this discussion has pointed to some profitable avenues of additional theoretical exploration. That will assist in the task of bringing the field's potential closer to full fruition.

Notes

1. See Lancy and Tindall (1976); Stevens (1977a); Salter (1978); H. B. Schwartzman (1980); Cheska (1981); Loy (1982); and Manning (1983). These volumes are presumed by Cheska and other anthropologists studying play and sport to be among, if not the embodiment of, the most significant and seminal works available in the subdiscipline.

2. Only provisional acceptance of this characterization may be granted at this point because, although it is both manageable and simple, as Ritzer (1980) has pointed out, this definition "is of such a general nature that it would prove useless were we to try to apply it in any depth" (p. 4).

3. Although Friedrichs' work has indeed received much praise in the field, the reader interested in perusing a critically dissenting view is directed to Ritzer's (1980) criticism of the "inherent weaknesses" of his "highly limited," problematic, and "inadequate definition of a paradigm" pp 19-23). Ritzer contended that Friedrichs' free utilization of "a bewildering array of paradigms and would-be paradigms"—in addition to difficulties caused by equating theories with paradigms, as well as mistakenly assuming "that a paradigm must apply to a discipline as a whole" — caused him to adopt "an overly splintered conception of the state of sociology."

4. This definition is, in effect, a synthesis of the "three-fold typology" originally presented by Masterman (1970) under the rubic of "metaphysical paradigm" (Ritzer, 1980, p. 7). Masterman's characterization, in turn, was developed to accommodate Kuhn's multitude of uses of the paradigm concept.

5. In my opinion, the insightful efforts contained within the studies conducted by Masterman (1970), and especially Ritzer (1975, 1980), provide material sufficient to accomplish this task.

6. Most assuredly, a detailed and comprehensive scrutiny of the nature and utilization of any or all of the other three components that make up diverse paradigms would also yield beneficial results for comprehending and evaluating the field of study.

7. This identification or equation of play and game, echoed extensively throughout the literature, causes theoretical difficulties.

8. Once again, an indiscriminate utilization and/or collapsing of the categories of play and game causes problems. Caillois' writings seem to be the main source of this major confusion and its continued expression in the field.

9. This state of affairs also places in doubt Harris' (1981) contention that play is distinguishable from nonplay activities "on the basis of an accompanying subjective, cognitive perspective held by the players which involves a relatively *weak commitment to the attainment of goals*" (p. 27). This assertion is at least questionable, if not false. It would appear possible to dedicate oneself fully to the enterprise at hand without vitiating the play attitude or damaging play as a contextual category.

10. It is interesting to note that both Phillips (1973) and Ritzer (1975, 1980) chastised Kuhn for his "retreat" on the roles played by subjectivity and irrational factors in determining the emergence or dominance of a particular paradigm. That is, Kuhn's later "equivocation" notwithstanding, these two sociologists endorsed his earlier viewpoint that paradigms do indeed rise and fall largely as a result of subjective rather than objective factors such as, for example, endorsements attained by influential members of specific scientific communities. As a consequence, they asserted that Kuhn's disavowal of his original position, due to the ensuing criticism, was ill advised and detrimental. Indeed, Ritzer (1980) even contended that Kuhn, in his revised posture, "has disowned many of the original ideas that made his book most attractive to one interested in the sociology of science" (p. 10).

11. It should be noted, however, that Bamberg (1983) did vascillate somewhat in his position by postulating that games may be perceived as "ritualized play that follow particular mental plans and goals" (p. 139).

12. For an extended defense of this specific contention, see Meier (1981).

13. It should be noted, for example, that the sociology of sport literature does not fare appreciably better in terms of the specific conceptual question at hand. For a critical discussion of the deficiencies in that field of inquiry, as well as the delineation of a suggested path of rectification, see Meier (1981, pp. 85-91).

14. The three previously mentioned papers, unfortunately, all fail to provide any clear description or explanation, much less precise definition or conceptual model, of either of the two major terms. It is also disconcerting to discover the number of additional social scientists who simply assume that the two concepts, play in particular, are unproblematic and, consequently, present their material without an adequate conceptual foundation.

15. Other traits sometimes postulated as integral components of the "flow experience" include feelings of elation, moments of heightened concentration, loss of self-awareness, the institution of reflex action, and even feelings of transcendence.

16. However, it must be noted that Csikszentmihalyi (1981) later clearly repudiated the stance advocated here by asserting that "neither flow or playfulness should be confused with play forms or play behavior" (p. 25).

17. Bateson's response was published in the *TAASP Newsletter* (Spring, 1979). The quotation following in the text is Schwartzman's paraphrase of Bateson's comments.

18. It may be apparent to the careful reader that the reasoning employed in this statement is in jeopardy of violating Bateson's own warnings against mixing logical types. The nature of logical tests of validity is partially at stake here.

19. For example, the plethora of research studies clearly demonstrating the invalidity of the catharsis of aggression hypothesis has done relatively little to dissuade its promotion as either an organizational guide to structure violent contact sports or as a motivator for participation therein.

20. There are variations on this theme in the literature. In his discussion of the analytic distinctions contained within the conceptual model of play and games developed by the South African Basotho culture, Adams (1980), for example, noted that these two categories are placed in opposition not to work but to war (p. 151).

21. It should be noted that Sutton-Smith (1983) recognized and acknowledged this deficiency in his conclusions. "I am assuming that in these examples I am talking about play" (p. 108) However, unless justification is provided for this specific contention, this admission undermines Sutton-Smith's entire position for the reasons previously listed and provides support for a challenge along the lines herein suggested.

22. It is problematic to assume that if children have to engage in certain game or sports activities such as fighting to demonstrate social power or to achieve acceptance, such activities are proper examples of play rather than nonplay phenomena. In Berne's (1964) terms, most of the "games people play" demonstrate no manifestation of play whatsoever, but may be far more appropriately considered as status enhancement maneuvers.

23. I have defended this contention concerning the distinction between play and game or sport forms in considerable depth elsewhere (Meier, 1981, pp. 91-97).

24. This should not be interpreted as an invitation to engage in inter- and intra-paradigmatic political conflicts—particularly since affairs of this nature often have significantly "more negative than positive consequences," and often serve "to divide the discipline unnecessarily" (Ritzer, 1975, p. 164)—or in the verbal decimation of opposing theoretical structures. Rather, it is a call to move toward a serious critique, to present reasonable arguments, to reveal anomalies, etc., with the intention of revealing potential avenues of rectification.

25. Indeed, as La Fave pointed out, the analysis of play need not violate principles of "logical consistency or, for that matter, comprehensiveness, parsimony, falsifiability, contributiveness and precision" (paraphrased by Guilmette & Duthie, 1981, p. 37).

REFERENCES

Adams, C.R. (1980). Distinctive features of play and games: A folk model from Southern Africa. In H.B. Schwartzman (Ed.), *Play and culture* (pp. 150-162). West Point, NY: Leisure Press.

Bamberg, M. (1983). Metaphor and play interaction in young children. In F.E. Manning (Ed.), *The world of play* (pp. 127-143). West Point, NY: Leisure Press.

Bateson, G. (1978). Play and paradigm. In M.A. Salter (Ed.), *Play: Anthropological perspectives* (pp. 7-16). West Point, NY: Leisure Press.

Bateson, G. (1979). Gregory Bateson on play and work. *TAASP Newsletter, 4* (4), 2-4.

Beran, J.A. (1977). Attitudes toward play among Filipino children of Negroes Oriental, Philippines. In P. Stevens (Ed.), *Studies in the anthropology of play: Papers in memory of B. Allan Tindall* (pp. 81-87). West Point, NY: Leisure Press.

Berne, E. (1964). *Games people play.* New York: Grove Press.

Blanchard, K. (1980). Sport and ritual in Choctaw society: Structure and perspective. In H.B. Schwartzman (Ed.), *Play and culture* (pp. 83-90), West Point, NY: Leisure Press.

Bowen, W.P. (1909). The meaning of work and play. *Hygiene and physical education, 1*(5): 408-410.

Caillois, R. (1961). *Man, play and games.* New York: Free Press.

Cheska, A.T. (1978). The study of play from five anthropological perspectives. In M.A. Salter (Ed.), *Play: Anthropological perspectives* (pp. 17-35).

Cheska, A.T. (Ed.). (1981). *Play as context.* West Point, NY: Leisure Press.

Cheska, A.T. (1982). TAASP—A playful narrative of an 8-year-old. *TAASP Newsletter, 9* (1), 6-12.

Conn, S., & Marquez, J.B. (1983). The social context of pinball: The making of a setting and its etiquette. In F.E. Manning (Ed.), *The world of play* (pp. 66-77).

Csikszentmihalyi, M. (1981). Some paradoxes in the definition of play. In A.T. Cheska (Ed.), *Play as context* (pp. 14-26). West Point, NY: Leisure Press.

Daher, M. (1981). Leisure, play and labor in Thoreau. In A.T. Cheska (Ed.), *Play as context* (pp. 159-167). West Point, NY: Leisure Press.

Denzin, N.K. (1982). The paradoxes of play. In J. Loy (Ed.) *The paradoxes of play* (pp. 13-251). West Point, NY: Leisure Press.

Duthie, J.H. (1976). Play/non-play determinants. In D.F. Lancy & B.A. Tindall (Eds.) *The study of play: Problems and prospects* (pp. 207-210). West Point, NY: Leisure Press.

Duthie, J.H. (1980). Athletics: The ritual of a technological society? In H.B. Schwartzman (Ed.), *Play and culture* (pp. 91-97). West Point, NY: Leisure Press.

Edwards, H. (1973). *Sociology of sport.* Homewood, Il: Dorsey Press.

Fox, S.J. (1980). Theoretical implications for the study of interrelationships between ritual and play. In H.B. Schwartzman (Ed.), *Play and culture* (pp. 51-57). West Point, NY: Leisure Press.

Friedrichs, R.W. (1970). *A sociology of sociology.* New York: The Free Press.

Gorfain, P. (1983). Hamlet and the tragedy of ludic revenge. In F.E. Manning (Ed.), *The world of play* (pp. 111-124). West Point, NY: Leisure Press.

Grayzel, J.A. (1978). The functions of play and the play motif at a state penitentiary. In M.A. Salter (Ed.), *Play: Anthropological perspectives* (pp. 94-103). West Point, NY: Leisure Press.

Guilmette, A.M. (1976). Binocular resolution as a function of the play identification class. In D.F. Lancy & B.A. Tindall (Eds.), *The study of play: Problems and prospects* (pp. 211-216). West Point, NY: Leisure Press.

Guilmette, A.M., & Duthie, J.H. (1981). Play: A multiparadoxical phenomenon. In A.T. Cheska (Ed.), *Play as context* (pp. 36-42). West Point, NY: Leisure Press.

Guilmette, A.M., & Duthie, J.H. (1982). Playing to grow and growing to play. In J. Loy (Ed.), *The paradoxes of play* (pp. 86-91). West Point, NY: Leisure Press.

Handelman, D. (198). Re-thinking Naven: Play and identity. In H.B. Schwartzman (Ed.), *Play and culture* (pp. 58-69). West Point, NY: Leisure Press.

Harris, J.C. (1981). Beyond Huizinga: Relationships between play and culture. In A.T. Cheska (Ed.), *Play as context* (pp. 26-36). West Point, NY: Leisure Press.

Humphrey, R.L. (1981). Play as life: Suggestions for a cognitive study of the Meso-American ball game. In A.T. Cheska (Ed.), *Play as context* (pp. 134-149). West Point, NY: Leisure Press.

Huizinga, J. (1955). *Homo ludens: A study of the play element in culture.* Boston: Beacon Press.

Jorgensen, M. (1983). Anti-school parodies as speech play and social protest. In F.E. Manning (Ed.), *The world of play* (pp. 91-102). West Point, NY: Leisure Press.

Kuhn, T.S. (1962). *The structure of scientific revolutions* Chicago: University of Chicago Press.

Kuhn, T.S. (1970). *The structure of scientific revolutions* (2nd ed.). Chicago: University of Chicago Press.

Lancy, D.F. (1976). The play behavior of Kpelle children during rapid cultural change. In D.F. Lancy & B.A. Tindall (Eds.) *The study of play: Problems and prospects* (pp. 72-78). West Point, NY: Leisure Press.

Lancy, D.F., & Tindall, B.A. (Eds.). (1976). *The study of play: Problems and prospects.* West Point, NY: Leisure Press.

Loy, J. (Ed.). (1982). *The paradoxes of play.* West Point, NY: Leisure Press.

Manning, F.E. (Ed.). (1983). *The world of play.* West Point, NY: Leisure Press.

Masterman, M. (1970). The nature of a paradigm. In I. Lakatos & A. Musgreave (Eds.), *Criticism and the growth of knowledge.* Cambridge: Cambridge University Press.

Mergen, B. (1977). From play to recreation: The acceptance of leisure in the United States, 1880-1930. In P. Stevens (Ed.), *Studies in the anthropology of play: Papers in memory of B. Allan Tindall* (pp. 55-64). West Point, NY: Leisure Press.

Mergen, B. (1978). Work and play in an occupational subculture: American shipyard workers. In M.A. Salter (Ed.), *Play: Anthropological perspectives* (pp. 187-199). West Point, NY: Leisure Press.

Meier, K.V. (1981). On the inadequacies of sociological definitions of sport. *International Review of Sport Sociology, 16* (2), 79-102.

Mouledoux, E.C. (1976). Theoretical considerations and a method for the study of play. In D.F. Lancy & B.A. Tindall (Eds.), *The study of play: Problems and prospects* (pp. 38-50). West Point, NY: Leisure Press.

Mouledoux, E.C. (1977). The development of play in childhood: An application of the classifications of Piaget and Caillois in developmental research. In P. Stevens (Eds.), *Studies in the anthropology of play: Papers in memory of B. Allan Tindall* (pp. 196-209). West Point, NY: Leisure Press.

Nardo, A.K. (1982). The poetry of John Donne's liminal play. In J. Loy (Ed.), *The paradoxes of play* (pp. 34-42). West Point, NY: Leisure Press.

Norbeck, E. (1976). The study of play: Johan Huizinga and modern anthropology. In D.F. Lancy & B.A. Tindall (Eds.), *The study of play: Problems and prospects* (pp. 1-10). West Point, NY: Leisure Press.

Olofson, H. (1976). Playing a kingdom: A Hausa meta-society in the walled city of Zaria, Nigeria. In D.F. Lancy & B.A. Tindall (Eds.), *The study of play: Problems and prospects* (pp. 156-163). West Point, NY: Leisure Press.

Phillips, D. (1973). Paradigms, falsification and sociology. *Acta Sociologica, 16*, 13-31.

Post, D. (1978). Piaget's theory of play: A review of the critical literature. In M.A. Salter (ed.), *Play: Anthropological perspectives.* West Point, NY: Leisure Press.

Ritzer, G. (1975). Sociology: A multiple paradigm science. *The American Sociologist, 10* (August), 156-167.

Ritzer, G. (1980). *Sociology: A multiple paradigm science* (rev. ed.) Boston: Allyn and Bacon.

Robinson, C.E. (1978). The uses of order and disorder in play: An analysis of Vietnamese refugee children's play. In M.A. Salter (Ed.), *Play: Anthropological perspectives* (pp. 137-145). West Point, NY: Leisure Press.

Sack, A.L. (1977). Sport: Play or work? In P. Stevens (Ed.), *Studies in the anthropology of play: Papers in memory of B. Allan Tindall* (pp. 186-195). West Point, NY: Leisure Press.

Salamone, F. (1976). Religion as play: Bori, a friendly "witchdoctor." In D.F. Lancy & B.A. Tindall (Eds.), *The study of play: Problems and prospects* (pp. 147-155). West Point, NY: Leisure Press.

Salter, M.A. (1977). Meteorological play-forms of the eastern Woodlands. In P. Stevens (Ed.), *Studies in the anthropology of play: Papers in memory of B. Allan Tindall* (pp. 16-27). West Point, NY: Leisure Press.

Salter, M.A. (Ed.). (1978). *Play: Anthropological perspectives.* West Point, NY: Leisure Press.

Schwartzman, H.B. (Ed.). (1980). *Play and culture.* West Point, NY: Leisure Press.

Schwartzman, H.B., & Barbera, L. (1976). Childrens play in Africa and South America: A review of the ethnographic literature. In D.F. Lancy & B.A. Tindall (Eds.), *The study of play: Problems and prospects* (pp. 11-20). West Point, NY: Leisure Press.

Schwartzman, J. (1980). Paradox, play and post-modern fiction. In H.B. Schwartzman (Ed.), *Play and culture* (pp. 38-48). West Point, NY: Leisure Press.

Schwartzman, J. (1981). Play: Epistemology and change. In A.T. Cheska (Ed.), *Play as context* (pp. 52-59). West Point, NY: Leisure Press.

Schwartzman, J. (1982). Playing around with words: Humor and post-modern fiction. In J. Loy (Ed.), *The paradoxes of play* (pp. 50-57). West Point, NY: Leisure Press.

Shapere, D. (1964). The structure of scientific revolutions. *Philosophical Review, 73*, 383-394.

Stevens, P. (Ed.). (1977a). *Studies in the anthropology of play: Papers in memory of B. Allan Tindall.* West Point, NY: Leisure Press.

Stevens, P. (1977b). Laying the groundwork for an anthropology of play. In P. Stevens (Ed.), *Studies in the anthropology of play: Papers in memory of B. Allan Tindall* (pp. 237-249). West Point, NY: Leisure Press.

Stevens, P. (1980). Play and work: A false dichotomy? In H.B. Schwartzman (Ed.), *Play and culture* (pp. 316-323). West Point, NY: Leisure Press.

Stewart, L.H., & Stewart, C.T. (1981). Play, games and affects: A contribution toward a comprehensive theory of play. In A.T. Cheska (Ed.), *Play as context* (pp. 42-52). West Point, NY: Leisure Press.

Sutton-Smith, B. (1971). Piaget on play: A critique. In R.E. Herron & B. Sutton-Smith (Eds.), *Child's play* (pp. 226-236). New York: John Wiley.

Sutton-Smith, B. (1983). Play theory and cruel play of the nineteenth century. In F.E. Manning (Ed.), *The world of play* (pp. 103-110). West Point, NY: Leisure Press.

Townshend, P. (1980). Games and strategy: A new look at correlates and cross-cultural methods. In H.B. Schwartzman (Ed.), *Play and culture* (pp. 217-225). West Point, NY: Leisure Press.